Meat and
2 *Veggies*

Ple

Meat and 2 Veggies

How to combine meat and vegetarian meals without having to cook separate dishes

Sharon Buthlay

SPRING HILL

Published by Spring Hill

Spring Hill is an imprint of
How To Books Ltd
Spring Hill House
Spring Hill Road
Begbroke
Oxford
OX5 1RX
Tel: (01865) 375794
Fax: (01865) 379162

info@howtobooks.co.uk
www.howtobooks.co.uk

The right of Sharon Buthlay to be identified as author of this work has been asserted by her in accordance with the Copyright, Designs and Patents Act 1988.

© Copyright 2007 Sharon Buthlay

British Library Cataloguing in Publication Data
A catalogue record of this book is available from the British Library

ISBN13: 978-1-905862-05-4

Cover Design by Mousemat Design Ltd

Produced for How To Books by Deer Park Productions, Tavistock
Designed and typeset by Mousemat Design Ltd
Printed and bound by Cromwell Press, Trowbridge, Wiltshire

NOTE: The material contained in this book is set out in good faith for general guidance and no liability can be accepted for loss or expense incurred as a result of relying in particular circumstances on statements made in the book. Laws and regulations are complex and liable to change, and readers should check the current position with relevant authorities before making personal arrangements.

Contents

Introduction

As a busy but conscientious mum, responsible for feeding my growing family, two of whom are vegetarian, I searched high and low for a book that would show me how to adapt our favourite family recipes to provide a meat and a vegetarian version of the same meal. When I couldn't find the book I needed, I decided to write one – and this is it!

The purpose of this book is to make life easier for those cooks, like me, who are required to provide meals for meat eaters and vegetarians at the same table. Whether you are providing meals on an everyday basis for the family, or occasionally for guests, you will be delighted to discover many quick, easy to prepare meals that work for both vegetarians and non-vegetarians. The recipes include a step by step guide to enable you to prepare the traditional meat, fowl or fish dish and its vegetarian alternative.

Using the quick, effective formulas I have designed, you will be able to effortlessly adapt all the family favourites, such as shepherd's pie, spaghetti bolognaise, roast beef and Yorkshire pudding and classic dishes such as beef bourgignon and coq au vin.

Meat and 2 Veggies also includes plenty of practical tips and common-sense advice, which I have amassed over the years from experience and from my research, on how to eat well and cook wholesome, healthy meals for your family and friends.

During the 30 years that I have been cooking I have collected a large and varied assortment of recipes and cookery books. My predilection for cookery books is well known and on Christmas Day you will generally find me poring over my latest acquisitions, presents from my nearest and dearest. Whilst I enjoy drooling over designer cookery books full of glossy photos and exotic foods, I have deliberately avoided that type of presentation here because I don't find that type of cookery book to be very practical or user-friendly for everyday cooking. The recipes are often fiddly and time-consuming, too rich for everyday use, and call for ingredients that are not easily available. As the old saying goes 'there is more to life than stuffing a mushroom' or for that matter a quail's egg.

The recipes and cookery books I use most frequently are those that I bought years ago, when I was still learning to cook; dog-eared, common-sense books with no-fail recipes and few photos. When writing *Meat and 2 Veggies* I set out to adopt that same common-sense attitude. The recipes are adaptions of popular classic dishes and family favourites, which call for familiar, easy to find, fresh and seasonal ingredients wherever possible.

The majority of the recipes are quick and easy to prepare and cook. By using the step by step instructions even the novice cook will be able to produce tempting and healthy meals that meet current nutritional guidelines, without being faddy or over complicated.

For many of us the traditional set meal times for breakfast, lunch and dinner have become a thing of the past. Our busy lives dictate that meals are taken as and when possible. Few have the time for formal entertaining, and cooking for friends and family has become a more relaxed affair, perhaps a barbeque, with all the joys of eating al fresco, or a spicy curry shared with friends on a cold winter's evening. The recipes in *Meat and 2 Veggies* reflect the changes that have taken place over the past few years in the way we eat and entertain. You will find recipes for the most popular traditional meals, Sunday lunches, holiday entertaining, barbeques, curries, pasta, pizza, Mexican and much, much more.

In today's busy, stressful world many of us lead such demanding lives that we may overlook our nutritional needs. Breakfast consists of a hastily snatched piece of toast or an apple eaten in the car on the way to work. Lunch is a quick sandwich or chocolate bar devoured in front of the computer, and our children routinely munch on crisps, burgers and fries while guzzling gallons of fizzy drinks. Health-related problems such as obesity, diabetes, heart disease and many forms of cancer are on the increase because of our failure to eat fresh, healthy food in the correct quantities.

Like many women today I juggle a family and a career and, although I enjoy cooking, I don't have much time to spend reading cookery books, shopping for exotic ingredients or preparing unfamiliar dishes during a busy working week. I tend to reserve my attempts at more exotic fare for when I am entertaining, or at holiday times, and stick to what I know the rest of the time. This doesn't mean that I adhere rigidly to traditional British food, quite the contrary. A typical week's menu in our house could include pasta dishes from Italy, perhaps a curry dish from India, a salad Niçoise from France, fajitas from Mexico, a tortilla from Spain or a quick but tasty stir fry from Thailand or China and all of our favourites are here for you to enjoy.

To maintain optimum health it is important to eat a varied and balanced diet every day. In addition to main course meals, *Meat and 2 Veggies* also includes recipes for healthy, appetising breakfasts, lunches and snacks, that can be quickly prepared in advance and used for packed lunches, picnics, evening snacks or just for when the kids come grazing after work or school.

It is particularly important to make sure that vegetarian children eat the correct balance of foods to provide a sufficient intake of protein, iron, vitamins and minerals. The recipes in *Meat and 2 Veggies* have been carefully planned to do just that. You can relax in the knowledge that every main meal, and many of the breakfasts and lunches, provide a healthy balance of protein, carbohydrates and plenty of the essential vitamins and minerals. They are also low in fat, salt and sugar and high in fibre to accord with current healthy eating guidelines.

Scientists are constantly working to discover the effects of different types of food on the body and our health. As a result of this we are bombarded with reports of 'new scientific discoveries', that are often unproved, and dire warnings about food and how it affects our health. This type of alarmist reporting can cause confusion and unnecessary stress to those cooks who are conscientious enough to want to provide a healthy diet for their family. Indeed, it almost seems that if the medicinal properties of food continue to be promoted as aggressively as they are at present, we shall probably need a prescription for the weekly food shop!

Clever manufacturers and marketers are seizing upon the insecurity brought about by this alarmist style of reporting. Processed food, which has been stripped of its natural goodness, is being artificially fortified with vitamins, minerals, omega 3 and 6 and much more, and then marketed as 'healthy' food.

It should be unnecessary for us to purchase foods that have been artificially fortified or to take vitamin tablets provided we eat a well balanced diet made up of fresh, natural ingredients. I do not include in this description certain foods, such as white flour, that are fortified with vitamins and minerals by law. It is more important than ever to be aware of what constitutes a healthy diet and you will find laid out in Chapter 1 the current government guidelines for a healthy diet.

As one in 15 people is now following a vegetarian diet, it follows that many of us have to cook for a friend or family member who is a vegetarian. In order to remain healthy vegetarians must learn to replace the foods they omit from their diets with suitable, healthy alternatives. Today there are many healthy food substitutes for meat in the diet and you will find a comprehensive list of these foods, together with an explanation as to how protein is found in the vegetarian diet, in Chapter 1.

It has become so much easier to shop for and cook delicious and healthy vegetarian meals. There are now many different types of meat substitute that can be prepared and cooked in exactly the same way as meat. I have checked every ingredient I have used and have been able to find all of them in my local supermarkets. Those ingredients that were difficult to find I have substituted with an easy to find alternative. I promise that you won't have to trawl around health food shops, buying stuff that looks as if it should line the bottom of a bird cage, nor will you have to boil dried beans for hours at a time.

You will also find in Chapter 1 a list of common meat products to avoid when cooking for vegetarians. There really is no point in cooking a beautiful vegetarian dish and then ruining it with gravy made from the meat juice or with a splash of Worcester sauce (which contains anchovies).

For those of you who are too hard pressed to plan ahead, you will find in Chapter 9 a four-week menu plan of delicious main meals that are healthy, varied and exciting. There is a weekly shopping list for each plan that you can simply photocopy and take to the supermarket or, even better, use to order online.

Chapter 7 is devoted to recipes and menu suggestions for family celebrations such as Easter, Hallowe'en, Fireworks night, Christmas, New Year, picnics, barbeques and entertaining.

The advice contained in this book follows current recommended guidelines for good nutrition; however you should always consult your own doctor before embarking on any change to your diet.

Bon appétit.

Sharon Buthlay

CHAPTER 1

VEGETARIANS AND THE VEGETARIAN DIET

There are currently four million vegetarians in the UK alone. In the past ten years the number of vegetarians has doubled and is increasing at the rate of 5,000 every week. Vegetarianism is no longer seen as the choice of a few cranks or sandal-wearing hippies, but as a sensible, modern way of eating that fits in with current health guidelines.

What is a vegetarian?

A vegetarian chooses not to eat meat, fish, poultry or any animal by-products. Most vegetarians are lacto-ovo vegetarians; this means that although they exclude meat, fish and fowl from their diet, they still eat dairy products and eggs. Vegans are vegetarians who also choose to exclude dairy products and eggs from their diet.

WHY DO PEOPLE CHOOSE TO BECOME A VEGETARIAN?

There are numerous reasons for becoming a vegetarian. For many people it is a moral decision not to eat animals that have been reared and killed for food. Today's modern farming practices produce meat and fish more cheaply than ever before, but this mass production of edible flesh comes at the expense of the animals, who are often reared in harsh conditions and fed chemicals and hormones that can end up in our bodies.

Others choose to exclude meat from their diet because they have been alarmed at the recent health scares associated with eating meat, fish and animal products. In recent years it has been shown that humans can be infected by eating certain animal products, and problems have included BSA, CJD and salmonella poisoning. More recently there have been concerns about the levels of mercury found in certain types of fish, such as shark, swordfish and marlin, and about the additives that are routinely fed to farmed fish.

More and more people are adopting a meat-free diet simply for health reasons because it is a low fat, high fibre way of eating.

Historically, many countries and cultures have excluded meat from their diet because it is scarce, or for religious reasons.

Eating vegetarian food is also friendlier to the environment because growing crops for food is economically more efficient, and has less impact on the world around us. For instance, a field of soya beans will yield 30 times as much protein as the same field which is used for rearing cattle.

The Vegetarian Diet

The old stereotype of the pale, unhealthy vegetarian, anaemic due to a dietary deficiency in iron, has long since been proved to be incorrect. A vegetarian diet, provided it is varied and well balanced, meets the current nutritional guidelines for a low fat, high fibre diet and includes sufficient amounts of protein and iron. In fact, medical research indicates that vegetarians are less likely to suffer from heart disease, certain types of cancer and many other diseases that are caused by our western diet of too much animal fat, sugars and processed food.

Protein in the Vegetarian Diet

THE PROTEIN MYTH
The need for protein is vastly overestimated and many people eat far too much. The Department of Health states that in order to remain healthy we should get around 15% of our calories each day from protein. Current government guidelines recommend that the average woman needs about 45 grams of protein a day and the average man needs about 55 grams. Pregnant women, young children and very active people need slightly more protein.

It is easy to include sufficient protein in your diet. For example, a bowl of cereal with milk for breakfast will provide around 12 grams of protein, a cheese sandwich for lunch provides around 15 grams of protein, and for dinner a 225 grams baked potato topped with chilli non carne, made from soya mince and kidney beans, provides around 35 grams of protein. The total daily intake of protein for these three simple, but nutritious, meals amounts to 62 grams of protein, more than sufficient for the average man or woman.

Protein is necessary for the growth and repair of body tissues and is also a source of energy. Protein is found in meat, offal, fish, eggs and dairy products. In the vegetarian diet protein can be found in nuts, seeds, pulses, grains cereals, mycoprotein and soya products.

It is necessary to eat protein every day because it cannot be stored by the body. Including some protein at every meal will ensure that you obtain a sufficient amount for your dietary needs.

HOW WE OBTAIN PROTEIN FROM PLANT FOODS
Meat, fish and fowl all provide a complete protein without the addition of any other ingredient. In the vegetarian diet we must obtain protein from plant-based foods. Protein is made up of a combination of amino acids. Plant foods contain amino acids, but no one single plant food contains all the amino acids needed, in the correct proportions, to provide a perfect protein.

There are 22 amino acids in all; most can be produced naturally in the body and are called 'non-essential' amino acids. There are nine amino acids that our body cannot produce and which must be provided in our diet. These are called 'essential' amino acids.

Perfect proteins are found in meat, fish and fowl. A range of building blocks is found in different plant foods, so by eating a wide variety of these you can obtain 'prefect protein' from plant foods.

FOOD COMBINING TO CREATE A PERFECT PROTEIN

It is necessary to mix different types of plant foods together at the same meal to create a perfect protein. Research has shown that the body creates a reservoir of amino acids to make up any deficiencies in our diet, so we don't have to worry about combining complementary protein foods all the time, provided our diet is generally varied and well balanced.

Examples of food combinations that provide a perfect protein are shown below.
- Grains and beans – as in beans on toast.
- Rice and peas or beans – as in paella or pilaf.
- Pulses with nuts and seeds – as in hummus.
- Dairy products with whole grains – as in a cheese sandwich.
- Cereals/grains and nuts – as in muesli.
- Cereals with cheese – as in macaroni cheese.
- Cereals with eggs – as in vegetable quiche.
- Oats with milk – such as porridge.

Approximate protein content in grams in 100 grams of common foods

Beef	20.5
White fish	17.5
Egg	11
Whole cow's milk	3.2
Tinned beans	4.8
Kidney beans	12 grams per 150 grams
Soya beans (cooked)	14
Rice	2.2
Wholemeal flour	12.7
White flour	9.4

High Protein Providers for Vegetarians

MEAT SUBSTITUTES

Meat substitutes are generally low in fat and high in protein. They can be bought in their raw state, or as manufactured products that mimic meat, such as burgers, sausages, mince, chicken portions, lamb steaks, meaty chunks or meatballs; in fact the list is as endless and as varied as that for manufactured meat products. Always check the label as some commercially manufactured products contain a high fat content and additives.

TOFU
Tofu is made from soya milk. It is a very good source of protein and calcium and is low in fat. Tofu is best marinated before use, as it does not have much natural flavour, but readily absorbs other flavours in a dish. Tofu is also sold in a silken form which can be used to make mayonnaise, desserts and sauces.

SOYA
This is produced from the soya bean and is also a good source of protein and is low in fat. Soya is very useful in replacing dairy products for those who are lactose intolerant and can be used to produce soya milk, soya yoghurt, soya cheese and as a meat replacement product.

TVP
Textured vegetable protein is made from soya. It is usually sold as soya mince or soya chunks. You can buy it either in a dried form, which has to be reconstituted with liquid, or as a chilled or frozen product which is ready to use.

QUORN
Quorn is a mycoprotein made from the fermentation of a fungus mixed with egg white. It doesn't sound that appetising but, in fact, it is very tasty. It is low in fat and high in fibre and is extremely versatile. Quorn is sold as various flavoured steaks, chunks, mince, sandwich slices, sausages, burgers and in many ready meals.

PULSES
Pulses are more commonly known as beans, peas and lentils. They can be bought dried or canned. They are a good source of protein, vitamins and minerals, and are also high in fibre and complex carbohydrates. Many dried pulses need to be soaked overnight before cooking, and red kidney beans must be fast boiled for at least ten minutes after soaking, and then cooked according to the pack instructions. Canned pulses are more convenient, but often have salt and sugar added during the manufacturing process. It is therefore best to drain and rinse canned pulses before use.

EGGS
Eggs are a powerhouse of nutrition, high in protein and packed with vitamins and minerals, they are also low in calories. Most vegetarians will only eat free range eggs. Current nutritional advice is to limit your intake of eggs to a maximum of four per week. Eggs should not be served raw and should be properly cooked to avoid the risk of salmonella poisoning.

VEGETARIAN CHEESE

Vegetarian cheese is produced with plant rennet rather than animal rennet. Cheese is high in protein, calcium, zinc and vitamin B12. Full fat cheese contains a high level of saturated fat which current nutritional guidelines advise us to avoid. Most supermarkets offer an excellent range of vegetarian cheeses, including low fat varieties that are suitable for vegetarians.

How to achieve a balanced diet as a vegetarian

Follow the guidelines below to achieve a balanced diet that includes the correct daily amount of protein, carbohydrates, vitamins and minerals.

- **Bread, pasta, cereals and grains** Three to four servings of cereals/grains. Try to use wholemeal or wholegrain versions of breads, pasta and rice as often as possible and avoid adding too much fat. These foods give us carbohydrates for energy, fibre, protein, and some vitamins and minerals.
- **Fruit and vegetables** Four to five servings of fruit and vegetables. You can include fresh, frozen, juiced, tinned or dried. Fruit and vegetables are a particularly good source of vitamins, minerals and fibre. It is important to include vitamin C with every meal, because the iron found in plant based foods, such as dark leafy vegetables, nuts, seeds and cereals, can only be released for use in the body when vitamin C is also present at the same meal.
- **High protein foods** Two to three servings of high protein foods. Make sure your diet includes a wide variety of pulses such as beans, lentils, peas and chickpeas, nuts, seeds, soya, mycoprotein (Quorn), and wheat proteins to give you plenty of protein, minerals and vitamins.
- **Dairy and soya foods** Two servings of dairy/soya products. These include milk, yoghurt, vegetarian cheese, free range eggs or soya products. These are good sources of calcium, protein and some vitamins. If you are avoiding dairy foods, choose fortified soya, rice or oat drinks, or make sure that you eat other foods that are high in calcium such as dark green leafy vegetables, nuts, pulses and seeds.
- **Fats and oils** Good fats are important in the diet. Include a small amount of vegetable oil or vegetarian margarine in your daily intake. Try to avoid saturated fats which are contained in fatty meat but also in full fat dairy products, butter, palm oil, some margarines and egg yolks. Fats are often hidden in processed foods such as pastries, pies, biscuits, cakes, cereal bars, desserts etc and it is wise to keep these processed foods to a minimum to ensure a healthy diet. Your fat intake should come from good fats such as olive, soya, sunflower, corn or rapeseed oils and margarines, avocados, nuts and nut butters.
- **Yeast extract** Some yeast extract such as Marmite, or cereals are fortified

with vitamin B12. Try to include this in your diet everyday as B12 is not easily found in the vegetarian diet.

Shopping for Vegetarian Food

If you are unused to shopping for vegetarian food you will, at first, need to read the labels to ensure the product is suitable for vegetarians. Beware of hidden animal ingredients in foods. See below for common animal products added to foods and suggested vegetarian alternatives.

Anchovies – small fish. Found on pizza, Caesar salad and in some brands of sauce such as Worcester sauce.	Anchovies are used to give a savoury, salty flavour to food. Try replacing this with a dash of soy sauce, yeast extract or some chopped olives.
Animal fat, found in biscuits, stock, suet, pastry and some margarine.	Replace with vegetarian shortening or suet for baking and vegetarian margarine.
Aspic – savoury jelly derived from meat or fish.	There are several vegetarian alternatives that can be used as thickeners for soups and stews or to make sweet or savoury jellies. These include carrageen, agaragar and Gelozone. You may have to visit a health food store to buy these.
Chitin – produced from crab and shrimp.	This is used in the manufacturing process of certain foods. Avoid.
Cochineal – E120 made from crushed insects. Used as a food colouring and found in sweets and some alcoholic drinks.	This is used in the manufacturing process of certain foods. Choose vegetarian boiled sweets and alcoholic beverages.
E542 – edible bone phosphate	Avoid.
Gelatine – a gelling agent derived from animal ligaments, skins, tendons, bones. Found in jellies, yoghurts, wine, boiled sweets, capsules.	Use one of the gelling agents described above or arrowroot. Look out for vegetarian yoghurt, wine, sweets and capsules.
Isinglass – a fining agent derived from the swim bladders of tropical fish. May be used in making alcohol.	Choose vegetarian wine. Most supermarkets and off-licences now have a choice of vegetarian wines.

Calf rennet – an enzyme taken from the stomach of a newly-killed calf. Used in making cheese	Choose vegetarian cheeses that have been made with vegetarian rennet.
Pepsin – an enzyme from a pig's stomach used like rennet.	As above.
Whey and whey powder are usually by-products of the cheese-making process which may contain animal rennet. Can be used in crisps as a flavour carrier.	Whey is used in the manufacture of many different food products. Look for vegetarian choices.

Fig 1. Common hidden animal products to watch out for in food.

WHERE TO SHOP FOR VEGETARIAN FOOD

You will find a wide variety of vegetarian food in most local shops and food markets. The major supermarkets stock all of the items you will need to provide a healthy, vegetarian diet. The choice of organic fruit and vegetables is increasing all the time, as is the range of exotic produce from other countries that enable us to prepare healthy, interesting and exciting meals.

Nearly every high street has a health food shop and these can be a good source of nuts, dried pulses and cereals, which are often sold loose, and can be cheaper than buying the same pre-packaged goods in the supermarket. Health food stores also stock more unusual vegetarian goods such as the thickening and gelling agents referred to above.

FOOD LABELLING

Many foods are now labelled as suitable for vegetarians – this is usually shown as a **V** sign or as a green tick sign. There is no internationally recognised standard for labelling vegetarian food, as yet, and it is still wise to check the ingredients to ensure that no animal fats or additives are included.

The Vegetarian Society

If the label states that the product has been approved by the Vegetarian Society and displays their seedling trademark it is suitable for vegetarians. More than 2,000 products have been licensed by the Vegetarian Society. You can use the database on their web site www.vegsoc.org to search for a product and check whether it meets their requirements.

CHAPTER 2

USING THE RECIPES

To make life easier for you I have included both metric and imperial measures. Use one or the other, but not a mixture of the two. All spoon sizes given are for a level teaspoon (5ml) or a level tablespoon (15 ml). If you don't own a set of cook's spoons you can use the little medicine spoons and pots as these are usually 5 ml, 10ml and 15 ml. Try to use fresh herbs and spices wherever possible, substitute with dried if fresh are unavailable; generally speaking one teaspoon of dried herbs is the equivalent of two tablespoons of fresh; the quantities are given in the recipes. Always buy the best ingredients you can afford, choose fresh fruit and vegetables in season and buy organic produce wherever possible – it really does improve the flavour and is much healthier. Wash all fruit and vegetables before use.

Substituting ingredients and Quick tips

Although it is nice to make a meal from scratch it is not always possible and so I have given 'Quick tips' where possible. These tips will enable you to produce a similar dish, using ready prepared or commercially-bought sauces and flavourings. I have included an ingredients list for each menu, but many of the recipes can be adapted to suit your personal taste using different combinations of herbs, spices and vegetables.

Conversion charts

The conversions listed below and in the recipes are approximate conversions. The slight variations will not affect the recipe, but it is important to use either all imperial or all metric measurements.

OVEN TIMINGS AND TEMPERATURES

I have included the oven temperatures for centigrade, fahrenheit and gas. If you are using a fan assisted oven or an Aga you will need to adjust the cooking time and temperature according to the manufacturer's instructions.

Gas mark	Fahrenheit	Centigrade
1	275	140
2	300	150
3	325	170
4	350	180
5	375	190
6	400	200
7	425	220
8	450	230
9	475	240

Fig 2. Oven temperatures.

WEIGHTS AND MEASURES

Ml	Fl oz	Pints
15	½	
30	1	
50	2	
75	2 ½	
120	4	
150	5	¼
175	6	
250	8	
300	10	½
400	14	
450		¾
600		1
1 litre		1¾ pints
1.2 litres		2 pints

Fig 3. Liquid measures.

Gram	Ounces	Pounds
10	½	
25	1	
40	1½	
50	2	
60	2½	
75	3	
110	4	
125	4½	
150	5	
175	6	
200	7	
225	8	
250	9	
275	10	
350	12	
450	16	1
700	24	1½
900	32	2

Fig 4. Weights.

American conversion charts

American recipes tend to be measured in cups and English recipes can be confusing for the American cook.

Dried goods

	Cups	Metric	Imperial
Flour	1	150 grams	5 oz
Sugar	1	225 grams	8 oz
Fats (butter, margarine)	1	225 grams	8 oz
Rice (uncooked)	1	200 grams	7 oz
Cheese (grated)	1	110 grams	4 oz
Pasta: Spaghetti (uncooked)	3.75	450 grams	16 oz or 1 lb
Meat (raw)	2	450 grams	16 oz or 1 lb
Potatoes (raw)	2.5	450 grams	16 oz or 1 lb
Tuna (tinned)	2.25	450 grams	16 oz or 1 lb
Tomatoes (chopped)	2.8	450 grams	16 oz or 1lb

Liquids

1 teaspoon	5 ml	1 teaspoon
½ fl oz	15 ml	1 tablespoon
¼ cup	60 ml	4 tablespoons
1¼ cups	275 ml	½ pint
16 fl oz or 1 pint	450 ml	¾ pint
2½ pints or 5 cups	1.2 litres	2 pints

Fig 5. Cups/metric/imperial. measures.

Running a well organised kitchen

Do you dream of being able to whip up a healthy, tasty meal at short notice earning compliments from friends and family? In reality does shortage of time or lack of essential ingredients mean that, yet again, you slam a pizza in the oven or rely upon expensive and calorie-laden takeaways? This chapter shows you how to stock up on basic ingredients to ensure that a quick, appetising meal is always to hand.

STOCKING YOUR LARDER

There is an art to keeping a well stocked larder, and you will find that if you keep your store cupboard, fridge and freezer well provisioned you will always be able to prepare a nutritious meal or snack at short notice. Naturally, you would not buy everything listed every week. The idea is to build up a basic store cupboard of useful ingredients and to keep the fridge and freezer stocked with seasonal, organic meat, fish, vegetarian products, dairy products, fruit and vegetables.

It is useful to prepare a weekly menu plan and shopping list, to ensure that you have all the ingredients necessary for your recipes and to avoid waste. See Chapter 9 for a whole month of menus and shopping lists. You may find that cooking vegetarian dishes means that you store more dried goods than before. To save space in your cupboards display rice, pasta, beans and lentils in attractive glass canisters on open shelves.

BASIC STORE CUPBOARD INGREDIENTS:
Dried goods
- Rice – basmati, medium grain, brown rice, wild rice and arborio rice (for risotto).
- Pasta – no-cook lasagne, pasta shapes, tagliatelli, spaghetti and gnocchi.
- Flour – wholemeal, white flour and cornflour. (Once opened flour should be stored in the fridge to prevent flour weevils.)
- Sugar – brown and caster sugar.
- Dried pulses and grains – red, yellow and green lentils, beans, chickpeas, couscous, bulgur wheat, dried split peas and barley.
- Cereals – oats, organic muesli.
- Nuts – unsalted chopped mixed nuts, almonds, cashews, Brazil nuts, walnuts and pine nuts.
- Seeds – sunflower, sesame, poppy.
- Stock cubes, gravy mix and bouillon mix.
- Vinegars – malt, cider, balsamic, white wine and red wine.
- Bottled sauces and mustards - a selection including soy sauce, Worcester sauce, chilli sauce, mint sauce, horseradish, cranberry, tabasco, English mustard, and Dijon mustard.
- Oils – olive oil, extra virgin for salad dressings and mild olive oil for cooking, sunflower oil, rapeseed oil, nut oils.
- Condiments – sea salt, salt, ground white pepper, black peppercorns.
- Dried herbs – a selection including: oregano, basil, rosemary, thyme, parsley, sage, coriander.
- Dried vegetables – shiitake and oyster mushrooms and sun dried tomatoes.
- Dried spices – a selection including: garam masala, cumin, paprika, chilli powder, cinnamon, turmeric, nutmeg, cardamom pods.
- Tea – your favourite breakfast tea, plus some fruit or herb teas.
- Coffee – freshly roasted ground coffee or coffee beans that you can grind yourself.
- Breads and biscuits – these breads will keep for a short period in the store

cupboard or fridge: taco shells, tortilla wraps, pitta bread, part-baked rolls or baguettes, dried breadcrumbs, bread sticks, croutons for soups and salads, wholemeal crackers for cheese, ice cream wafers and macaroons (useful for instant desserts and trifles).

Miscellaneous

- Dried yeast and a jar of yeast extract.
- Vegetarian suet.
- Baking powder.

Jars/sachets

- Tomato purée, sun dried tomato purée, basil pesto, garlic paste.
- Mixed peppers/roasted vegetables in olive oil.
- Curry pastes.
- Chinese stir fry pastes, Thai cooking pastes.
- Lazy garlic (fresh garlic chopped and preserved (useful for when you run out).
- A selection of olives, good chutneys, pickles.
- A selection of honey, pure fruit jams and marmalades and a good fruit purée for pouring over ice cream.

Tins

- Vegetables – chopped tomatoes, sweetcorn.
- Beans – a selection including organic baked beans in tomato sauce, butter beans, red kidney beans, chickpeas and borlotti beans.
- Fruit – buy in juice rather than syrup include: apricots, mandarins, grapefruit, pineapple rings and peaches, (these are useful for breakfasts and desserts when fresh fruit in season is in short supply).
- Fish – include tuna, salmon, sardines, pilchards and anchovies.

Frozen

- Vegetables – peas, whole sweetcorn, fine green beans and oven chips (low fat).
- Meat – your usual selection including some chicken portions, lean steaks and chops, lean minced meat.
- Fish – your usual selection including some wild salmon, cod steaks, tuna steaks, whole prawns.
- Vegetarian – Quorn fillets, chunks and mince, vegetarian sausages and vegetarian hot dogs.
- Desserts – good quality vegetarian ice cream, bags of frozen mixed fruit (useful for dessert toppings and smoothies).
- Bread – a selection of bread and rolls (if you are unable to buy fresh every day).
- Pastry – ready to roll puff, short crust and filo pastry.

Fridge

- Dairy – a selection of cheeses including vegetarian cheeses, organic free range eggs, organic yoghurts, organic milk, vegetarian margarine, butter,

organic natural yoghurt, Greek yoghurt, crème fraiche.
- Meat – bacon, sausages, cold meats for sandwiches etc, fresh meat.
- Vegetarian – tofu, soya products, Quorn deli slices for sandwiches, vegetarian bacon, steaks or burgers.
- Other – hummus, fresh salsa dip, fresh herbs.

FRESH VEGETABLES
- Buy organic where possible and buy what you need for a couple of days only. Include everyday staples such as lettuce, tomatoes, cucumber, spring onions, bean sprouts, celery, beetroot, radishes, watercress or rocket, mixed red, yellow and green peppers, red onions and Spanish onions, fresh garlic, ginger and chillies, courgettes, squash, aubergines, green beans and cauliflower.
- Root vegetables such as carrots, parsnips, sweet potatoes, swede, baking potatoes, new potatoes, etc, will keep well for several days in a cool dark place.
- Dark green leafy vegetables should be bought in season and used on the day of purchase, if possible. Broccoli, curly kale, red, white and green cabbages will keep fresh longer than the more tender varieties such as spinach, watercress and rocket.

FRESH FRUIT
- Buy fresh fruit in season every couple of days. Hard fruits, such as apples and pears, and citrus fruits, last longer than soft fruits in the fruit bowl. In summer melons, pineapples, nectarines, peaches, etc, can be bought unripe and ripened at home. Soft fruit such as ripe peaches, nectarines, grapes and berries should be stored in the fridge and eaten within a day or two of purchase.

Kitchen equipment and gadgets

Are you a complete gadget hound? Or do you always find yourself without the necessary basic kitchen tools? Read on to discover the basic kitchen equipment you need to become an efficient cook.

If you are like me you will have acquired a hotchpotch of kitchen equipment gradually over the years. For those of you who are setting up a kitchen for the first time, or about to renew your kitchenware, I have listed below the items I find most useful. If you already have a well stocked kitchen you may simply need to buy an extra wok or frying pan, an extra saucepan and a couple of extra baking tins and casserole dishes, in which to cook the alternative meat/vegetarian dish.

When cooking for vegetarians it is important not to contaminate the dish by using the same chopping board and cooking utensils as used for meat products.

SAUCEPANS

Your needs will be dictated by the number of people you cook for and by preference. Recently, I have tended to buy stainless steel saucepans with stainless steel handles and glass lids. I find that these are light and easy to clean; the handles do not catch fire or fall off, although they can get hot and you sometimes need to hold them with a cloth. The transparent lids mean that I can see how the food is cooking without having to lift the lid.

Basic saucepans

- One or two large, double handled saucepans with a heavy base for cooking pasta, soups and stews.
- Two medium sized saucepans for potatoes and vegetables.
- A small saucepan for boiling eggs and making sauces.
- A wok for stir fries.
- Two non-stick frying pans for pancakes and omelettes.
- A non-stick griddle pan.
- An egg poacher.

Other

- A deep, stainless steel colander for draining pasta and vegetables.
- A vegetable steamer (the sort you can put in the saucepan to steam vegetables).
- A fine mesh sieve for washing rice and lentils and sifting flour, etc.
- A salad spinner.
- A metal oven dish for the turkey or Sunday joint. Ensure it is deep enough to hold a full-sized bird, but not too large for your oven.
- A shallow, metal roasting tray for roast potatoes, roasted vegetables, etc.
- Two casserole dishes of the size you need (for instance, if you are cooking a casserole for two vegetarians and two meat eaters you would need two casserole dishes that would each serve two).
- Two square or oval gratin dishes for cooking lasagne, moussaka, etc. Again you will need to select the size you require.
- A selection of non-stick baking tins including a minced pie tin, a Yorkshire pudding tin, a loaf tin (useful for nut roasts, terrines and meat loaf), a flan tin for quiches (buy the one with the loose base that you can remove), a cake tin, a flat baking tray and a pizza tray (the best ones have perforations in the bottom which allow the dough to cook and become crispy).

ELECTRICAL GOODS

For a gadget to be of use it should be easy to clean, use and store. Frustratingly, many gadgets are fiddly things, which take more time to clean than they save, and are bulky and difficult to store. The gadgets I find useful are as follows.

- Food processor. Buy the best you can afford. The most important thing is to have a powerful motor, otherwise it simply burns out after a year or so. The best accessories are a dough maker, chopping blade, blender, juicer, shredder, slicer and grinder (for coffee beans, nuts and whole spices). Look for models that are simple to use and easy to clean.
- An electric hand blender and whisk. Useful for small jobs when you don't want to get the food processor out. Also allows you to whisk sauces and blend soups in the saucepan. Mine also has a small attachment for chopping small amounts of herbs, garlic, etc.
- Digital weighing scales with a flat surface (so that you can use your own bowls/plates, etc. to weigh your ingredients).
- A toaster – the most useful ones are those that allow you to cook on several different heat and width settings. Useful for bagels, pitta bread, etc.
- An electric kettle.
- A microwave oven.

COOKING IMPLEMENTS
- A set of cook's measuring spoons.
- A selection of wooden spoons.
- A set of cooking implements. The most useful include a fish slice, a spatula, a soup ladle, a potato masher, a large slotted spoon, a long handled spoon for basting, a hand whisk, and a spaghetti spoon for lifting and serving pasta.
- A turkey baster.
- A selection of knives. You will need a serrated bread knife, a sharp chopping knife for vegetables, a meat cleaver, a carving knife and fork, small knives for peeling vegetables and fruit, and a palette knife (useful for pancakes and omelettes).
- A vegetable peeler – these are useful not only for peeling but to cut hard vegetables into long strips.
- An apple corer and a melon baller.
- A vegetable brush for scrubbing vegetables.
- A pastry brush.
- A selection of kitchen scissors.
- A pizza wheel – also good for chopping herbs.
- A hand grater (useful for small amounts when you don't want to get the food processor out). Choose one that has a coarse grater at one end and a fine grater (for lemon rind, nutmeg, etc) at the other end.
- A selection of measuring jugs.
- A selection of cookie cutters (useful for mince pies, mini pizzas, etc).

- A rolling pin.
- A tin opener, a bottle opener and a corkscrew.
- Metal and wooden skewers.
- A chopping board for meat and a separate chopping board for vegetables. The toughest and most hygienic are the glass ones.
- A timer (if you don't have one on your cooker).
- A glass cafetière – buy the size you need. I have two, one that serves two and one that serves four.

Cleanliness is next to godliness

Or so it is said. I am a firm believer in keeping a clean kitchen – there is not much point in producing a healthy, nutritious meal if you are going to give everyone food poisoning. Here are some tips for keeping your kitchen clean and your food free from infection.

FOOD HANDLING
Storing food.
Always check the sell-by date on food before using and if it is out of date throw it away. Perishable goods should be stored in the fridge or freezer. Once opened, products such as jams, marmalades, bottled sauces, relishes, pickles, flour, etc should be stored in the fridge. Potatoes and onions should be removed from their polythene bags and stored in a cool dark place.
Defrosting frozen food.
It is best to defrost food overnight in the fridge. Once defrosted, food should be used up within 24 hours. Never cook food that is not properly defrosted.
Fresh fruit and vegetables.
These should be thoroughly washed before use. Wash fruit before putting it into the fruit bowl.
Ready-washed salads and vegetables. Always wash ready made salads and vegetables. Bacteria can build up in the bag and has been shown to cause food poisoning.
Meat.
Fresh meat should be stored in a sealed container on the bottom shelf where it cannot drip onto other food. Cooked meat should always be kept separate from raw meat to avoid cross infection. Store all meat, whether fresh or cooked, in separate, sealed containers. A large joint should be thoroughly wrapped in foil and put on a plate or in a dish before placing in the fridge.
Poultry, fish and seafood
These are the main culprits when it comes to food poisoning – particularly in the summer when barbeques are popular. It is important to cook chicken

thoroughly until the juices run clear. Always test by piercing the thickest part of the meat with a skewer or knife – if any pink shows it is not cooked enough. Mussels should be closed when you cook them and open after they are cooked. Any that do not behave in this way should be discarded. Other seafood should be eaten on the day it is purchased or as soon as it is defrosted.

Eggs.

Try to buy free range eggs with the British lion mark. Check the sell-by date and store in the fridge. If you spill egg on your hands or the work surface wash immediately to avoid infection.

EQUIPMENT

Work surfaces and sink.

Clean your work surfaces and sink before and after every meal using an antibacterial product.

Chopping boards.

Keep at least two chopping boards, one for meat and one for vegetables. Wooden and plastic chopping boards can become scarred with use and harbour germs. The safest are the glass chopping boards. Wash before and after use with antibacterial cleaner.

The fridge.

It is best to clean the fridge at least once a week. I usually do this just before I do the main food shop. Remove the shelves and salad baskets and wash in a solution of hot water and bicarbonate of soda (this cleans without creating a smell). Then wash the inside of the fridge in the same way. Use a new sponge or cloth and dry with kitchen paper.

The cooker.

Cleaning the cooker has to be the worst job in the kitchen, but is best done regularly to avoid build up of grease that attracts bacteria. Hobs should be cleaned after each use.

The dishwasher.

Dishwashers can harbour bacteria if not thoroughly cleaned. Once a week run the dishwasher on empty and add an appropriate dish washer cleaner.

3

QUICK START BREAKFASTS

It is well documented that breakfast is the most important meal of the day. Eating a proper breakfast balances our blood sugar levels, gives the metabolism a kick start and ensures that we receive a good supply of essential protein, carbohydrates, vitamins and minerals. Breakfast is also the ideal time to incorporate some fruit into our diet as it is quick to prepare and easy to digest.

A healthy breakfast is especially important for growing children and it is worth getting up a little earlier, or taking some time to prepare the night before, to ensure that children start the day with something more wholesome than white toast or sugary, processed cereals. The breakfasts listed in this chapter can all be prepared and cooked in less than 30 minutes.

Muesli and fresh fruit sundae

TIME TO PREPARE: 10 MINUTES
SERVES: 4

This is a fun breakfast that most children can't resist because it looks so much like a dessert. You can vary the flavour of the yoghurt and the type of fruit or cereal used according to preference.

Ingredients

¼ pint (150 ml) apple juice
4oz (110 grams) organic muesli
8 fl oz (250 ml) of organic,
   vanilla flavoured yoghurt
12 oz (350 grams) mixed berries
2oz (50 grams) chopped mixed nuts

Health note

Low in fat and salt and provides carbohydrates for energy, some protein and calcium, and a good mix of vitamins and minerals. Look for good quality, organic, unsweetened yoghurt. Children should be fed full fat milk and yoghurts.

Method

Step one:
Put the muesli and apple juice in a mixing bowl, stir and leave to soak for a couple of minutes (this can be left to soak overnight if you prefer).

Step two:
Wash and drain the fruit, reserve four whole berries.

Step three:
Take four sundae glasses and layer the fruit, yoghurt and muesli, finish with a swirl of yoghurt, sprinkle with chopped nuts and top with a berry.

Fruity pancakes

TIME TO PREPARE: 10 MINUTES
TIME TO COOK: 5 MINUTES
BASIC PANCAKE MIXTURE (MAKES 12 PANCAKES)

Once you get the knack of them, pancakes are quick and easy to make, so don't just save them for Shrove Tuesday.

Ingredients

6 oz (175 grams) plain white flour
2 large organic free range eggs
10 fl oz (300 ml) skimmed milk
2 oz (50 grams) unsalted butter
Pinch of salt

Health note

Pancakes provide carbohydrates for energy, fibre, some protein, calcium, B vitamins, folate and iron. The fillings provide additional vitamins and minerals.

Method

Step one:
Put a large pan of water on to boil. Lightly grease a dinner plate and place over the boiling water. Sieve the flour and the salt into a large mixing bowl.

Step two:
Break the eggs into a cup or bowl and mix lightly with a fork.

Step three:
Make a well in the centre of the flour and gradually whisk the eggs in until all the egg is incorporated.

Step four:
Slowly add the milk, continuing to whisk until the mixture is smooth, free from lumps and the consistency of single cream.

Step five:
Melt the butter in a non-stick frying pan over a gentle heat. Leave enough melted butter in the pan to coat the base and sides and pour the excess melted butter into a small dish or cup.

Step six:
Return the frying pan to the hob and turn the heat to a low to medium setting. Add enough batter to coat the pan; about 4-5 large tablespoons

Continued on next page

should be enough, depending on the size of your pan. Swirl the batter around the pan to ensure it is completely covered with a thin layer of batter. Using a palette knife gently lift the edges of the pancake to prevent sticking.

Step seven:
When the first side is golden brown you can either flip the pancake (if you are feeling lucky), or take the frying pan off the heat and, using a palette knife, carefully slide the pancake onto a plate cooked side down. Next, place the frying pan over the plate and turn the plate upside down to tip the pancake back into the frying pan. The uncooked side should now be on the bottom. Each side should not take more than about 15–20 seconds.

Step eight:
When cooked, put the pancake on the warm, greased plate, cover with foil and keep warm by placing the plate over the pan of boiling water (you may need to top up the water). Place a layer of greased foil or greaseproof paper between each pancake while keeping warm to prevent them sticking together.

Step nine:
When the pancakes are ready simply spread them with your chosen filling and either roll up or fold in half and then half again to create a triangle.

Serving suggestion

When you have cooked and filled the pancakes top them with some chopped nuts, some chopped or sliced fruit and a dollop of crème fraiche or Greek yoghurt.

Quick tip

You can prepare the batter and the fruit fillings the evening before to save time in the morning. Alternatively, you can buy ready made pancakes and simply warm through and fill.

Fruit fillings

BANANA AND HONEY

You will need to make this just before you use it otherwise the bananas will discolour.

Ingredients

4 large bananas
4 tablespoons (60 ml) of runny honey

Method

Mash the banana, and honey together and spread over the cooked pancakes.

CREAMY APRICOT

Ingredients

1lb (450 grams) fresh apricots halved and stone removed (you can use tinned or frozen apricots if fresh are unavailable)
2 tablespoons (30 ml) runny honey
10 fl oz (300 ml) crème fraiche
2 oz (50 grams) chopped almonds

Health note

Apricots and almonds are an excellent source of calcium, iron and zinc.

Method

Step one:
Put the apricots in a pan, add just enough boiling water to cover them and add the honey. Bring to the boil and simmer on a low heat for 10 minutes until the fruit is soft.

Step two:
Drain off any excess liquid and then add the crème fraiche to the apricots and blend with a hand blender or food processor.

Step three:
When blended stir in the chopped almonds.

Step four:
Spread the apricot and almond mixture over the cooked pancakes, roll or fold them and serve immediately.

CHERRY SURPRISE

Ingredients

1lb (450 grams) fresh cherries, stone removed (you can use cherries canned in natural juice or frozen if fresh are unavailable)
2 tablespoons (30 ml) runny honey
Chocolate spread

Method

Step one:
Place the fresh or frozen cherries in a pan and add just enough boiling water to cover the base of the pan (if using tinned cherries put them in the pan in their own juice).

Step two:
Add the honey and bring to the boil, lower the heat and simmer for 5 minutes until the fruit is soft.

Step three:
Drain any excess liquid from the cooked cherries and mash lightly.

Step four:
Spread each pancake with the chocolate spread and the cooked cherries, roll or fold and serve immediately.

OTHER SUGGESTIONS FOR PANCAKE FILLINGS:
Lemon and sugar
Serve the pancakes rolled or folded, and top with a squeeze of lemon and a sprinkling of brown sugar.
Apple and cinnamon
Chop a crisp green apple and stir into a carton of natural yoghurt with a pinch of cinnamon. Spread over the pancake, roll or fold and serve.
Greek yoghurt with honey
Spread the cooked pancake with Greek honey and add a dollop of Greek yoghurt, roll or fold and serve immediately.
Fresh berries
Mix together some fresh chopped berries, put 2 tablespoons (30 ml) of fruit on each pancake, roll or fold, sprinkle with a little crunchy, brown sugar and serve.

Quick bake peach muffins

TIME TO PREPARE: 10 MINUTES
TIME TO COOK: 20 MINUTES
MAKES 12 LARGE MUFFINS OR 40 MINI MUFFINS

These muffins make a deliciously moist and sweet breakfast that can, if necessary, be eaten on the move. You can substitute the peach with dried fruit, fresh berries or other chopped fresh fruit if desired.

Ingredients

5 oz (150 grams) plain white flour
5 oz (150 grams) wholemeal flour
1 teaspoon (5 ml) baking powder
2 large free range eggs
½ teaspoon salt
3 oz (75 grams) caster sugar
4 oz (110 grams) butter
8 fl oz (250 ml) fortified soya milk
8 oz (225 grams) fresh or tinned peaches

Health note

A good source of fibre and complex carbohydrates, calcium, iron, folate, vitamins A, B and C. For extra goodness use soya milk that is fortified with vitamin B12.

Method

Step one:
You can either use a proper muffin tin or buy paper muffin cases (which saves on washing up). If using a tin, grease it first with a little sunflower oil.

Step two:
Melt the butter and allow it to cool. Chop the peaches into small dice. Sift the flour, baking powder and salt into a large bowl.

Step three:
In a separate bowl mix together the egg, milk, sugar and melted butter.

Step four:
Sift the dry ingredients again straight onto the egg mixture. Using a large spoon, gently fold the flour into the egg mixture and then gently fold in the peaches.

Step five:
Spoon the mixture into the prepared tin or muffin cases and bake on the top

Continued on next page

shelf of the oven at 200C/400F/gas mark 6 for 20 minutes if cooking the mini muffins, or 30 minutes if cooking the large muffins. To test if cooked, pierce the muffins with a knife, if it comes out clean they are cooked.

To Serve

These are best served warm, drizzled with a little honey, but can also be made in advance and warmed through quickly in the oven or microwave, and are perfect for packed lunches, birthday parties and picnics.

Quick tip

The muffins can be made and stored for up to two days in an airtight container. You can use any fresh fruit such as nectarines, apricots, apples, pears, etc, or dried fruit such as raisins and sultanas.

Super smoothies

Smoothies can be made from any soft fruit, such as berries, bananas, ripe nectarines, peaches and melons. You will need a blender or juicer. Simply combine the fruit of your choice with some organic, natural yoghurt, whole organic milk, soya milk, or use fruit juice if you are avoiding dairy foods.

Quick tip

Any leftover smoothie mixture can be made into a super healthy treat. Simply pour into an ice lolly mould or an empty yoghurt carton, add an ice lolly stick and freeze.

Health note

These smoothies provide protein, calcium, zinc and vitamins A, B, C and D, and are perfect for those who cannot stomach food before lunch time.

MIXED BERRY SMOOTHIES

TIME TO PREPARE: 5 MINUTES
MAKES 4 SMOOTHIES

Ingredients

1lb (450 grams) fresh mixed berries
   (if you can't get fresh you can
   use frozen, simply defrost before using)
10 fl oz (300 ml) carton of organic, natural yoghurt
10 fl oz (300 ml) cranberry juice
4 tablespoons (60 ml) runny honey

Health note

A good source of vitamin C, calcium and protein and low in fat.

Method

Step one:
Hull the fruit and remove any pips or stones.

Step two:
Place the fruit in the blender with the yoghurt and blend until smooth.

Step three:
Add the fruit juice and the honey and blend until creamy.

Step four:
Serve immediately in tall glasses, over crushed ice.

APRICOT AND BANANA SMOOTHIES

TIME TO PREPARE: 5 MINUTES
MAKES 4 SMOOTHIES

Ingredients

4 medium size bananas
8 oz (225 grams) fresh apricots
10 fl oz (300 ml) carton of organic,
   vanilla flavoured yoghurt
5 fl oz (150 ml) soya milk
2 teaspoons (10 ml) cocoa powder

Health note

A good source of vitamin B6, protein,
calcium, iron and zinc.

Method

Step one:
Peel the bananas and chop into chunks.

Step two:
Remove the stones from the apricots.

Step three:
Put the fruit in a blender and add the yoghurt and the soya milk. Blend until
smooth and creamy.

Step four:
Pour into tall glasses and sift a little cocoa powder over each smoothie. Serve
immediately.

Quick tip

The little chocolate shakers you find in Capuccino packs are perfect for
sprinkling small amounts of cocoa powder.

ST CLEMENTS SMOOTHIE

TIME TO PREPARE: 10 MINUTES
MAKES 4 SMOOTHIES

Ingredients

10 fl oz (300 ml) freshly
    squeezed orange juice
Juice and zest of a lemon
Juice and zest of a lime
2 grapefruit
2 large oranges
4 tablespoons (60 ml) honey

Health note

An excellent source of vitamin C and folic acid.

Method

Step one:
Peel the grapefruit and the oranges, remove the pith and the seeds and divide into segments.

Step two:
Place the fruit segments into a blender with the orange juice, the honey, the lemon and lime juice and the zest.

Step three:
Blend until smooth. You can sieve this, before drinking, to remove the pulp and 'bits' if you prefer a smooth drink.

Summer pudding Greek yoghurt

TIME TO PREPARE: 10 MINUTES
DEFROSTING TIME: 30 MINUTES
SERVES: 4

This is a pleasantly cooling summer breakfast which must be made the night before as the dish is eaten partially frozen like ice cream. It also makes a healthy dessert.

Ingredients

1 lb (450 grams) mixed berries
4 tablespoons (60 ml) runny honey
2 fl oz (50 ml) water
10 fl oz (300 ml) carton of Greek yoghurt

Health note

A good source of vitamin C, protein, calcium and fibre.

Method

Step one:
Place the fruit and honey in a saucepan and add the water. Bring to the boil and simmer for five minutes until the fruit is cooked.

Step two:
Allow the fruit to cool and then stir in the Greek yoghurt.

Step three:
Place the mixture into four individual serving dishes and freeze.

Step four:
Remove from the freezer 30 minutes before serving.

French toast with cinnamon and apples

TIME TO PREPARE: 15 MINUTES
TIME TO COOK: 15 MINUTES
SERVES: 4

This recipe is ideal for those cooler autumn days when something a little more warming and substantial is needed. It is better to use bread that is a day or two old.

Ingredients

2 large cooking apples
1 oz (25 grams) unsalted butter
1 teaspoon (5 ml) cinnamon
2 tablespoons (30 ml) honey
4 x 2" (5 cm) thick slices wholemeal bread
2 medium size free range eggs
5 fl oz (150 ml) milk
1 oz (25 grams) caster sugar

Health note

Contains fibre, carbohydrates, vitamins A, B C and D, protein, iron, calcium, zinc and magnesium.

Method

Step one:
Peel, core and roughly chop the apples. Put a large, foil-lined plate in the oven on the lowest setting to keep warm.

Step two:
Melt the butter in a non-stick saucepan over a low heat.

Step three:
Add the apples, the honey and the cinnamon to the pan and cook for 5 minutes until the apples are softened, but have not lost their shape. Remove from the heat and reserve.

Step four:
Beat the eggs, milk and caster sugar together in a large mixing bowl.

Step five:
Take a slice of bread and carefully cut a slit halfway through the side of the bread to form a pocket. Stuff each bread pocket with the apple mixture. At this point the bread slices can be individually wrapped in foil and refrigerated overnight.

Continued on next page

Step six:
To cook, place a large non-stick frying pan over a medium heat and brush with a little melted butter.

Step seven:
Dip a stuffed bread pocket into the egg mixture and cook in the frying pan over a medium heat for about 3–4 minutes on each side.

Step eight:
Put the cooked toast onto the warmed plate, sprinkle with a little cinnamon, if liked, and cover with foil to keep warm while you cook the remainder of the toasts.

Quick tip

This dish can be partly prepared the evening before to save time in the morning. Simply follow the instructions to step five, then wrap each toast in foil and refrigerate overnight.

English muffin pizzas

TIME TO PREPARE: 10 MINUTES
TIME TO COOK: 5 MINUTES
SERVES: 4

These savoury little pizzas are popular with children and adults alike, ideal for when you want a cooked breakfast but don't have time to prepare the full English.

Ingredients

4 wholemeal English breakfast muffins
5 fl oz (150 ml) pizza sauce (see p. 345)
4 large beef tomatoes
8 large flat mushrooms
1 tablespoon (15 ml) sunflower oil
2 oz (50 grams) grated Cheddar cheese
Salt and black pepper to taste

Health note

Rich in complex carbohydrates, vitamins A, B and C, protein, calcium, iron, folate and carotene.

Method

Step one:
Pre-heat the grill on high.

Step two:
Slice each muffin in half and toast the uncut side until light brown and crispy.

Step three:
When toasted remove from under the grill and spread the untoasted side of each muffin with a tablespoon (15 ml) of the pizza sauce.

Step four:
Put a large non-stick frying pan on the hob and heat the oil gently, add the mushrooms to the pan and cook for 2 minutes each side.

Step five:
Cut the ends off the tomatoes and discard. Cut each tomato into 2 thick slices and place under the hot grill for 2 minutes.

Step six:
Place one slice of tomato and a mushroom on each muffin and top with grated cheese.

Continued on next page

Step seven:
Place the muffin pizzas back under the hot grill until the cheese has melted. Season with salt and black pepper to taste.

To serve

For non-vegetarians the pizzas can be garnished with some chopped, cooked bacon. For a change you can omit the cheese and replace with a lightly poached egg.

Quick tip

For those who eat breakfast on the move, these muffins can be wrapped in greaseproof paper and then foil.

Kedgeree

TIME TO PREPARE: 10 MINUTES
TIME TO COOK: 20 MINUTES
SERVES: 6 (3 FISH AND 3 VEGGIE)

Once made, kedgeree can be kept warm without spoiling and is perfect for a late breakfast/early brunch, allowing guests to rise when they please and help themselves.

Ingredients

12 oz (350 grams) basmati rice
1 pint (600 ml) water
8 oz (225 grams) smoked haddock fillets (skin removed)
1 tablespoon (15 ml) sunflower oil
½ teaspoon (2.25 ml) cayenne pepper
½ teaspoon (2.25 ml) turmeric
8 spring onions
2 tablespoons (30 ml) fresh chopped chives
2 tablespoons (30 ml) fresh chopped parsley
2 tablespoons (30 ml) lemon juice
2 oz (50 grams) frozen peas
4 large free range eggs
Salt and pepper

Health note

Fish is an excellent, low fat source of protein. The mixture of rice and peas also creates a perfect protein.

Method

Step one:
Preheat the oven to 180C/350F/gas mark 4. Place the haddock fillets in an ovenproof dish and add sufficient water to cover them. Put the haddock into the oven and cook for 15-20 minutes until the fish is cooked through and flakes easily.

Step two:
While the haddock is cooking put a large saucepan on the hob. Add the oil and warm gently over a medium heat.

Continued on next page

Step three:
Chop the spring onions finely and add to the oil, then add the cayenne, the turmeric and the chopped chives. Cook gently for 2-3 minutes until the onion has softened.

Step four:
Boil the water in a kettle. Add the rice to the pan and then pour on the boiled water. Bring to the boil and then turn the heat to the lowest setting and cover. Cook for 20 minutes until all the water has been absorbed and the rice is tender.

Step five:
While the rice and the haddock are cooking, hard boil the eggs (to hard boil eggs cook for 8–10 minutes). When the eggs are cooked remove them from the heat and, leaving them in the saucepan, run them under the cold tap for 2-3 minutes (this stops the eggs cooking further and makes them easy to peel). When cold peel the eggs and cut into quarters.

Step six:
Cook the peas in boiling water for 5 minutes. When cooked drain off any surplus water.

Step seven:
When the haddock is cooked remove it from the oven. Drain off any remaining liquid and flake the haddock into small flakes.

Step eight:
When the rice is cooked divide it between two bowls.
Add the haddock, a tablespoon of parsley and a tablespoon of lemon juice to one bowl of rice, season with salt and pepper and stir through.

Step nine:
Add the peas, a tablespoon of parsley and a tablespoon of lemon juice to the other bowl of rice, season with salt and pepper and stir through.

To serve

Garnish with the quartered eggs and a little more parsley.

Full English breakfast

TIME TO PREPARE: 15 MINUTES
TIME TO COOK: 30 MINUTES
SERVES: 4 (2 MEAT AND 2 VEGGIE)

There is a knack to cooking the traditional English breakfast. Careful timing is necessary to ensure that each ingredient is cooked to perfection and arrives at the table piping hot. It is easy to cook a gorgeous vegetarian alternative as you will see below.

Ingredients

4 large organic free range eggs
2 slices lean, unsmoked back bacon
2 slices vegetarian 'bacon'
2 lean pork sausages
2 vegetarian sausages
14 oz (400 grams) tin organic baked beans
4 large mushrooms
4 large tomatoes
8 hash browns (see recipe below)
4 thick slices of wholemeal bread
2 tablespoons (30 ml) sunflower oil

Health note

Although fat has been kept to a minimum, by grilling and baking instead of frying, you should bear in mind that this is still a high fat/high calorie breakfast to be enjoyed as an occasional luxury. You could always compensate for the calories by taking everyone for a long walk afterwards.

For the Hash Browns

TIME TO PREPARE: 15 MINUTES
TIME TO COOK: 25 MINUTES

These hash browns contain much less fat than the commercially prepared variety and are cooked in the oven, rather than deep fried, which reduces the fat content further.

Ingredients

1lb (450 grams) potatoes
1 small onion
2 tablespoons (30 ml) chopped chives
    (use a teaspoon [5 ml] of dried if fresh is unavailable)
Salt and black pepper to taste
1 large organic free range egg

Continued on next page

Method

Step one:
Pre-heat the oven to 190C/375F/gas mark 5.

Step two:
Grease two large baking sheets.

Step three:
Peel the potatoes but leave them whole, place them in a pan of boiling, salted water and cook for 10 minutes. Remove the potatoes from the heat then drain and rinse with cold water until cooled.

Step four:
Using a coarse grater, grate the potatoes into a mixing bowl.

Step five:
Peel and grate the onion and add it to the potato.

Step six:
Chop the chives and mix them into the grated potato, adding salt and pepper to taste.

Step seven:
Beat the egg and add to the potato mix and stir well.

Step eight:
Flour your hands and then take a large tablespoon of the mixture and roll into a ball. Place each ball on the baking tray and pat down to form eight individual rounds. At this point the hash browns can be covered with foil and refrigerated overnight, ready for use in the morning.

Step nine:
Brush the hash browns with a little sunflower oil and bake in the oven for 25 minutes.

Quick tip

The hash browns can be prepared the evening before and refrigerated overnight, or they can be cooked and frozen for later use.

Method for full English breakfast

Step one:
If making the homemade hash browns start by preparing those. Pre-heat the oven to 190C/375F/gas mark 5.

Step two:
Get the eggs, bacon, sausage, mushrooms and tomatoes out of the fridge. Pre-heat the grill to high. Cut the tomatoes in half widthways and place them with the mushrooms on an oiled non-stick baking tray, brush with a little sunflower oil and season with salt and pepper to taste.

Step three:
Place the pork sausages and the vegetarian sausages on separate oiled non-stick trays and brush each sausage with a little oil. (This will give three separate trays in the oven.)

Step four:
Lay the table with knives, forks, condiments, milk jug, sugar bowl, a jug of fresh orange juice and glasses. Fill the kettle and get the teapot or mugs ready.

Step five:
Countdown – set the cooker timer to 25 minutes.

Step six:
25 minutes left from serving time – put the hash browns in the oven (if using frozen check the manufacturer's cooking time and adjust accordingly). Open the beans and pour into a small saucepan and place on the hob (don't turn the heat on yet).

Step seven:
20 minutes left – place the sausages and veggie sausages in the oven. Get out a large non-stick frying pan and brush with a little sunflower oil and place on the hob (don't turn on the heat yet).

Step eight:
15 minutes left – put the mushrooms and tomatoes in the oven. While doing this turn the hash browns and the sausages and baste again if needed.

Step nine:
10 minutes left – place the vegetarian bacon under the grill and grill for 2 minutes on each side. Put on a warmed plate, cover with foil and put in the

Continued on next page

bottom of the grill to keep warm. Next grill the remaining bacon for 2–3 minutes on each side and keep warm as before.

Step ten:
5 minutes left – turn the heat on under the beans and cook until they bubble, then stir and turn the heat down to low.

Step eleven:
4 minutes left – turn the oven to low, make sure everything is cooked and turn if necessary. Put the bread in the toaster or under the grill and, when toasted, butter it and cut into triangular halves, arrange on a plate and cover with foil. Put the plate of toast on the bottom shelf of the oven or grill to keep warm. Put four large plates in the bottom of the oven or grill to warm.

Step twelve:
3 minutes left – put the heat on under the frying pan, brush with a little oil and crack the eggs into the pan. Cook on a medium heat until the eggs are set. Make the tea or coffee. Serve immediately (hopefully to a round of applause).

Continental breakfast

TIME TO PREPARE: 15 MINUTES
SERVES: 4 TO 6

Warm, lazy summer days call for a decadent continental breakfast that can be prepared and served in minutes. Just remember that all those delicious croissants and brioche can be surprisingly high in fats and calories. Leave the baking to the French and concentrate instead on preparing some steaming, aromatic freshly ground coffee and serving the breads with some homemade fruit spreads.

Ingredients

4 croissants or pain au chocolate
1 brioche loaf
1 French baguette
Pure fruit strawberry spread
    (see recipe on p. 342)
Pure fruit apricot spread
    (see recipe on p. 343)
1 large cantaloupe melon, 2 nectarines,
    2 peaches, small bunch of black grapes,
    small punnet of strawberries
A platter of continental cheeses
    including vegetarian brie, Edam
    or Gouda, cottage cheese, etc
A jug of freshly squeezed orange juice
Large cafetière of perfect French coffee
    (see below)

Health note

The whole breakfast provides carbohydrates, fibre, calcium, zinc, protein, vitamins A, B, C, iron and folate.

Method

Step one:
Pre-heat the oven to 150C/300F/gas mark 2.

Step two:
Put the croissants/pain au chocolat on to a large non-stick baking tray.

Step three:
Slice the brioche into 2″ (5cm) thick slices and place on the baking tray.

Continued on next page

Step four:
Slice the baguette diagonally into 2" (5cm) thick slices and place on the baking tray.

Step five:
Lay the table.

Step six:
Prepare a large platter or basket for the baked goods. Warm the platter and line with an attractive serviette.

Step seven:
Prepare a large platter of fresh fruit by slicing the melon in two, discard the seeds and slice each half into four. Halve the peaches and the nectarines and remove the stones. Hull the strawberries and leave the grapes in little bunches – arrange the fruit attractively on the platter.

Step eight:
Arrange your cheese selection on another platter or cheeseboard.

Step nine:
Prepare the coffee and leave to infuse (see below).

Step ten:
Place the croissants/pain au chocolate, brioche and baguette into the oven for 3– 4 minutes until warmed through but not dried out.

Method for perfect French coffee

Buy freshly roasted coffee or grind freshly roasted beans yourself. The type of coffee you use will depend upon your own personal preference, but true French coffee is made using darkly roasted beans.

Step one:
Warm the cafetière by filling it with hot water and then emptying it.

Step two:
Add the correct amount of coffee for the number of cups you wish to make, according to the instructions on the pack, and then add the correct amount of hot but not boiling water.

Step three:

Put the lid on the cafetière but do not push down the plunger. Leave to infuse for 4–5 minutes.

Step four:

When the coffee is ready, plunge (I always put the cafetière in the sink before pushing down the plunger to avoid accidents). Serve immediately to avoid a stewed taste.

To serve the breakfast

Serve the warmed baked goods and bread on a large platter/basket with little dishes of fruit spreads. Serve the fruit on another large platter and the cheese on a separate platter. Serve the coffee piping hot in the cafetière with a jug of warm milk and a bowl of brown sugar. You may also, like the French, wish to offer hot chocolate as well as coffee. Then simply let your family/guests help themselves.

Quick and healthy breakfasts

When you really are pushed for time it is still possible to prepare and eat a nutritious breakfast. Buy breads that have seeds and whole grains added as these are a useful source of nutrients. Listed below are ideas for breakfasts that can be prepared in less than 5 minutes.

QUICK HOT BREAKFASTS:
Organic beans on wholemeal toast
Poached or scrambled egg on granary toast
Bacon/vegetarian bacon and tomato sandwich
Edam or Gouda cheese and tomatoes on toast
Hot porridge oats with milk/soya milk, raisins and honey

QUICK COLD BREAKFASTS
Organic muesli with dried fruit, nuts and organic or fortified soya milk
Fresh fruit in season with organic yoghurt
Wholemeal or granary sandwich filled with low fat soft cheese and homemade fruit spread
Organic peanut butter and banana sandwich
Toasted wholemeal bagel topped with soft cheese and smoked salmon

4

LIGHT MEALS AND LUNCHES

Warming Lunches for Winter Days

Filled jacket potatoes

What could be more comforting on a cold winter's day than a steaming jacket potato, with its contrast of dark brown crispy skin and fluffy white potato, topped with a savoury filling?

JACKET POTATOES

TIME TO COOK: 1 HOUR
SERVES: 4

Ingredients

4 large baking potatoes

Health note

High in fibre and carbohydrates, low in fat and salt and a good source of vitamin C.

Method

Step one:
Pre-heat the oven to 200C/400F/gas mark 6.

Step two:
Scrub the jacket potatoes well and pat dry with kitchen roll. Prick the skins with a fork in three or four places. Place the potatoes in a baking dish and put into the oven.

Step three:
Cook for 1 hour until the skin is crispy and the inside is soft (test with a metal skewer to check – if not soft enough just cook for longer). Alternatively, if you want to go out for a couple of hours leaving the potatoes to cook slowly, simply cook on high for 20 minutes and then turn the oven down to 150C/300F/gas mark 2. You can then leave the potatoes to cook for up to 2 hours – you will get a very crunchy skin by cooking the potatoes long and slow.

Quick tip

You can cook the potatoes in the microwave to save time. If you prefer a crispy skin, part cook in the microwave on high for 5–7 minutes, and then simply finish cooking in a hot oven for the last 10–15 minutes.

TUNA AND SPICY BEAN MIX/CHEESY SPICY BEAN MIX TOPPING

SERVES: 4 (2 TUNA AND 2 CHEESE)
TIME TO PREPARE: 10 MINUTES
TIME TO COOK: 10 MINUTES

The bean mixture can be prepared in advance (without the tuna) and kept in the fridge for 2–3 days.

Ingredients

1 tablespoon (15 ml) sunflower oil
1 small red onion
1 small red or green chilli (or 2 teaspoons [10 ml] mild chilli powder)
2 cloves of garlic
16 oz (450 grams) tin butter beans
16 oz (450 grams) tin red kidney beans
8 oz (225 grams) fine green beans
6oz (175 grams) tin tuna in brine
   or water
2oz (50 grams) grated Cheddar cheese
Salt and freshly ground black pepper
   to taste

Health note

The tuna, cheese and beans all provide protein. Although the cheese is high in fat it provides a valuable source of calcium. Tuna is a good source of Omega 3 fatty acids which are thought to help prevent heart disease.

Method

Step one:
Trim the green beans, chop into 2" (5cm) pieces and cook in boiling water for 5-7 minutes until tender, drain and reserve.

Step two:
Drain the tinned butter beans and the kidney beans.

Step three:
Peel and finely chop the onion and garlic.

Step four:
Put a large frying pan on the hob over a medium heat and add the oil. When the oil is hot add the onions and garlic and cook over a low heat for 5 minutes until softened but not browned.

Continued on next page

Step five:
Remove the seeds from the chilli and chop finely (I always remove chilli seeds under cold, running water to avoid burns and irritation from the seeds). Add the chopped (or dried) chilli to the pan and cook for a further minute.

Step six:
Add the drained butter beans, kidney beans and green beans. Fry the bean mixture over a low heat for a further 5 minutes, mashing lightly with a fork to break up some but not all of the beans.

Step seven:
When the beans are cooked divide the mixture into two bowls.

Step eight:
For the tuna mix drain the tinned tuna and stir through the beans.

Step nine:
For the cheese mix stir the grated cheese through the beans.
Season with salt and black pepper to taste.

To serve

Split the cooked potatoes in half and top two of the potatoes with the tuna mix and two with the cheese mix. In addition to a potato topping this mixture can also be spread on a warmed tortilla.

Quick tip

You can save time by using a tin of mixed beans in spicy sauce or a tin of Mexican refried beans. Omit steps 1-7 and simply warm the beans through in a saucepan before adding the tuna or cheese at Step eight.

PRAWN CRUNCH/COTTAGE CHEESE AND HERB CRUNCH TOPPING

TIME TO PREPARE: 5 MINUTES
SERVES: 4 (2 PRAWN AND 2 COTTAGE CHEESE)

Ingredients

6 oz (175 grams) plain cottage cheese
6 oz (175 grams) cooked prawns
2 celery stalks
1 oz (25 grams) washed raw bean sprouts
1 large green pepper
1 large red pepper
2 spring onions
2 oz (50 grams) salted peanuts
2 tablespoons (30 ml) chopped chives
2 tablespoons (30 ml) finely chopped flat leaf parsley
2 tablespoons (30 ml) tofu mayonnaise (see recipe on p. 91)
Salt and freshly ground black pepper to taste

Health note

An excellent source of protein and calcium and low in fat and salt.

Method

Step one:
Chop the celery and the peppers into small dice. Top and tail the spring onions and chop finely.

Step two:
Break the peanuts into small pieces by putting them in a plastic bag and beating with a rolling pin.

Step three:
Snip the chives into small pieces and finely chop the parsley.

Step four:
Combine all the vegetables, herbs and nuts in a large mixing bowl and add a pinch of salt and freshly ground black pepper to taste.

Step five:
Divide the vegetable mixture between two bowls, add the prawns to one bowl and the cottage cheese to the other and stir thoroughly. Add the mayonnaise to the prawns and stir.

Continued on next page

Split the cooked potatoes in half and top two with the cheese mix and the remaining two with the prawn mix. In addition to a potato topping this mixture makes a healthy, low fat lunch when served with a crisp salad and some toasted pitta bread.

Quick tip

You can substitute low fat mayonnaise for the tofu mayonnaise to save time.

CREAMY CHICKEN/TOFU TIKKA TOPPING

SERVES: 4 (2 CHICKEN AND 2 TOFU)
TIME TO PREPARE: 5 MINUTES + 30 MINUTES MARINATING TIME
TIME TO COOK: 20 MINUTES

This mixture can be prepared the day before and marinated in the fridge overnight.

Ingredients

2 boneless, skinless chicken breasts
4 oz (110 grams) firm tofu
8 fl oz (250 ml) natural yoghurt
2 tablespoons (30 ml) tikka paste
2 tablespoons (30 ml) mango chutney
Salt and black pepper to taste

Health note

Chicken, tofu and yoghurt are a good source of protein, and are low in fat and salt.

Method

Step one:
Pour the yoghurt into a mixing bowl, add the tikka paste and the mango chutney and mix. Divide the mixture between two shallow baking dishes.

Step two:
Chop the chicken into 1" (2.5cm) pieces. Put the chopped chicken into one of the baking dishes and stir into the yoghurt mix. Cover the chicken mixture with foil and chill in the fridge for 30 minutes.

Step three:
Cut the tofu into 1″ (2.5cm) cubes and place in the remaining baking dish with the yoghurt mix – stir well until all the tofu is coated. Cover the tofu mix with foil and chill in the fridge for at least 30 minutes.

Step four:
Pre-heat the oven to 200C/400F/gas mark 6. Put the two foil covered dishes into the oven and cook for 20 minutes.

To serve

Split the cooked potatoes in half and top with the tikka mix. In addition to a potato topping this mixture can be served on its own with a crisp green salad, or used as a sandwich or pitta bread filling.

Made in a minute Pizzas

QUICK FRENCH BREAD PIZZA WITH MOZZARELLA CHEESE, GARLIC AND OLIVE TOPPING

TIME TO PREPARE: 5 MINUTES
TIME TO COOK: 5–7 MINUTES
SERVES: 4

This is an excellent recipe for using up stale French bread – it also works well with stale ciabatta bread.

Ingredients

1 wholemeal or granary baguette
4 fl oz (120 ml) pizza sauce
   (see recipe on p. 345)
4 oz (110 grams) vegetarian mozzarella
   cheese (this recipe works well with other
   cheeses such as Gruyère or Cheddar if preferred)
4 cloves garlic
2 oz (50 grams) black olives (stone removed)
2 teaspoons (10 ml) dried oregano

Health note

A good source of fibre and carbohydrates, protein and calcium.

Method

Step one:
Pre-heat the oven to 200C/400F/gas mark 6.

Step two:
Peel the garlic and chop three of the cloves finely, reserving one whole one. Chop the olives.

Step three:
Cut the baguette in half lengthways and then cut each half into two widthways, so that you end up with four long slices. Rub the cut side of each pizza with the whole garlic clove and then top each slice with a quarter of the pizza topping.

Step four:
Grate the cheese and mix with the garlic and the chopped olives. Put one quarter of the cheese mix on each pizza and sprinkle each with half a teaspoon of the oregano.

Step five:
Place the pizzas on a large non-stick baking tray and bake in the oven on 200C/400F/gas mark 6 for 5–7 minutes until the cheese is melted and bubbling. When cooked sprinkle each pizza with a little olive oil and a few more chopped olives.

To serve

Serve as a light lunch with a crisp salad or cut the pizzas into finger slices and serve as party food.

WHOLEWHEAT PITTA PIZZA WITH MELTED RED LEICESTER CHEESE, TOMATO AND GREEN PEPPER TOPPING

TIME TO PREPARE: 10 MINUTES
TIME TO COOK: 5 MINUTES
SERVES: 4

Wholemeal pitta bread makes a fast, healthy alternative to the usual oil and calorie-laden pizza base.

Ingredients

4 wholemeal pittas
4 tablespoons (60 ml) pizza sauce
 (see recipe on p. 345)
4 oz (110 grams) red Leicester cheese
2 large vine ripened tomatoes
2 large green peppers
Salt and black pepper to taste

Health note

The pitta provides fibre and carbohydrate; peppers and tomatoes are a good source of vitamin C; the cheese provides protein and calcium.

Method

Step one:
Line the grill pan with foil and preheat to a medium heat.

Step two:
Spread each pitta with a tablespoon (15 ml) of the pizza sauce.

Step three:
Chop the tomatoes into fine dice and sprinkle half the chopped tomato onto each pitta.

Continued on next page

Step four:
Grate the cheese and sprinkle one quarter over each pitta.

Step five:
De-seed the green peppers then slice them into thin lengthways strips. Place the strips of pepper in a criss cross pattern on top of the pittas.

Step six:
Place the pittas on the lined grill pan and cook under the grill for 5 minutes until the cheese is melted and bubbling.

To serve

Serve as a light lunch with salad or allow the pizzas to cool, cut each pitta into four and serve as party food.

Omelettes with a difference

The omelette must be the ultimate fast food, prepared and cooked in moments.

Health note

Eggs contain protein, calcium, iron and vitamins A, D and B12, which can be difficult to find in a vegetarian diet. Current health guidelines recommend we limit our intake of eggs to no more than four per week.

SPANISH OMELETTE

TIME TO PREPARE: 10 MINUTES
TIME TO COOK: 5 TO 10 MINUTES
SERVES: 4 (2 VEGGIE AND 2 NON VEGGIE)

The Spanish omelette is a savoury mix of eggs, meat, fish and vegetables and is an excellent way of using up leftovers. I usually use potatoes, peppers, onions and tomatoes, but you can include virtually any chopped, cooked vegetables such as courgettes, mushrooms, leeks, etc.

Ingredients

6 medium organic free range eggs
4 cooked new potatoes cut into 1" (2.5 cm) slices (you can use old potatoes cut into
    1" cubes and cooked)
1 red pepper
1 green pepper
1 medium red onion (or 2 chopped spring onions)
2 large, ripe tomatoes
3 oz (75 grams) cooked fish or meat (eg cooked prawns, spicy sausage, chopped ham
    or bacon – whatever you have to hand)
2 oz (50 grams) grated cheese
2 cooked vegetarian sausages
1 teaspoon (5 ml) paprika
2 tablespoons (30 ml) sunflower oil
Salt and freshly ground black pepper

Method

Step one:
Remove the grill pan and preheat the grill.

Continued on next page

Step two:
Make the vegetarian omelette first. De-seed the peppers and chop into small dice. Chop the tomatoes into small dice. Peel and finely chop the onion.

Step three:
Put a frying pan on the hob over a medium heat and add half the cooking oil.

Step four:
Add half the potatoes to the pan and cook gently for a minute or so until the potato has browned slightly, turn the potatoes over and cook for a further minute to brown the other side.

Step five:
Slice the vegetarian sausages into 1" (2.5cm) slices and add to the pan with half the tomatoes, peppers and onion. Sprinkle over half the paprika and black pepper to taste. Cook the vegetable mixture for 2 minutes, stirring gently to prevent sticking.

Step six:
Crack three of the eggs into a bowl and beat lightly with a fork, season with salt and pepper and add to the vegetable mixture in the pan. Cook for about 3 minutes until the underside of the omelette is set but the top is still runny.

Step seven:
Sprinkle the top of the omelette with the grated cheese and place the pan under the hot grill until the omelette has set and the cheese is melted and bubbling.

Step eight:
Using a palette knife, loosen the edges and gently slide the omelette onto a warmed plate. Serve immediately or cover with foil and keep warm while you cook the second meat/fish omelette.

Step eight:
For the meat/fish omelette wipe the pan clean with a paper towel and put back on the heat. Pour in 1 tablespoon (15 ml) of oil. Follow the same steps as for the vegetarian omelette, but add the cooked fish or meat at Step four and cook for an extra 3 minutes until the fish or meat is heated through and piping hot. Omit the cheese at Step seven and continue to Step eight.

Cut each omelette into four quarters, and serve each person with two quarters plus some crusty French bread and a side salad. This omelette can be served cold, cut into fingers or wedges as party or picnic food.

LUXURY FRESH HERB OMELETTE

TIME TO PREPARE: 5 MINUTES + 30 MINUTES STANDING TIME
TIME TO COOK: 5 TO 6 MINUTES
SERVES: 4

Use only fresh herbs to make this luxurious tasting omelette. This makes a light yet sophisticated summer lunch when served with a tomato and onion salad.

Ingredients

8 medium organic free range eggs
2 oz (50 grams) unsalted butter
1 tablespoon (15 ml) finely chopped chives
1 tablespoon (15 ml) finely chopped flat leaf parsley
2 tablespoons (30 ml) fresh single cream
Salt and freshly ground black pepper to taste

Method

Step one:
Crack the eggs into a mixing bowl and beat lightly with a fork.

Step two:
Add the chopped herbs, cover with cling film and allow the mixture to stand for 30 minutes to allow the flavour of the herbs to infuse the eggs.

Step three:
Place a large frying or omelette pan on the hob over a medium heat, add the butter and heat gently until melted. Swirl the butter around the sides and base of the pan to completely cover it, and tip the remainder of the melted butter and the cream into the eggs, then stir lightly to mix. Season with salt and pepper and add half the mixture to the pan. Cook on a low heat, tilting the pan from time to time and lifting the edges of the omelette with a palette knife to allow the uncooked egg to run onto the base of the pan.

Continued on next page

Step four:
When the underside of the omelette is lightly browned, gently lift one side with the palette knife and fold in half, whilst still in the pan, and continue to cook on a low heat. The finished omelette should be just firm, light golden on the outside and still slightly runny in the middle. Serve immediately or cover with foil to keep warm while you cook the remaining omelette.

To serve

Cut each omelette in half, garnish with some chopped herbs and serve with french fries or a fresh tomato salad (see recipe on p. 88). Non-vegetarians may like to add some chopped smoked salmon to the omelette at Step four.

MIXED MUSHROOM OMELETTE

TIME TO PREPARE: 5 MINUTES
TIME TO COOK: 3 TO 4 MINUTES
SERVES: 1

This omelette is the ideal emergency dish to serve at a dinner party where you have been advised that one of your guests is vegetarian at the moment of their arrival. It is rich and luxurious but can be prepared and cooked in moments.

Ingredients

3 large free range eggs
1 oz (25 grams) butter
2 tablespoons (30 ml) single cream
1 tablespoon (15 ml) cognac
2 oz (50 grams) mixed fresh mushrooms
2 tablespoons (30 ml) chopped fresh parsley
2 tablespoons (30 ml) chopped fresh chives
1 clove of garlic
2 teaspoons (10 ml) grated vegetarian cheese
Salt and black pepper to taste

Method

Step one:
Peel the garlic, crush and chop finely. Thinly slice the mushrooms. Finely chop the herbs.

Step two:
Crack the eggs into a mixing bowl and mix lightly with a fork. Stir in a tablespoon (15 ml) of cream, and season well with salt and pepper.

Step three:
Put a small frying pan on the hob over a medium heat and add the butter. Heat gently until the butter is melted but not browned, add the mushrooms, cognac, garlic and herbs and cook gently for 2 minutes. Stir the remaining tablespoon (15 ml) of cream into the mushroom mixture.

Step four:
Tip the mushroom mixture onto a warmed plate, wipe the pan with kitchen paper and add a little more butter to oil the pan.

Step five:
Tip the egg mixture into the pan and cook gently, tilting the pan and pulling back the edges of the omelette with a palette knife to allow the uncooked mixture access to the base of the pan. The omelette should take about 3 minutes to cook.

Step six:
When the omelette is cooked slide it gently onto a plate. Add the mushroom mixture to one half of the omelette only, then using a palette knife or fish slice, carefully fold the other half over on top of the mushrooms. Sprinkle with cheese and serve immediately.

To serve

Garnish with chopped fresh herbs and serve with sauté potatoes, seasonal vegetables or salad.

MEXICAN TORTILLA

TIME TO PREPARE: 10 MINUTES
TIME TO COOK: 10 MINUTES
SERVES: 4

This spicy Mexican omelette is quick and easy to prepare, and makes a tasty and interesting brunch or supper.

Ingredients

2 small packs lightly salted tortilla chips
1 tablespoon (15 ml) of sunflower oil
1 small onion
6 large organic free range eggs
Small bunch of flat leaf parsley
2 teaspoons (10 ml) paprika
1 teaspoon (5 ml) dried cumin
Salt and black pepper to taste

Method

Step one:
Remove the grill pan and preheat the grill on high.

Step two:
Put the cooking oil into a large frying pan and heat over a medium heat.

Step three:
Peel and finely chop the onion and add to the oil in the pan. Cook for one minute until softened but not browned.

Step four:
Chop the parsley and add to the pan, then add the spices and the tortilla chips. Stir and cook for a further minute.

Step five:
Crack the eggs into a mixing bowl, beat lightly and season with salt and freshly ground black pepper. Add the eggs to the pan and swirl around to ensure the pan is completely covered with the egg mixture.

Step six:
Cook over a low to medium heat for 3–4 minutes until the underside of the omelette is lightly browned. Lift the edges gently with a palette knife to ensure the underside is cooked.

Step seven:
Place the pan under the pre-heated grill until the top of the omelette is set and golden.

To serve

Cut into quarters and serve with some extra tortilla chips and some fresh tomato sauce or salsa (see p. 272 for recipe).

Quick tip

You can use commercially-made tomato sauce or salsa to save time.

Satisfying Soups

Soup is quick and easy to prepare and makes a cheap and nutritious lunch or starter. Try to use fresh vegetable stock where possible as the taste is infinitely better than stock cubes. If you don't have time to make fresh vegetable stock the next best thing is organic Swiss bouillon stock powder.

Health note

Soup is an excellent way of adding vegetables to our daily diet in an easy to digest way. Home-made vegetable stock contains much less salt than stock cubes.

VEGETABLE STOCK

TIME TO PREPARE: 10 MINUTES
TIME TO COOK: 20 TO 30 MINUTES
MAKES: 2 PINTS (1.2 LITRES)

Ingredients

2 pints (1.2 litres) water
1 large leek
1 small onion
2 carrots
2 sticks celery
1 bay leaf
2 tablespoons (30ml) chopped fresh parsley
Salt and black pepper to taste

Method

Step one:
Put a large, heavy based saucepan on the hob, add the water and turn the heat to high.

Step two:
Peel and finely chop the carrots and celery. Peel the leek and the onion and slice finely.

Step three:
Add the vegetables and herbs to the water and season with salt and pepper.

Step four:
Bring the stock to the boil and then turn down the heat. Simmer the stock gently for about 20 minutes. Allow to cool.

Step five:
Remove the vegetables with a slotted spoon or pour the stock into a container through a metal sieve. Cover and chill or freeze.

Quick tip

The stock will keep well in the fridge for 4–5 days or can be frozen for future use. I find that the best way to freeze stock is to place a freezer bag inside a rigid plastic container. Pour the amount of stock you wish to freeze into the bag, seal, label and freeze. When the stock is frozen you can then remove the container.

SPICY PARSNIP AND APPLE SOUP WITH TOASTED SEEDS

TIME TO PREPARE: 15 MINUTES
TIME TO COOK: 25 MINUTES
SERVES 4 TO 6

The toasted seeds add a satisfying crunch to this creamy soup.
Health note: Seeds are an excellent source of protein, vitamins and minerals.

Ingredients

1 oz (25g) unsalted butter
1 large white onion
1 lb (450 grams) parsnips
1 large cooking apple
1½ Pints (900 ml) vegetable stock
1 teaspoon (5 ml) ground cumin
1 teaspoon (5 ml) turmeric
Small bunch fresh coriander
10 fl oz (300 ml) organic milk
1 oz (25 grams) mixed seeds

Continued on next page

Method

Step one:
Peel and chop the onion finely. Chop the coriander. Peel the parsnips and the cooking apple and chop into small chunks.

Step two:
Place a large, heavy based saucepan on the hob over a low heat and add the butter. Heat gently until the butter is melted.

Step three:
Add the onion and the spices to the pan and fry gently for 5 minutes until softened but not browned. Do not allow the spices to burn as this will spoil the taste of the soup.

Step four:
Add the chopped parsnips, apple and coriander to the pan and stir.

Step five:
Add the vegetable stock to the pan and season with salt and black pepper. Bring to the boil and then reduce to a low to medium heat. Put the lid on and simmer the soup gently for about 20 minutes until all the vegetables are tender.

Step six:
Remove the pan from the heat and add the milk.

Step seven:
Blend the soup to a purée with a hand blender or in a food processor and return to the saucepan to keep warm.

Step eight:
To toast the seeds simply put them in a non-stick frying pan and toss them over a gentle heat for about 5 minutes – they will darken and develop a lovely nutty taste and a crunchy texture.

To serve

Serve warm, garnished with the toasted seeds and a little more chopped coriander.

SATURDAY MINESTRONE WITH WARM CIABATTA ROLLS

TIME TO PREPARE: 10 MINUTES
TIME TO COOK: 20 MINUTES
SERVES: 4 TO 6

I call this Saturday minestrone as I often prepare it on Saturday mornings before doing my weekly shop. It is an excellent way to use up leftover vegetables, beans and cheese and a welcome reward when I struggle home with all those carrier bags.

Ingredients

1 tablespoon (15 ml) olive oil
1 medium white onion
1 large leek (or 3 to 4 spring onions)
2 cloves garlic
2 sticks celery
2 carrots
1 red pepper
1 green pepper
¼ green cabbage (savoy is best but use what you have – spinach is good)
14oz (400 grams) tin cooked beans
14oz (400 grams) tin chopped tomatoes
2 tablespoons (30 ml) fresh basil
2 tablespoons (30 ml) fresh flat leaf parsley
1 teaspoon (5 ml) dried oregano
1 teaspoon (5 ml) smoked paprika
2 pints (1.2 litres) vegetable stock (see recipe on p. 64 or use stock cubes or powder)
2 oz (50 grams) grated cheese (parmesan works best, but use what you have)
2 oz (50 grams) small pasta shapes or vermicelli broken into small pieces (you can substitute the pasta with rice if you prefer)
Salt and black pepper to taste

Health note

This is a good all-rounder. The vegetables supply a mixture of vitamins and minerals, the pasta provides carbohydrates and fibre, the beans provide both fibre and protein, and the cheese provides yet more protein and calcium.

Method

Step one:
Peel and chop the onion and the garlic. Slice the leek thinly. Chop the carrots and the celery into small dice. De-seed the peppers and chop into small dice. Shred the cabbage thinly. Chop the herbs.

Continued on next page

Step two:
Place a large, heavy based saucepan on the hob over a medium heat and add the oil. Heat through until just hot.

Step three:
Add the onion, leek, paprika and garlic and cook for about 2 minutes until softened but not browned.

Step four:
Add the carrots, celery, peppers, herbs, beans, tinned tomatoes and the stock. Bring to the boil, add the pasta or rice, cover and simmer for at least 20 minutes.

Step five:
10 minutes before you wish to serve the soup add the cabbage and season with salt and black pepper to taste and cook for a further 10 minutes.

To serve

Spoon the soup into large soup bowls and sprinkle with the cheese. Serve with warmed ciabatta rolls.

RED LENTIL AND CARROT SOUP WITH SESAME SEED TOAST

TIME TO PREPARE: 10 MINUTES
TIME TO COOK: 20 MINUTES
SERVES: 4 TO 6

This appetising and nutritious soup is easy to prepare, and ready to serve in just 30 minutes. The freshly grated ginger and black pepper give it a bit of a zing without overwhelming the fresh natural flavours of the vegetables.

Ingredients for the soup

1 tablespoon (15 ml) sunflower oil
4 oz (110 grams) dried red lentils
Large Spanish onion
1lb (450grams) carrots
6 oz (175grams) potatoes
1" (2.5cm) fresh root ginger
1¾ pints (1 litre) vegetable stock
Large bay leaf
Salt and black pepper
Ingredients for the sesame seed toast:
4–6 thick slices wholemeal bread
2 medium organic free range eggs
1 oz (25 grams) sesame seeds
1 tablespoon (15 ml) soy sauce

Health note

High in fibre and protein, a rich source of vitamins and low in fat.

Method for the soup

Step one:
Pour the oil into a large saucepan and heat over a medium heat until the pan and oil are warm, but not hot.

Step two:
Peel and chop the onion finely and add to the pan, turn the heat to a low setting and cook for 5 minutes.

Step three:
While the onions are sweating, peel the potatoes and carrots and chop into small dice.

Step four:
Peel the ginger and grate it directly into the pan, add the potatoes and carrots to the pan and stir.

Step five:
Wash and rinse the lentils and add to the vegetables in the pan. Cook on a low heat for about 5 minutes, stirring from time to time to prevent sticking and burning.

Step six:
Add the stock and the bay leaf, and season with salt and freshly ground black pepper to taste. Bring to a gentle boil and then reduce the heat to a low simmer, cover and cook for a further 15 minutes until the vegetables are tender.

Step seven:
Remove the pan from the heat, remove and discard the bay leaf and blend the soup with a hand blender.

Method for the toast

Step one:
Line the grill tray with greased tin foil. Pre-heat the grill to high.

Step two:
Mix the sesame seeds with the soy sauce and put them on the grill tray, making sure they are evenly spaced. Grill the sesame seeds on high for 3–4 minutes.

Step three:
Put the eggs in a mixing bowl and beat lightly.

Step four:
Cut each slice of bread into four even triangles. Dip one side of each triangle into the egg mixture and then dip the same side into the toasted seeds.

Step five:
Place the bread seed side up on a well oiled baking tray and cook in the oven on 190C/375F/gas mark 5 for 8–10 minutes until golden and crispy.

To serve

Serve the soup with a swirl of crème fraiche, a sprinkle of chopped parsley and the sesame seed toast.

Quick tip

If you don't have time to make the sesame seed toast serve instead with some chunky granary bread with whole grains and seeds.

CHICKEN/SPRING VEGETABLE SOUP WITH WHOLEGRAIN GARLIC CROUTONS

TIME TO PREPARE: 15 MINUTES
TIME TO COOK: 20 MINUTES
SERVES: 4 TO 6 (2 TO 3 CHICKEN AND 2 TO 3 VEGGIE)

This is a beautifully clear soup full of fresh, young spring vegetables. The garlic croutons add a hint of spice and a satisfying crunch.

Ingredients

2 tablespoons (30 ml) light olive oil
4 oz (110 grams) shredded, cooked chicken
Large Spanish onion
2 baby leeks
4 baby carrots
2 baby courgettes
2 oz (50 grams) frozen petit pois
2 pints (1.2 litres) fresh vegetable stock
A bouquet garni made up of a sprig of curly parsley, rosemary, thyme, a bay leaf
    and a few basil leaves
Salt and black pepper to taste
For the croutons (see recipe on p. 348)

Health note

The chicken is high in protein and low in fat. This soup is rich in vitamins and antioxidants and low in fat.

Method

Step one:
Make the bouquet garni by tying the fresh herbs together with a piece of string.

Step two:
Put a large heavy based pan on the hob over a medium heat. Add the olive oil and warm through until just hot.

Step three:
Peel and finely chop the onion and add to the pan. Cook over a gentle heat for 5 minutes until the onion is soft and transparent.

Continued on next page

Step four:
Scrub the carrots and leave whole, cut the leeks and courgettes into thin slices.

Step five:
Add the stock to the pan and then add the peas, carrots, leeks, courgettes and the bouquet garni. Season the soup with salt and black pepper to taste.

Step six:
If you are making both the chicken and the vegetable soup you now need to divide the soup between two saucepans. Add the chicken to one saucepan only.

Step seven:
Bring the soup to a gentle boil, then lower the heat and cover. Simmer on a low heat for 10–15 minutes until the vegetables are tender (and if using chicken until the chicken is piping hot).

Step eight:
Remove the bouquet garni and serve warm with the garlic croutons.

To serve

Serve the soup in individual bowls garnished with a little fresh parsley and the croutons.

Quick tip

The garlic croutons can be made in advance and stored in an airtight polythene box for 2–3 days.

CHUNKY TOMATO AND BASIL SOUP WITH GNOCCHI

TIME TO PREPARE: 10 MINUTES
TIME TO COOK: 35 MINUTES
SERVES: 4 TO 6

This fresh tomato soup is full of flavour and colour. The addition of gnocchi to the soup makes for a hearty and filling lunch or light supper when served with crusty French bread.

Ingredients

2 pints (1.2 litres) fresh vegetable stock
2 lb (900 grams) ripe plum tomatoes
2 tablespoons (30 ml) olive oil
1 medium white onion
2 cloves garlic
3 tablespoons (45 ml) sun dried tomato purée
1 tablespoon (15 ml) basil pesto
1 teaspoon (5 ml) dried paprika
2 tablespoons (30 ml) fresh chopped basil
6 oz (175 grams) pack of fresh gnocchi
 (if you can't find fresh use dried, but cook it
 according to pack instructions before adding it to the soup)
Salt and pepper

Health note

Tomatoes contain vitamin C, antioxidants and betacarotene. The gnocchi provides fibre and carbohydrates.

Method

Step one:
Put a large heavy based saucepan on the hob over a medium heat and add the oil. Heat gently, but do not allow to burn.

Step two:
Peel and finely chop the onion and garlic and add to the pan. Stir and cook on a low heat for 5 minutes until the onion is soft and transparent.

Step three:
While the onions are cooking place the tomatoes in boiling water for 2–3 minutes. Remove the tomatoes from the hot water with a spoon, allow them to cool a little before peeling and then chop into chunky dice.

Continued on next page

Step four:
Add the chopped tomatoes, the tomato purée, the basil pesto and paprika to the pan. Stir through and simmer gently for 5 minutes until the mixture resembles a thick sauce.

Step five:
Add the stock, the fresh basil and the gnocchi to the pan and season well with salt and black pepper. Bring to the boil and simmer gently for 20 minutes.

To serve

Garnish the soup with a few torn basil leaves and serve with fresh, crusty French breach.

Quick tip

While fresh tomatoes produce the best results, you can use good quality tinned plum tomatoes in place of the fresh to save time.

Lazy Lunches
for Summer Days

New York Caesar salad/with chicken

TIME TO PREPARE: 10 MINUTES + 30 MINUTES CHILLING
SERVES: 4 (2 CHICKEN AND 2 VEGETARIAN)

Salads make a satisfying lunch or supper when served with lots of fresh, crusty bread. The key to producing the perfect salad dish is to ensure that each ingredient is fresh, ripe and of the finest quality. The classic Caesar salad, when well made, is one of my favourite salads. It is such a simple dish of crisp lettuce and freshly grated parmesan with its creamy dressing and crunchy croutons.

Ingredients

1 large romaine or cos lettuce
4 oz (110 grams) fresh vegetarian
   parmesan cheese, shaved into thin slices
2 cooked chicken breasts sliced into 2"
   (5cm) thick slices
4 fresh anchovy fillets
4 oz (110 grams) garlic croutons
   (see recipe on p. 349)
Caesar salad dressing:
6 tablespoons (90 ml) extra virgin olive oil
2 cloves garlic
1 teaspoon (5 ml) dry English mustard
4 tablespoons (60 ml) lemon juice
2 large free range egg yolks cooked until hard
Salt and black pepper to taste

Health note

The original recipe for Caesar dressing calls for raw egg yolks. Because of the risk of salmonella poisoning I use cooked egg yolks in my recipe. The dressing is rich and quite thick, like a mayonnaise. If you prefer a lighter dressing you can thin it down by adding a little water until you achieve the desired consistency, or use the recipe for tofu mayonnaise, (see recipe on p. 91) which also works well with this salad.

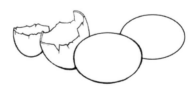

Method

Step one:
Wash and drain the lettuce and dry with kitchen paper. Chop the lettuce into 2" (5cm) pieces. Put in a bowl, cover with cling film and refrigerate for 30 minutes to allow the lettuce to crisp.

Step two:
While the lettuce is crisping get two salad bowls out. Press the garlic with the flat blade of a knife to release the oil and rub the base and sides of each bowl with a clove of garlic.

Step three:
Chop two of the anchovy fillets and add to the bowl you will be using for the chicken salad only. Mash the anchovy fillets against the sides and base of the bowl.

Step four:
Put the olive oil, lemon juice, cooked egg yolks, sauce, and mustard powder into a blender, and blend until you have a thick, creamy dressing. Add salt and black pepper to taste.

Step five:
When the lettuce is crisp, divide it between the two bowls and pour half the dressing over each.

Step six:
Add half the croutons and half the parmesan cheese to each bowl and toss the salad ingredients with the dressing.

Step seven:
Top the chicken Caesar salad with the cooked chicken and garnish with the remainder of the fresh anchovies.

Quick tip

The dressing and the croutons can be made up to one day in advance. Store the dressing in the fridge and the croutons in an airtight polythene box.

To serve

Serve immediately with some fresh crusty bread.

Greek salad

TIME TO PREPARE: 10 MINUTES
SERVES: 4

This classic Mediterranean salad is made with fat, ripe tomatoes, cool cucumber and salty feta cheese.

Ingredients

4 large ripe tomatoes
Small cucumber
2 oz (50 ml) kalamata olives
1 small red onion
1 green pepper
4 oz (110 grams) feta cheese
For the dressing:
4 tablespoons (60 ml) extra virgin olive oil
2 tablespoons (30 ml) lemon juice
1 clove garlic
½ teaspoon (2.5ml) dried oregano
Salt and black pepper

Health note

Olive oil is a mono-unsaturated fat. Mono-unsaturated fats are thought to help lower cholesterol levels, so reducing the likelihood of heart disease.

Method

Step one:
Cut each tomato into quarters and place in a large salad bowl.

Step two:
Peel the cucumber, cut in half lengthways and scoop out the seeds. Cut into 1" (2.5cm) cubes and add to the salad bowl

Step three:
Peel the onion, chop it in half and then slice thinly. Add the onion slices to the salad bowl.

Step four:
Drain the feta cheese and cut into 1" (2.5cm) cubes and add to the salad bowl.

Step five:
Peel and chop the garlic. Make the dressing by placing all the ingredients in a screw top jar or blender. Shake vigorously or blend to combine, season with salt and pepper to taste.

Step six:
Pour the dressing over the salad and toss the ingredients to combine.

Step seven:
De-seed the pepper and cut into thin strips, scatter the pepper over the salad and then scatter the olives on top.

To serve

Serve with crusty bread for a simple summer lunch, in individual dishes as a starter, or as an accompaniment to meat or fish dishes at a barbeque.

American chef's salad

TIME TO PREPARE: 10 MINUTES
SERVES: 4 (2 MEAT AND 2 VEGGIE)

This is another of those dishes that is handy for using up all the odds and
ends in the fridge. Use your imagination to create a hearty main course salad.

Ingredients

Large bowl of mixed salad leaves
4 spring onions or one red onion
2 peppers
8 cherry tomatoes
8 radishes
½ cucumber
4 oz (110 grams) cooked green beans
4 oz (110 grams) cooked new potatoes
4 oz (110 grams) cooked button mushrooms
2 large free range eggs
4 oz (110 grams) cheese
For the dressing:
5 fl oz (150 ml) low fat crème fraiche
1 clove garlic
2 tablespoons (30 ml) low fat or tofu
    mayonnaise (see recipe on p. 91)
½ teaspoon (2.5ml) English mustard powder
2 tablespoons (30 ml) extra virgin olive oil
1 tablespoon (15 ml) white wine vinegar
1 tablespoon (15 ml) lemon juice
Salt and pepper
For the meat version:
2 oz (50 grams) cooked bacon or ham
2 oz (50 grams) cooked chicken or turkey

Health note

Another good all-rounder. The vegetables
provide a mixture of vitamins, minerals
and antioxidants; the eggs and cheese
provide protein and calcium; the potatoes
provide fibre and carbohydrate. A tasty
low fat dressing replaces the usual high
fat, high calorie mayonnaise.

Method

Step one:
If you are making both the meat and vegetarian versions you will need two large salad bowls. Divide the salad leaves between the two bowls.

Step two:
Hard boil the eggs and allow them to cool under running water for a couple of minutes. Peel the eggs and cut into quarters.

Step three:
Peel and chop the onion finely, de-seed the peppers and dice, cut the tomatoes in half, slice the radishes thinly, cut the cucumber in half lengthways, remove the seeds and cut into 1" (2.5cm) dice, cut the green beans into 1" (2.5cm) lengths and slice the potatoes into 1" (2.5 cm) thick slices.

Step four:
Divide the salad vegetables between the two bowls.

Step five:
Make the dressing by putting all the ingredients into a screw top jar or blender and shaking vigorously or blending, to combine, season with salt and pepper to taste. Pour one half of the dressing over each bowl of salad.

Step six:
Chop the cooked ham, chicken, etc into 1" (2.5cm) dice and add to one of the bowls. Toss to combine and garnish with four egg quarters.

Step seven:
Cut the cheese into 1" (2.5cm) cubes and add to the vegetarian bowl. Toss to combine and garnish with four egg quarters.

To serve

Serve as a main course with some crusty bread, new potatoes or a jacket potato. There is no end to the combinations of ingredients you can use in this salad – try including chickpeas and add some mint to the dressing, or you could include chopped nuts and fruit – the secret is to use ingredients that combine well and not so many that they overwhelm the dish.

Salade Niçoise/salade du jardin

TIME TO PREPARE: 20 MINUTES
SERVES: 4 (2 FISH AND 2 VEGGIE)

This strongly flavoured salad from Nice typically uses fresh, local ingredients. The goat's cheese makes a tangy alternative to the tuna for the vegetarian version. The salad should be beautifully arranged on individual plates.

Ingredients

4 large ripe tomatoes
1 lb (450 grams) new potatoes
8 oz (225 grams) fine green beans
1 large red onion
½ large cucumber
1 cos or romaine lettuce
2 oz (50 grams) black pitted olives in olive oil
4 large free range eggs
4 anchovy fillets or a small tin of anchovies
2 tablespoons (30 ml) capers
2 lightly grilled tuna steaks or an 8 oz (225 grams) tin of tuna that has been drained
2 oz (50 grams) goat cheese (the round type)
For the dressing:
2 large cloves of garlic
1 teaspoon (5ml) of Dijon mustard
4 tablespoons (60 ml) extra virgin olive oil
2 tablespoons (30 ml) white wine vinegar
Juice of 1 lemon
1 tablespoon (15 ml) finely chopped fresh flat leaf parsley
1 tablespoon (15 ml) finely chopped fresh tarragon, or 1 teaspoon (5 ml) Herbes de Provence or mixed herbs
Salt and pepper

Health note

High in protein, low in fat, contains 'good' fats and vitamins A, B and C, fibre and carbohydrates.

Method

Step one:
Scrub the new potatoes, place them in a large saucepan and cover with boiling water. Boil for 20 minutes or until tender.

Step two:
Top and tail the green beans and place in a metal steamer. Cook over the

potatoes for 10 minutes until tender.

Step three:
8 minutes before the potatoes are cooked, put the eggs into the saucepan with the potatoes and boil for 8 minutes. When cooked, remove the eggs from the heat and run under a cold tap for 2–3 minutes, (this makes removing the shell easier). Leave to cool.

Step four:
Chop the lettuce leaves into 2" (5cm) chunks. Peel the cucumber, cut it in half lengthways and remove the seeds then cut it into 2" (5 cm) chunks. Cut each tomato into 8 wedges. Peel the onion and slice thinly.

Step five:
When the green beans are cooked drain them and rinse with cold water. When the potatoes are cooked drain them, rinse with cold water and cut in half lengthways.

Step six:
You will need four large plates. Line each plate with some lettuce and put a spoonful of the cucumber in the centre of each. Arrange the potato in a circle around the cucumber and then arrange the tomatoes in a circle around the potatoes.

Step seven:
Place the cooked or tinned tuna in the centre of two of the plates.

Step eight:
Slice the Goat's cheese into 1" (2.5 cm) rounds and arrange in the centre of the other two plates.

Step nine:
Arrange the green beans on the plates to form a criss-cross pattern, sprinkle each plate with the sliced red onion, the capers and a few of the olives.

Step ten:
Place all of the ingredients for the dressing into a screw top jar or blender and shake vigorously, or blend until combined, season with salt and pepper to taste. Pour the dressing carefully over the salad and serve immediately.

To serve

This has to be served with lots of warm, crusty French baguette.

Tonno et fagioli (tuna and white bean)/white bean and onion salad

TIME TO PREPARE: 10 MINUTES
SERVES: 4 (2 TUNA AND 2 VEGETARIAN)

This is another rustic, strongly flavoured salad that is perfect for eating out of doors on a warm sunny day. It also makes a punchy starter to serve before a light main course. The salad is most attractive when served in individual dishes.

Ingredients

6 oz (175 grams) tin tuna in oil
4 oz (110 grams) cooked butter beans
4 oz (110 grams) cooked cannellini beans
(tinned beans work perfectly well in this dish)
1 large red onion
2 little gem lettuces
4 tablespoons (60 ml) fresh chopped parsley (or 2 teaspoons [10 ml] of dried parsley)
2 lemons cut into wedges
For the dressing:
2 tablespoons (30 ml) white wine vinegar
6 tablespoons (90 ml) light olive oil
1 tablespoon (15 ml) lemon juice
1 teaspoon (5 ml) Dijon mustard
Salt and pepper to taste

Health note

High in protein, a source of 'good fats', iron, B vitamins, zinc and magnesium.

Method

Step one:
Break the leaves off the lettuce, leave them whole and arrange them on four shallow dishes.

Step two:
Drain the tuna and reserve the oil. Drain the beans and mix them together.

Step three:
Peel and thinly slice the onion.

Step four:
Mix half the beans with the tuna and divide the tuna mixture between two of the dishes, spooning it into the centre of the lettuce leaves. Spoon the remaining beans into the lettuce leaves on the remaining two dishes.

Step five:
Sprinkle each dish with some of the onion and the chopped parsley.

Step six:
Make the dressing by placing all the ingredients in a screw top jar or blender and shake vigorously, or blend, to combine.

Step seven:
Pour half the dressing over the vegetarian salads. Combine the reserved tuna oil with the remainder of the dressing and shake or blend to mix. Pour the tuna dressing over the tuna salads.

To serve

Garnish with lemon wedges and serve with fresh Italian bread such as focaccia or ciabatta.

Warm bacon/lentil and rice salad

TIME TO PREPARE: 15 MINUTES
TIME TO COOK: 40 MINUTES
SERVES: 4 (2 MEAT AND 2 VEGGIE)

This warm, savoury salad makes a tasty and filling winter lunch or light supper dish when salad vegetables are out of season.

Ingredients

16 oz (450 grams) cooked green lentils
   (tinned lentils work perfectly well
   in this dish)
8 oz (225 grams) brown rice
10 fl oz (300 ml) vegetable stock
   (see recipe on p. 64)
2 large red onions
2 large leeks
4 cloves garlic
4 oz (110 grams) chopped, cooked gammon
5 fl oz (150 ml) olive oil
4 tablespoons (60 ml) finely chopped fresh coriander
   (or use 2 teaspoons [10 ml] dried)
1 teaspoon (5 ml) each of paprika, cumin, ground ginger and garam masala
Salt and black pepper to taste

Health note

The mixture of lentils and rice creates a perfect protein. This dish is high in protein, fibre, iron and complex carbohydrates and low in fat.

Method

Step one:
Put the rice in a large saucepan and fill the pan two thirds full with boiling water. Add a teaspoon of salt and bring to the boil. Simmer gently for 30 minutes until the rice is tender.

Step two:
Put the oil in a large frying pan or wok and heat through until hot. Peel the onions, leeks and garlic and chop finely. Add the onions, garlic, leeks and spices to the pan. Cook over a low heat for 5 minutes until the onion has softened.

Step three:
When the rice is cooked, drain it thoroughly and add it to the frying pan. Add

the lentils, the chopped coriander and the stock, season with salt and pepper and stir through thoroughly.

Step four:
If making both the bacon and the vegetarian salad you will need to divide the mixture into two and pour one half into another pan. Add the chopped cooked bacon to one pan and stir. Cook both salads on a gentle heat for a further 10 minutes or until the stock has been absorbed.

 To serve

This salad is delicious served simply with a crisp, green salad.

Tomato and onion salad with vinaigrette dressing

TIME TO PREPARE: 10 MINUTES
SERVES: 4

Spanish onions are mild and sweet so are perfect for this recipe, or red onions make a colourful and tasty alternative.

Ingredients

4 large beefsteak tomatoes
1 large Spanish onion
1 large free range egg, hard boiled
A few fresh basil leaves
For the dressing:
6 tablespoons (90ml) extra virgin olive oil
2 tablespoons (30 ml) white wine vinegar
1 large clove garlic
1 teaspoon (5 ml) English mustard powder
Salt and black pepper to taste

Health note

The onion family contains an anticoagulant called cycloallin which helps to keep our hearts healthy. Onions also provide vitamins B and C, calcium, iron and potassium.

Method

Step one:
Slice the tomatoes thinly widthways. Discard the ends of the tomato.

Step two:
Peel the onion, leave it whole and slice it thinly. Carefully break each ring apart into separate rings. Tear the basil leaves and rub between your fingers to release the oil.

Step three:
Take four dinner plates and place a layer of tomatoes on each, then a layer of onions on top of the tomatoes and finish with another layer of tomatoes.

Step four:
Peel the egg and chop it finely. Sprinkle a little of the egg into the centre of each plate.

Step five:
Place all the ingredients for the dressing into a blender or screw top jar and blend thoroughly.

Step six:
Just before serving, pour the vinaigrette dressing over the salad and scatter with the basil leaves.

To serve

Serve with crusty French bread to mop up the juices.

Crunchy red cabbage and apple salad with walnut dressing

TIME TO PREPARE: 15 MINUTES
SERVES: 4

This vibrantly coloured salad with its rich, nutty dressing is a welcome addition to both the summer and winter table. As it keeps well, it is an ideal salad to serve at a barbeque or party.

Ingredients

1 small red cabbage
4 Cox's or Braeburn apples
4 oz (110 grams) shelled walnuts
Juice and zest of a lemon
For the dressing:
6 fl oz (175 ml) walnut oil
2 fl oz (50 ml) balsamic vinegar
2 fl oz (50 ml) apple juice
Salt and pepper to taste

Health note

Cabbage is rich in vitamin C, folic acid and antioxidants. Walnuts are a source of protein, Omega 3 fats, iron, magnesium and vitamin E.

Method

Step one:
Cut the cabbage in half and slice thinly. Place it in a large salad bowl.

Step two:
Core the apples. Cut them in half and slice thinly lengthways. Place them in the bowl with the cabbage and pour over the lemon juice. Mix thoroughly.

Step three:
Add the chopped walnuts and the lemon zest to the salad and mix thoroughly.

For the dressing:
Place all the ingredients for the dressing in a screw top jar or blender and shake vigorously or blend.

To serve

Just before serving pour the dressing over the salad and mix thoroughly.

Traditional coleslaw salad

TIME TO PREPARE: 15 TO 20 MINUTES

This mixture of crisp, raw vegetables with creamy mayonnaise is simple and inexpensive to prepare and far superior to the shop-bought versions.

Ingredients

1 small white cabbage
2 large Spanish onions
4 large carrots
2 tablespoons (30 ml) sesame seeds
1 tablespoon (15 ml) caraway seeds
For the tofu mayonnaise:
2 oz (50 grams) silken tofu
2 tablespoons (30 ml) sunflower oil
The zest and juice of half a lemon
The zest and juice of a half a lime
1 tablespoon (15 ml) honey
Salt and black pepper to taste

Health note

The mixture of raw cabbage, carrot and onions delivers a powerful mix of vitamins and minerals. The tofu mayonnaise contains protein, calcium and soy isoflavones, which are rich in the natural antioxidants that are thought to help us to fight cancer.

Method

Step one:
Cut the cabbage in half and slice thinly. Place in a large salad bowl.

Step two:
Peel the onion, cut it in half and slice thinly. Add to the cabbage.

Step three:
Roughly grate the carrots and add to the salad bowl.

Step four:
Add the seeds to the salad and mix the ingredients together thoroughly.

For the dressing:
Place all the ingredients in a blender or food processor and blend until smooth and creamy, season with salt and black pepper to taste.

To serve

Add the dressing to the vegetables and mix thoroughly. Cover and chill. This recipe makes a large quantity of salad which keeps well in the fridge for 2–3 days.

Creamy spinach and new potato salad

TIME TO PREPARE: 15 MINUTES
TIME TO COOK: 20 MINUTES
SERVES: 4 TO 6

This recipe is a lighter, more sophisticated version of the classic potato salad and is an ideal accompaniment to a summer barbeque or buffet table.

Ingredients

1 lb (450 grams) new potatoes
8 oz (225 grams) fresh spinach
4 large radishes
Large bunch fresh flat leaf parsley
Bunch spring onions
For the dressing:
¾ pint (450 ml) carton low fat crème fraiche
Large bunch fresh mint
Juice and zest of 1 lemon
Salt and pepper to taste

Health note

Potatoes are a good source of fibre and carbohydrates; also provide vitamins A, B and C, calcium, potassium and iron.

Method

Step one:
Scrub the potatoes and place in a pan of boiling, salted water. Boil rapidly for 20 minutes, or until tender, then rinse under the cold tap until cool.

Step two:
Top and tail the onions and chop finely. Top and tail the radishes and slice thinly.

Step three:
Slice the cooled potatoes in half lengthways.

Step four:
Layer one half of the spinach onto a serving plate, scatter half the chopped onion over the spinach then add a layer of the cooked potato. Add another layer of spinach, then another layer of potato. Sprinkle the top with the chopped parsley, the remainder of the onion and the radish slices.

For the dressing:
Retain a few mint leaves for garnish and chop the remainder very finely. Stir the mint into the crème fraiche with the zest and juice of the lemon. Add seasoning to taste and stir thoroughly to mix.

To serve

Just before serving spoon the dressing over the salad and garnish with some chopped mint leaves.

Mexican rice salad

TIME TO PREPARE: 10 MINUTES
TIME TO COOK: 30 MINUTES
MAKES A LARGE BOWL ENOUGH TO SERVE 4 TO 6 AS A MAIN COURSE
ACCOMPANIMENT OR AS A LIGHT LUNCH

This fragrant and spicy salad is equally delicious served warm or cold. Leftover rice salad makes a quick and tasty filling for stuffed peppers. You can omit the chillies if you prefer a less spicy salad or if cooking for children.

Ingredients

1 lb (450 grams) plum tomatoes
1 tablespoon (15 ml) olive oil
2 tablespoons (30 ml) tomato purée
12 oz (350 grams) wholegrain brown rice
1¾ pints (1 litre) vegetable stock
2 cloves garlic
Small bunch fresh, flat leaf parsley
Small bunch fresh coriander
1 medium red onion
2 red or green chillies de-seeded and finely chopped
4 oz (110 grams) frozen peas
4 oz (110 grams) frozen sweetcorn
4 oz (110 grams) carrots
1 small green pepper
1 small red pepper
Salt and pepper to taste

Health note

Wholegrain brown rice is an important source of fibre, iron, magnesium and vitamin B1. The mixture of rice and peas makes a perfect protein.

Method

Step one:
Pour the olive oil into a large, heavy based saucepan and heat over a medium heat.

Step two:
Peel the garlic and onion and chop finely. Add the garlic, onion and chillies to the oil in the pan and cook on a low heat for 2–3 minutes until softened.

Step three:
Add the rice to the pan and stir thoroughly. Add the stock to the pan and turn the heat to high, stirring frequently. When the liquid boils turn the heat to the lowest setting, then put the saucepan lid on and simmer for 25 minutes.

Step four:
Pre-heat the grill. Place the tomatoes under the pre-heated grill until the skin is charred and blackened. Allow the tomatoes to cool and then peel off the skin and discard it. Roughly chop the tomatoes.

Step five:
Cut the carrots into small dice. Chop the parsley and coriander. De-seed the peppers and chop into small dice.

Step six:
When the rice has been cooking for 15 minutes, remove the lid and check to ensure there is sufficient cooking liquid – if not top up with a little more stock or water. Add the tomatoes, peas, sweetcorn, peppers, carrots, herbs and tomato purée to the pan. Add seasoning to taste, stir thoroughly and put the lid back on. Cook for a further 10 minutes or until the rice is tender, all the liquid is absorbed and the vegetables are cooked but still crisp.

To serve

Serve as an accompaniment to a main meal, topped with a little sour cream and chives or, for a buffet, serve in a large salad bowl garnished with a little fresh coriander and some sliced tomatoes.

Spanish pasta salad

TIME TO PREPARE: 10 MINUTES
TIME TO COOK: 30 TO 35 MINUTES
SERVES: 6 TO 8 (3 TO 4 MEAT AND 3 TO 4 VEGGIE)

I first made this salad when on holiday with friends in Spain many years ago; there were lots of hungry mouths to feed and not much cash. This versatile dish can be served hot or cold and keeps well for several days in the fridge.

Ingredients

4 tablespoons (60 ml) olive oil
2 x 14 oz (400 grams) tins chopped tomatoes
1 lb (450 grams) pasta shapes
1 large onion
5 cloves garlic
4 large beefsteak tomatoes
2 green peppers
2 red peppers
4 oz (110 grams) pitted black olives
Bunch fresh basil
2 teaspoons (10 ml) dried oregano
1 teaspoon (5 ml) smoked paprika (or mild chilli powder)
4 vegetarian frankfurters or vegetarian sausages
4 oz (110 grams) Spanish sausage or 4 large pork sausages
Salt and pepper

Health note

The peppers and tomatoes are good sources of vitamin C. Tomatoes also contain lycopene, an antioxidant that is thought to combat cancer. The pasta provides fibre and carbohydrates for energy.

Method

Step one:
Pour the oil into a large heavy based saucepan and heat on a medium heat.

Step two:
Peel and finely chop the onion and garlic and add to the pan. Cook on a low heat for 5 minutes until golden.

Step three:
De-seed the peppers and chop into small dice. Place the tomatoes in boiling water for a couple of minutes (this makes them easier to peel). Peel and roughly chop the tomatoes and add them to the pan with the peppers, the olives and the paprika. Cook for a further 5 minutes over a low heat.

Step four:
Chop the basil and add it to the pan with the oregano and the tinned tomatoes, stir thoroughly and season to taste, bring to the boil and then simmer, uncovered, over a low heat for 20 minutes.

Step five:
While the sauce is cooking put the pasta into a pan of boiling, salted water and cook it for 12–15 minutes.

Step six:
While the pasta is cooking (separately) pre-cook the sausages and the veggie sausages, under the grill or in the oven for 10–15 minutes. If using veggie frankfurters or Spanish sausage these do not require pre-cooking.

Step seven:
When the pasta sauce has been cooking for 15 minutes pour half into another saucepan. Slice the Spanish or pre-cooked pork sausages into 1" (2.5 cm) slices and add to one pan. Slice the veggie frankfurters or pre-cooked veggie sausages into 1" (2.5 cm) slices and add to the other pan. Return both pans to the heat and cook on medium for a further 5–10 minutes. The sausages should be heated through and piping hot, and the sauce should be rich and thick.

Step eight:
Drain the pasta. Mix one half of the pasta with the meat dish and the other half with the veggie dish. Stir thoroughly.

To serve

Serve hot as a main course with garlic bread or French bread. Alternatively, allow to cool and store in the fridge until needed as a salad.

Jewelled summer tabbouleh

TIME TO PREPARE: 30 MINUTES
SERVES: 4 AS A MAIN COURSE

This combination of crisp summer vegetables, aromatic herbs and bulgur wheat makes a mouth-watering light lunch or snack. It can also be served as an accompaniment to main course dishes such as the Turkey and Mediterranean kebabs (see recipe on p. 159) or as part of a buffet, as it is quick and inexpensive to prepare. Be warned, this salad grows and grows so make sure you use a large saucepan, or at the point of mixing tip the ingredients into a large bowl to mix thoroughly.

Ingredients

8 oz (250 grams) cracked bulgur wheat
24 fl oz (700 ml) water
7 oz (200 grams) fine green beans
7 oz (200 grams) frozen peas
2 medium red onions
12 oz (350 grams) tomatoes
1 lemon
1 lime
3 tablespoons (45 ml) chopped flat leaf parsley
3 tablespoons (45 ml) chopped fresh mint
3 tablespoons (45 ml) chopped fresh coriander
Salt and black pepper to taste
Honey and mustard dressing:
3 tablespoons (45 ml) extra virgin olive oil
2 tablespoons (30 ml) white wine vinegar
1 teaspoon (5 ml) honey
1 tablespoon (15 ml) dark French mustard
Salt and black pepper to taste

Health note

The combination of the bulgur wheat and peas creates a perfect protein and provides fibre, calcium, iron, vitamins B and C and folate.

Method

Step one:
Put the bulgur wheat into a large saucepan with the water and bring to the boil stirring occasionally. When the water has boiled, reduce the heat to a low simmer and cook for a further 8–10 minutes, until the bulgur wheat has absorbed all the water and the grains appear fluffy and separated.

Step two:
While the bulgur wheat is cooking, top and tail the green beans and cut into one inch (2.5cm) pieces. Place the beans in a saucepan with the frozen peas and enough water to cover them. Bring to the boil then reduce the heat to medium and cook for a further 2–3 minutes. When cooked, drain the vegetables.

Step three:
Peel the red onions and chop them finely. Chop the tomatoes into small dice. Grate the rind of the lemon and the lime into a small dish and squeeze the juice into a separate dish. Roughly chop the herbs.

Step four:
Add the cooked vegetables, the red onions, tomatoes, herbs, lemon and lime zest and juice to the bulgur wheat and stir thoroughly with a fork to mix. Add a little salt and pepper to taste.

Honey and mustard dressing:
Place all of the ingredients in a screw top jar or blender and shake or blend well to mix.

To serve

While the bulgur wheat salad is still warm pour over the dressing and mix thoroughly. If serving as a main course serve on a bed of crisp, green lettuce leaves and garnish with quartered hard boiled eggs and some fresh chopped mint or parsley.

Sandwiches, Rolls and Wraps

Sandwiches are the ultimate convenience food, easy to prepare and portable, ideal for packed lunches, picnics and parties. The following recipes prove that fast food can be both tasty and nutritious. In addition to the traditional baguette and crusty bloomer, try experimenting with ciabatta and focaccia bread, soda bread, pitta bread, tortilla wraps, and bagels. With so much to choose from, lunch need never consist of a boring, soggy sandwich again!

Filled baguettes

TIME TO PREPARE: 5 MINUTES
TIME TO COOK: 5 MINUTES
SERVES: 4 (2 MEAT AND 2 VEGGIE)

BRIE WITH BACON/VEGGIE BACON AND AVOCADO

The luxurious mixture of ingredients in this sandwich is quite rich, so no butter or margarine is necessary. It is best eaten soon after it is made as the avocado blackens when exposed to the air.

Ingredients

1 large French baguette
2 tablespoons (30 ml) extra virgin olive oil
2 oz (50 grams) fresh spinach
2 ripe avocados
2 slices lean, unsmoked back bacon
2 slices veggie bacon
4 oz (110 grams) vegetarian brie
4 tomatoes
Salt and pepper to taste

Health note

Although quite high in calories, this recipe is bursting with healthy ingredients such as spinach and tomatoes. The avocados are also a good source of monounsaturated fats.

Method

Step one:
Grill the bacon and the veggie bacon (separately) for about 5 minutes until the rind is crisp and brown.

Step two:
Cut the baguette lengthways into four equal portions then cut each portion almost, but not quite, in half widthways.

Step three:
Drizzle half a tablespoon (7.5 ml) of the olive oil onto the cut side of each baguette.

Step four:
Layer the spinach along the baguette.

Step five:
Peel the avocado, cut it in half and remove the stone. Cut each half into thin slices and layer them along the baguette.

Step six:
Slice the tomatoes and layer the tomato slices on top of the avocado. Season the vegetables with salt and freshly ground black pepper.

Step seven:
Slice the brie into eight thin slices lengthways and place two slices along the length of each baguette.

Step eight:
Place a bacon rasher on two of the baguettes and a veggie bacon rasher on the remaining two baguettes. Season to taste and serve immediately.

BRIE WITH GREEN APPLE AND BLACK GRAPES

TIME TO PREPARE: 5 MINUTES
SERVES: 4

The creaminess of the Brie is offset by the sharp tang of crisp green apple and the juicy black grapes. If you are not intending to serve this sandwich immediately, dip the apple slices in lemon juice to prevent them browning.

Ingredients

1 large wholemeal or granary baguette
2 granny smith apples
4 oz (110 grams) black grapes
4 oz (110 grams) vegetarian brie
4 tablespoons (60 ml) mango chutney

Health note

Apples and grapes are an important source of potassium, fibre and vitamin C. Brie is lower in calories than some hard cheeses such as Cheddar and is a good source of protein and calcium.

Method

Step one:
Cut the baguette into four equal portions lengthways, then cut each portion almost, but not quite, in half widthways.

Step two:
Spread each baguette with a tablespoon of the mango chutney.

Continued on next page

Step three:
Core the apples and slice thinly lengthways. Layer one quarter of the apple slices along each baguette.

Step four:
Slice the brie into eight thin slices. Layer two slices of brie lengthways onto each baguette.

Step five:
Wash the grapes, cut in half and remove any pips. Layer one quarter of the grapes along each baguette. Season to taste and serve immediately.

HUMMUS, ROCKET, ROASTED VEGETABLES AND CRACKED, BLACK PEPPER

TIME TO PREPARE: 10 MINUTES
TIME TO COOK: 20 MINUTES
SERVES: 4

This sandwich is a family favourite. The garlicky hummus and peppery rocket are perfectly complemented by the sweet roasted vegetables.

Ingredients

1 large French baguette
4 oz (110 grams) hummus (p. 275)
1 small bag fresh rocket
  (about 2 handfuls)
3 peppers (one each of green, red and yellow)
1 small red onion
2 tablespoons (30 ml) olive oil
Salt and freshly ground black pepper to taste

Health note

Hummus is made from chickpeas which contain protein, fibre, iron and zinc. The roasted vegetables are high in vitamin C.

Method

Step one:
De-seed the peppers and cut into quarters. Peel the onion and slice thinly. Put the vegetables into an oven dish and drizzle over the olive oil, season with salt and pepper to taste. Cover the dish with foil and cook in the oven at 190C/375F/gas mark 5 for 20 minutes. Allow to cool.

Step two:
Cut the baguette into four equal portions lengthways, then cut each portion almost, but not quite, in half widthways. Spread each baguette with 2 tablespoons (30 ml) of hummus.

Step three:
Layer the rocket along the baguette.

Step four:
Layer the roasted vegetables on top of the rocket and season well with salt and freshly ground black pepper.

To serve

Serve immediately or wrap in foil and chill until needed.

Quick tip

It is worth preparing a large tray of roasted vegetables and storing them in an airtight container in the fridge. They keep well for 2-3 days and can be used cold in sandwiches and salads.

HOT STEAK/VEGGIE STEAK BAGUETTE WITH WATERCRESS SALAD AND HERB BUTTER

TIME TO PREPARE: 10 MINUTES
TIME TO COOK: 10 TO 15 MINUTES
SERVES: 4 (2 MEAT AND 2 VEGGIE)

This savoury sandwich is a more sophisticated option at barbeques than the ubiquitous burger.

Ingredients

1 large French baguette
2 very thinly sliced lean sirloin steaks
2 Quorn peppered steaks
1 tablespoon (15 ml) olive oil
2 oz (50 grams) butter
Large bag watercress
Small bunch chives
Small bunch flat leaf parsley
1 clove garlic
Salt and pepper

Health note

Both the steak and the Quorn are high in protein and a good source of iron. Also they contain vitamins B, C and D. Choosing the leaner cuts of meat will reduce the fat content of this dish.

Method

Step one:
Pre-heat the grill to high. Brush the steaks on both sides with a little olive oil and season with salt and pepper. Grill the vegetarian steaks first for 7 minutes on each side. Remove from the grill, wrap in foil and keep warm in the oven. Grill the sirloin steaks for 5 minutes each side (or longer if you like them well cooked).

Step two:
Cut the baguette into four equal portions lengthways, then cut each portion almost, but not quite, in half widthways.

Step three:
Chop the chives and the parsley, peel and chop the garlic and mash the herbs and garlic into the butter. Butter the baguettes with the herb butter.

Step four:
Spread a layer of watercress along each baguette. Place a cooked sirloin steak in two of the baguettes and a cooked Quorn steak in the remaining two baguettes, season with salt, black pepper and add a little mustard if liked. Serve immediately.

Stuffed pittas

Crispy pitta breads, filled with a healthy, tasty salad, make a nutritious lunch and are ideal for lunch boxes and picnics. When making pittas that are to be eaten later, I always pack the salad in an airtight, polythene tub and wrap the toasted pitta bread in greaseproof paper. I fill them just before serving to avoid the pitta bread going soggy.

Health note

Wholewheat pittas are a good source of carbohydrates and fibre.

CHEDDAR AND APPLE SALAD

TIME TO PREPARE: 10 MINUTES
SERVES: 4

This mixture is very popular with children as it is quite sweet and crunchy.

Ingredients

4 wholemeal pitta breads
4 oz (110 grams) Cheddar cheese
2 apples
Juice and zest of 1 lemon
1 small iceberg lettuce
1 red onion
½ cucumber
4 tablespoons (60 ml) tofu mayonnaise
   (see recipe on p. 91) or use low fat mayonnaise
Salt and pepper to taste

Health note

The cheese is high in protein and calcium; apples contain fibre, vitamin C and potassium.

Method

Step one:
Pre-heat the grill. Toast the pitta breads for one minute.
Allow the pittas to cool and then carefully, using a thin, sharp knife, make a lengthways slit in each pitta.

Step two:
Thinly slice the lettuce, peel the cucumber, cut it in half lengthways and remove the seeds, chop into small dice. Peel and chop the onion into small dice. Grate the apples and the cheese.

Step three:
Put the vegetables, the cheese and the apples into a large mixing bowl with the lemon juice, zest and mayonnaise, stir thoroughly to mix and season to taste.

To serve

Stuff each pitta with some of the salad mixture and serve with the remaining salad.

TUNA AND SWEETCORN MIX

TIME TO PREPARE: 10 MINUTES
SERVES: 4

Ingredients

4 wholemeal pitta breads
1 small iceberg lettuce
2 tomatoes
4 spring onions
6 oz (175 grams) tin of tuna in brine
4 oz (110 grams) tin of sweetcorn
4 tablespoons (60 ml) tofu mayonnaise (see recipe on p. 91) or use low fat mayonnaise
Salt and pepper to taste

Health note

This popular mix is high in protein, low in fat and the tuna is a good source of Omega 3 fatty acids. The sweetcorn is a good source of fibre.

Method

Step one:
Pre-heat the grill. Toast the pitta breads for one minute.
Allow the pittas to cool and then carefully, using a thin, sharp knife, make a lengthways slit in each pitta.

Step two:
Slice the lettuce finely. Chop the tomatoes into small dice. Drain the tuna and the sweetcorn. Top and tail the spring onions and chop them finely.

Continued on next page

Step three:
Place the vegetables and the tuna into a large mixing bowl with the mayonnaise, stir thoroughly and season with salt and pepper to taste.

To serve

Spoon one quarter of the mixture into each pitta bread and serve with a crisp green salad.

HUMMUS AND SWEET PEPPER SALAD

TIME TO PREPARE: 10 MINUTES
SERVES: 4

Ingredients

4 wholemeal pitta breads
7 oz (200 grams) hummus (see recipe p. 275)
1 red pepper and 1 yellow pepper
1 small iceberg lettuce
1 small red onion
8 cherry tomatoes
Juice and zest of ½ lemon
Small bag mixed salad leaves (to serve)
Salt and pepper

Method

Step one:
Pre-heat the grill. Toast the pitta breads for one minute.
Allow the pittas to cool and then carefully, using a thin, sharp knife, make a lengthways slit in each pitta.

Step two:
Slice the lettuce thinly. De-seed the peppers and chop into small dice. Peel the onion and chop finely. Chop the tomatoes into small dice.

Step three:
Combine all the vegetables with the lemon zest and juice and the hummus in a large mixing bowl and season to taste.

Spoon one quarter of the mixture into each pitta. Serve on a bed of mixed salad leaves and garnish with quarters of lemon.

LAMB/AUBERGINE KEFTEDES

TIME TO PREPARE: 15 MINUTES
TIME TO COOK: 45 MINUTES
SERVES: 8 (4 LAMB AND 4 VEGGIE)

These savoury little meat/veggie balls are delicious when served as a pitta filling with some chopped, crisp lettuce and the mint and yoghurt dressing. They also make a tasty party snack.

Ingredients for the lamb keftedes

Ingredients for the Lamb keftedes:
1 lb (450 grams) lean, finely minced lamb
2 tablespoons (30 ml) olive oil
Large clove garlic
1 medium onion
1 tablespoon (15 ml) balsamic vinegar
1 teaspoon (5 ml) cumin
1 teaspoon (5 ml) oregano
1 tablespoon (15 ml) each of chopped fresh coriander and mint
   (or 1 teaspoon [5 ml] each of dried)
1 medium free range egg
4 oz (110 grams) breadcrumbs
To serve:
1 small iceberg lettuce
1 red onion
4 fl oz (120 ml) carton natural yoghurt
1 tablespoon (15 ml) chopped fresh mint
Salt and pepper to taste

Health note

The lamb is high in protein; fat is kept to a minimum by baking rather than the traditional deep frying.

Method

Step one:
Pre-heat the oven to 190C/375F/gas mark 5.

Continued on next page

Step two:
Pour the oil into a frying pan and warm through on a medium heat. Peel and chop the onion and the garlic and add to the frying pan with the cumin. Cook over a low heat for 5 minutes until the onion is softened and golden.

Step three:
Tip the onion mixture into a large mixing bowl and add all the other ingredients, mix thoroughly, and season with salt and freshly ground black pepper. Form the mixture into 16 2" (5 cm) balls.

Step four:
Line a shallow oven tray with greased foil and place the keftedes on the baking sheet. Cook at the top of the preheated oven for 15–20 minutes until cooked through.

Ingredients for the aubergine keftedes

4 medium sized aubergines
1 medium sized onion
4 oz (110 grams) self raising flour
4 tablespoons (60 ml) each of finely chopped fresh mint and parsley
   (Use 2 teaspoons [10 ml] each of dried if fresh are unavailable)
4 tablespoons (60 ml) olive oil
1 teaspoon (5 ml) each of cumin, cinnamon and mild chilli powder
Salt and black pepper to taste

Method

Step one:
Pre-heat the oven to 190C/375F/gas mark 5. Cut the aubergines in half and remove the seeds. Brush the cut halves with the olive oil and place on a greased baking sheet. Bake in the oven for 30 minutes until softened. Scoop the cooked flesh into a large mixing bowl and mash.

Step two:
Add the remaining ingredients to the bowl and mix thoroughly. Form the mixture into sixteen 2" (5 cm) balls.

Step three:
Line a shallow oven tray with greased foil. Place the keftedes onto the baking sheet and bake in the oven for 15 minutes.

To serve

Put four of the lamb keftedes into four of the pitta breads and four of the aubergine keftedes into the remaining four pitta breads. Add some chopped lettuce, and sliced red onion and season to taste. Mix the chopped mint into the natural yoghurt and spoon over the keftedes.

Quick tip

The keftedes can be made in advance. They will keep in the fridge for 2–3 days.

Wraps

Tortilla wraps can be made of either cornflour or wheatflour. I find the wheatflour tortillas are softer and nicer for making sandwich wraps.

Health note

High in fibre, calcium, iron, B vitamins and folate.

CHICKEN CAESAR/VEGETARIAN CAESAR

TIME TO PREPARE: 10 MINUTES
SERVES: 4 (2 CHICKEN AND 2 VEGGIE)

Ingredients

4 large tortilla wraps
1 small romaine or cos lettuce
3 oz (75 grams) shaved parmesan cheese
2 oz (50 grams) garlic croutons
  (recipe on p. 349)
4 tablespoons (60 ml) Caesar salad dressing
  (recipe on p. 76)
1 cooked chicken breast (skin removed)
Salt and freshly ground black pepper to taste

Health note

The chicken and cheese are high in protein.

Method

Step one:
Thinly slice the lettuce.

Step two:
Slice the chicken breast into ½" (1.25cm) slices.

Step three:
Spread each tortilla with a tablespoon (15 ml) mayonnaise; top this with a layer of lettuce, some croutons and 1 tablespoon (15 ml) of the parmesan cheese.

Step four:
Top two of the wraps with the chicken.

Step five:
Season the wraps with salt and freshly ground black pepper. To roll them, first fold over about 2″ (5 cm) at the top and the bottom, then, holding the folded parts down, carefully roll up so that you end up with a Swiss roll shape that is closed at each end. With a sharp knife cut each wrap in half.

To serve

Serve immediately with a little mixed salad and some extra croutons. To pack, tightly roll each half tortilla in greaseproof paper and then foil, and refrigerate until needed. These wraps should be eaten the day they are made.

PEPPERED BEEF/PEPPERED BEEF-STYLE SLICES – WITH HORSERADISH MAYONNAISE

TIME TO PREPARE: 10 MINUTES
SERVES: 4 (2 BEEF AND 2 VEGGIE)

Ingredients

4 large tortilla wraps
1 small iceberg lettuce
1 green pepper
2 thick slices peppered beef
4 slices Quorn peppered beef-style slices
4 tablespoons (60 ml) tofu mayonnaise
    (see recipe on p. 91) or use low fat mayonnaise
2 tablespoons (30 ml) horseradish
1 teaspoon (5ml) English mustard powder
Salt and freshly ground black pepper to taste

Health note

The beef and the Quorn are high in protein and a good source of iron, vitamins B and D and Omega 3 fatty

Method

Step one:
Cut the lettuce into thin slices. De-seed the pepper and cut into thin slices.

Step two:
Mix the mayonnaise, the horseradish and the mustard powder in a small bowl and season with salt and pepper.

Continued on next page

Step three:
Spread the tortilla wraps with 1 tablespoon of the mayonnaise mixture.

Step four:
Place a thin layer of lettuce and some chopped pepper onto each wrap.

Step five:
Place a slice of beef on two of the wraps and two Quorn beef-style slices on each of the remaining wraps.

Step six:
Season the wraps with salt and freshly ground black pepper. To roll them, first fold over about 2" (5 cm) at the top and the bottom, then, holding the folded parts down, carefully roll up so that you end up with a Swiss roll shape that is closed at each end. With a sharp knife cut each wrap in half.

To serve

Serve the wraps with a mixed salad and 1 teaspoon of the remaining mayonnaise mixture. If not using immediately, wrap tightly in greaseproof paper and then in foil and store in the fridge until needed. These wraps should be eaten the day they are made.

SALAMI/QUORN SMOKY HAM-STYLE SLICES WITH ROASTED VEGETABLE SALAD

TIME TO PREPARE: 15 MINUTES
TIME TO COOK: 20 MINUTES
SERVES: 4 (2 MEAT AND 2 VEGGIE)

The large range of commercially prepared vegetarian deli slices makes it much easier to prepare quick and tasty lunches for vegetarians.

Ingredients

4 large tortilla wraps
4 slices salami
4 slices Quorn smoky ham-style slices
1 red pepper, 1 green pepper,
1 courgette, 1 red onion
1 tablespoon (15 ml) olive oil

Health note

Salami is a high fat meat but as it is strongly flavoured, only a small amount is needed.

1 small iceberg lettuce
4 tablespoons (60 ml) low fat cream cheese
4 large green olives
Dash of chilli sauce
Salt and pepper to taste

Method

Step one:
Cut the lettuce into thin slices.

Step two:
Cut the peppers and courgettes into finger-length, ½" (1.25 cm) wide strips. Peel the onion and slice thinly. Put the vegetables into an oven dish and drizzle over the olive oil, then season with salt and pepper to taste. Cook the vegetables for 20 minutes on 190C/375F/gas mark 5. Allow to cool.

Step three:
Chop the olives and mix into the cream cheese. Add a dash of chilli sauce and mix.

Step four:
Spread a little of the cream cheese mix onto each wrap, add a thin layer of lettuce and a layer of roasted vegetables. Top two of the wraps with two slices of salami each and top the remaining wraps with two slices of ham-style each.

Step five:
Season the wraps with salt and freshly ground black pepper. To roll them first fold over about 2" (5 cm) at the top and the bottom, then, holding the folded parts down, carefully roll up so that you end up with a Swiss roll shape that is closed at each end. With a sharp knife cut each wrap in half.

To serve

Serve immediately with a mixed salad, some tomato salsa (see recipe on p. 272) and the remainder of the cream cheese mixture. If not serving immediately wrap tightly in greaseproof paper and then in foil and refrigerate until needed. These are best eaten the day they are made.

SMOKED SALMON/CREAM CHEESE WITH SUN DRIED TOMATO AND PIMENTO SALAD

TIME TO PREPARE: 10 MINUTES
SERVES: 4 (2 FISH AND 2 VEGGIE)

Ingredients

4 large tortilla wraps
4 oz (110 grams) cream cheese
4 oz (110 grams) jar sun dried tomatoes in oil
2 oz (50 grams) jar pimentos in oil
2 large slices smoked salmon
Small iceberg lettuce
1 lemon
Salt and black pepper to taste

Method

Step one:
Drain the tomatoes and the pimentos and chop them finely. Mix the tomatoes and pimentos into the cheese and season with salt and freshly ground black pepper.

Step two:
Spread one quarter of the cheese mixture onto each wrap.

Step three:
Place a slice of smoked salmon down the centre of two of the wraps.

Step four:
Season the wraps with salt and freshly ground black pepper. To roll them, first fold over about 2" (5 cm) at the top and the bottom, then, holding the folded parts down, carefully roll up so that you end up with a Swiss roll shape that is closed at each end. Cut each wrap into 2 "(5 cm) slices.

Step five:
Cut the lettuce into thin slices. Cut the lemon into four wedges.

To serve

Place a layer of lettuce on four plates. Arrange the wraps, cut side up so that the cheese and the salmon are showing, and serve garnished with the lemon wedges. Serve immediately.

Rolls

CHILLI HOT DOGS/VEGETARIAN CHILLI DOGS

TIME TO PREPARE: 10 MINUTES
TIME TO COOK: 10 MINUTES
SERVES: 4 (2 MEAT AND 2 VEGGIE)

The classic hot dog recipe is updated with a sweet and sour tomato sauce.

Ingredients

4 hot dog rolls
2 tablespoons (30 ml) sunflower oil
1 large Spanish onion
1 clove garlic
2 frankfurter sausages
2 vegetarian frankfurters
7 oz (200 grams) tin chopped tomatoes
1 teaspoon (5 ml) each of paprika and English mustard powder
1 tablespoon (15 ml) each of chilli sauce, tomato purée, white wine vinegar
2 teaspoons (10 ml) brown sugar

Health note

Veggie hot dogs are much lower in fat than the meat version.

Method

Step one:
Peel the onion and cut in half. Chop one half finely and slice the other half into ½″ (1.25 cm) slices. Peel and chop the garlic.

Step two:
Pour half the oil into a heavy based frying pan and add the garlic, the paprika, the mustard powder and the chopped onions. Cook over a medium heat for 3 minutes until the onion is softened.

Step three:
Add the chopped tomatoes, the tomato purée, the vinegar, the chilli sauce and the sugar to the onion mixture and stir well. Cook for a further 5 minutes, stirring frequently.

Step four:
Brush the frankfurters and the veggie frankfurters with the remainder of the

Continued on next page

oil. Grill separately under a hot grill, turning frequently, for about 4-5 minutes until they are cooked through and piping hot.

Step five:
Make a slit in each of the hot dog rolls (don't cut them through completely). Place a layer of sliced, raw onions along each roll. Then place a cooked frankfurter into each roll. Spoon 2 tablespoons (30 ml) of the tomato sauce on top of the frankfurters.

To serve

Wrap in a napkin and serve immediately.

CHILLIED SALAMI HERO/CHILLIED VEGGIE HERO

TIME TO PREPARE: 10 MINUTES
SERVES: 4 (2 MEAT AND 2 VEGGIE)

A hero is a long, submarine shaped, soft roll popular in the USA and now becoming known here.

Ingredients

4 wholemeal or granary torpedo rolls
2 tablespoons (30 ml) olive oil
2 teaspoons (10 ml) chilli sauce
2 ripe avocados
Juice of 1 lemon
4 slices salami
4 slices Quorn deli-style bacon
4 oz (110 grams) Edam or Gouda cheese
To serve:
1 bag mixed lettuce leaves
1 small punnet cherry tomatoes
Salt and freshly ground black pepper to taste

Health note

The wholemeal rolls are a good source of fibre and carbohydrates. The cheese and the Quorn are high in protein.

Method

Step one:
Slice the rolls lengthways almost, but not quite, in half. Drizzle ½ tablespoon (7.5 ml) of the olive oil and 1 teaspoon (5 ml) of the chilli sauce over the cut side of each roll.

Step two:
Peel the avocados, cut in half and remove the stone and then cut into thin slices. Dip the slices of avocado into the lemon juice. Slice the cheese into eight slices.

Step three:
Place a layer of avocado along each roll and top with two cheese slices per roll. Place two slices of salami into two rolls and two slices of Quorn deli-style bacon into the remaining two rolls then season with salt and pepper to taste.

To serve

Scatter the salad leaves over four plates. Cut each filled roll in half and place on top of the lettuce. Garnish with the cherry tomatoes. Serve immediately.

MOZZARELLA, BASIL AND TOMATO ON OLIVE FOCACCIA BREAD

TIME TO PREPARE: 5 MINUTES
SERVES: 4

This is a good sandwich to take on a picnic as it actually tastes better when the flavours have had the opportunity to develop and mingle.

Ingredients

4 soft olive focaccia rolls
4 tablespoons (60 ml) extra virgin olive oil
8 oz (225 grams) vegetarian mozzarella
Bunch fresh basil
4 large beef steak tomatoes
Salt and pepper to taste

Health note

Mozzarella is a high protein, medium fat cheese. Extra virgin olive oil is a good fat.

Method

Step one:
Slice each roll almost, but not quite, in half widthways.

Step two:
Open out the rolls and drizzle ½ tablespoon olive oil over the cut sides of each roll.

Step three
Slice the tomatoes thinly. Place a layer of tomatoes on each roll. Top the tomatoes with fresh basil leaves.

Step four:
Drain the mozzarella and slice into thin rounds. Place a layer of mozzarella on top of the tomatoes and basil, and season with salt and pepper.

Step five:
Place some more basil leaves on top of the mozzarella and then layer the remainder of the tomatoes on top of the basil. Season again.

To serve

If not serving immediately, pack in foil and refrigerate until needed. These are best eaten the day they are made.

Sandwiches

MATURE CHEDDAR CHEESE WITH QUICK APPLE CHUTNEY

TIME TO PREPARE: 10 MINUTES FOR THE SANDWICH
TIME TO COOK: 1 HOUR FOR THE CHUTNEY
SERVES: 4

The chutney can be prepared in advance and stored in the fridge for up to two weeks.

Ingredients

8 thick slices of wholemeal or granary
   bread from a fresh crusty loaf
4 oz (110 grams) mature vegetarian cheddar
For the chutney:
2 large Bramley cooking apples
1 onion
2 fl oz (50 ml) cider vinegar
2 oz (50 grams) brown sugar
1 tablespoon (15 ml) each raisins and sultanas
1 tablespoon (15 ml) grated orange rind
1 teaspoon (5 ml) each nutmeg and cinnamon
Salt and pepper to taste

Health note

The wholemeal bread provides fibre and carbohydrate and the cheese is high in protein and calcium.

Method

Step one:
Peel, core and roughly chop the apples. Peel and roughly chop the onion.

Step two:
Place the apple and onion in a large, heavy based saucepan with all the other ingredients for the chutney. Cook over a medium heat, stirring frequently until the mixture boils, then turn down the heat to the lowest setting, cover and simmer for 45 minutes.

Step three
Remove the lid, stir and cook uncovered for a further 10 minutes until the chutney is thickened and any excess liquid has been absorbed. Allow to cool and pour into sterilised jars or an airtight container and store in the fridge for up to two weeks.

FOR THE SANDWICH:

Method

Step one:
Grate the cheese.

Step two:
Spread each slice of bread with 1 tablespoon (15 ml) chutney then sprinkle the cheese onto four of the slices, top with the remaining four slices of bread.

To serve

These are nice served with a little salad garnish and some coleslaw (see recipe p. 91). If not serving immediately wrap in greaseproof paper, then foil and refrigerate until needed. These are best eaten the same day they are made.

Quick tip

The apple chutney also complements cold meat or cheese in salads and sandwiches.

SPICED EGG AND TOMATO

PREPARATION: 10 MINUTES
SERVES: 4

You can omit the spices if preferred or if making for children.

Ingredients

8 thick slices wholemeal or granary bread
4 medium free range eggs, hard boiled
4 ripe tomatoes
4 tablespoons (60 ml) tofu mayonnaise
  (see recipe on p. 91) or use
  low fat mayonnaise
2 oz (50 grams) Cheddar cheese
4 spring onions
1 teaspoon (5ml) garam masala
To serve: Small bag of rocket, punnet of
  mustard and cress and some thinly
  sliced radishes.

Health note

The wholemeal bread is a good source of fibre and carbohydrates. Try to use granary or seeded breads to increase the level of seeds and grains in your diet as these are a valuable source of nutrients.

Method

Step one:
Peel the eggs and place in a large mixing bowl. Mash lightly with a fork until thick and lumpy.

Step two:
Chop the tomatoes into small dice. Top and tail the spring onions and chop finely. Grate the cheese.

Step three:
Add the tomatoes, the mayonnaise, the cheese, the onions and the garam masala to the mixing bowl and stir well.

Step four:
Place one quarter of the mixture onto four of the bread slices, season well with salt and pepper and then cover with the remaining bread slices.

To serve

Cut each sandwich into four triangles and serve on a bed of rocket and mustard and cress and garnish with the radishes. These are best eaten the same day they are made.

TRADITIONAL CLUB/VEGETARIAN CLUB SANDWICH

TIME TO PREPARE: 15 MINUTES
SERVES: 4 (2 MEAT AND 2 VEGGIE)

The traditional club sandwich is lightly toasted and consists of three layers of bread with various fillings. It is best eaten immediately it is made.

Ingredients

12 medium slices wholemeal bread
2 oz (50 grams) vegetarian sunflower spread
2 oz (50 grams) cooked and shredded chicken breast
2 oz (50 grams) cooked Quorn lemon and black pepper bites
2 ripe tomatoes
½ cucumber
4 tablespoons (60 ml) tofu mayonnaise (see recipe on p. 91) or low fat mayonnaise
2 medium free range eggs, hard boiled
4 cocktail gherkins
Salt and pepper

Health note

High in fibre and protein and low in fat.

Method

Step one:
Toast the bread and leave to cool. When cool spread each slice thinly with a little sunflower spread.

Step two:
Slice the tomatoes thinly. Peel the cucumber and slice thinly. Peel the eggs, chop roughly and mix with 1 tablespoon (15 ml) mayonnaise. Chop the gherkins roughly and add to the egg, season with salt and pepper to taste.

Step three:
Take four dinner plates and place a slice of buttered toast, butter side up on each plate. Divide the chicken between two slices of toast and the Quorn between the other two, then top this with half the tomato and half the cucumber and season to taste.

Step four:
Take another four slices of buttered toast and put them, butter side down, on top of the chicken and vegetables. Spread the top of each sandwich with

mayonnaise. Next spread one quarter of the egg mixture onto each sandwich and top this with the remainder of the tomatoes and cucumber.

Step five:
Take the remaining four slices of buttered toast and lay them butter side down on top of the sandwich.

To serve

Cut each sandwich into four triangles and secure by placing a cocktail stick through the middle of each sandwich. Spike a slice of cucumber onto the top of the cocktail stick and do warn guests/children to remove the stick before consuming. Serve immediately.

CLASSIC BACON, LETTUCE AND TOMATO (BLT)/VEGETARIAN BLT

TIME TO PREPARE: 5 MINUTES
TIME TO COOK: 5 MINUTES
SERVES: 4 (2 BACON AND 2 VEGGIE)

Who can resist the classic BLT? Vegetarian bacon has improved enormously over the past couple of years and can be confidently included in this popular recipe.

Ingredients

8 thick slices wholemeal bread
2 tablespoons (30 ml) vegetarian
   sunflower spread
4 slices lean, unsmoked bacon
4 slices veggie bacon
1 small iceberg lettuce
4 ripe tomatoes
Salt and pepper
Tomato ketchup or mustard

Health note

I use unsmoked bacon as there is evidence that links smoked food to stomach cancer.

Method for the sandwich

Step one:
Spread each slice of bread with sunflower spread.

Continued on next page

Step two:
Thinly slice the lettuce and the tomatoes.

Step three:
Grill the bacon and the veggie bacon separately for 3–5 minutes until the rind is crisp and golden.

Step four:
Place a layer of lettuce on four of the bread slices and top with a layer of tomato, season with salt and pepper. Place two slices of bacon on top of the tomato on two of the bread slices and two slices of veggie bacon on the remaining two bread slices. If liked spread the remaining four slices of bread with a little tomato ketchup or mustard to taste. Place the remaining four bread slices on top of the bacon to complete the sandwich.

To serve

Cut each sandwich in half diagonally and serve with the remainder of the lettuce and some sliced tomatoes.

PEANUT BUTTER AND BANANA

TIME TO PREPARE: 5 MINUTES
SERVES: 4

This sandwich must be eaten immediately it is made or the banana will blacken. If you want to pack this for later, you will need to take along the separate ingredients (banana still in skin) and assemble just before eating.

Ingredients

8 thick slices wholemeal or granary bread
4 tablespoons (60 ml) smooth
   peanut butter
2 large bananas
2 granny smith apples
Juice of lemon

Health note

The peanut butter is a good source of protein; bananas contain magnesium, potassium, vitamin B6 and fibre, and are a superb energy booster.

Method

Step one:
Spread ½ tablespoon (7.5 ml) of peanut butter over each slice of bread.

Step two:
Peel the bananas and slice into ½" (1.25cm) slices. Dip the banana slices in the lemon juice.

Step three:
Core the apples, slice thinly and dip the slices in the lemon juice

Step four:
Place a layer of banana and a layer of apple on four of the bread slices and top with the remaining four bread slices.

To serve

Cut each sandwich into four triangles and serve immediately.

SMOOTH PATÉ/VEGETABLE PATÉ WITH RED ONION MARMALADE

TIME TO PREPARE: 10 MINUTES
TIME TO COOK: ONE HOUR FOR THE MARMALADE
SERVES: 4 (2 MEAT AND 2 VEGGIE)

The red onion marmalade can be made in advance and stored in the fridge for up two weeks.

Ingredients

8 slices thick wholemeal or granary bread
1 small cos or romaine lettuce
½ cucumber
2 ripe tomatoes
2 oz (50 grams) smooth liver paté
2 oz (50 grams) vegetarian smooth paté
For the marmalade:
2 tablespoons (30 ml) olive oil
1 lb (450 grams) red onions
2 tablespoons (30 ml) red wine vinegar
6 tablespoons (90 ml) red wine
1 tablespoon (15 ml) brown sugar
1 teaspoon (5 ml) allspice
Salt and pepper

Health note

Meat paté is generally high in fat and should be eaten sparingly. Its vegetarian counterpart is usually much lower in fat.

Method

For the marmalade:
Step one:
Peel the onions and slice them thinly. Put them in a heavy based saucepan with the olive oil and the allspice, and cook them over a low heat for about 15 minutes until softened.

Step two:
Add the red wine, red wine vinegar and sugar to the pan and gently bring to the boil, stirring frequently. Turn the heat down to medium, cover the pan and simmer gently for a further 15 minutes.

Step three:
Remove the pan lid, turn the heat down to the lowest setting and simmer the marmalade for a further 30 minutes. When cooked, season with salt and

pepper and allow to cool. Store in sterilised jars or an airtight container in the fridge.

For the sandwiches:
Step one:
Thinly slice the lettuce and tomatoes. Peel the cucumber and slice thinly.

Step two:
Spread the meat paté onto two slices of bread and the vegetarian paté onto another two slices of bread.

Step three:
Place a layer of cucumber on top of the paté and then top this with a layer of tomato. Next, place 2 tablespoons red onion marmalade onto each sandwich and top this with some lettuce. Season the sandwich with salt and pepper and then top with the remainder of the bread slices.

To serve

Cut each sandwich into four triangles and serve immediately with a salad garnish and a dollop of the red onion marmalade. If not serving immediately, wrap the sandwiches, uncut, in greaseproof paper then in foil and store in the fridge until needed. This sandwich is best served the day it is made.

Quick tip

The red onion marmalade is also good with sausages, chicken and pork and makes a good ploughman's lunch when served with cheese.

5

FAMILY FAVOURITE
MAIN COURSES

Poultry

Somerset chicken/savoury pie

TIME TO PREPARE: 15 MINUTES
TIME TO COOK: 25-30 MINUTES
SERVES: 4 (2 CHICKEN AND 2 VEGGIE)

Tender chicken or Quorn chunks in a savoury sauce bursting with vegetables and topped with a crisp, flaky pastry make these pies a real winner.

Ingredients

2 free range chicken breasts, skin
    and bone removed
2 Quorn chicken-style fillets, defrosted
2 tablespoons (30 ml) olive oil
2 bouquet garnis made of bay leaf, sprig
    of parsley and a sprig of thyme
1 pint (600 ml) dry Somerset cider
6 stalks celery
2 large leeks
2 medium sized onions
4 oz (110 grams) baby corn
4 oz (110 grams) fine green beans
2 carrots
1 pint (600 ml) organic milk
2 oz (50 grams) butter
2 oz (50 grams) plain flour
1 lb (450 grams) frozen puff pastry, defrosted
1 egg lightly beaten
Salt and freshly ground black pepper

Health note

High in fibre and protein, low in fat, rich in vitamins and antioxidants

Method

Step one:
Place the chicken breasts in a saucepan with half the cider and a bouquet garni and poach over a medium heat for 15 minutes until cooked through and tender. Remove from the heat and allow to cool.

Step two:
Peel the onions and slice thinly, scrub the carrots and chop into small dice, trim the celery and leeks, wash them thoroughly. Slice the celery and leeks in half lengthways and then into thin slices widthways. Cut the sweetcorn and green beans into ½" (1 cm) lengths.

Step three:
Pour the oil onto a large saucepan and warm it through over a medium heat. When hot add the onions and fry gently for 5 minutes. Add the carrots, sweetcorn, green beans, cider and bouquet garni, season well with salt and black pepper and cook for a further 5 minutes.

Step four:
Cut the cooked chicken into bite sized chunks, discard the cooking liquid. Cut the Quorn fillets into bite sized chunks using a different knife.

Step five:
Take two casserole or oven-proof dishes big enough to serve two each; add the cooked chicken to one dish and Quorn fillets to the other. Drain vegetables, reserving the cooking liquid, and the add half the vegetables to each dish and stir well. Discard the bouquet garni and return the cooking liquid to the hob. Bring to the boil and cook on a rapid boil until the liquid has reduced to about 4 tablespoons (60 ml).

Step six:
Put a medium sized saucepan on the hob over a low heat and add butter; heat gently until melted, then add the leeks and cook for 5 minutes. Stir in the flour, then gradually whisk in the milk and reduced vegetable stock and add some salt and freshly ground black pepper. Cook the sauce over a gentle heat for 5 minutes. Pre-heat the oven to 200C/400F/gas mark 6.

Step seven:
Pour half the sauce into each casserole dish and stir well. Divide the pastry in two and roll out each half until thin and big enough to cover your casserole dish. Gather up the pastry trimmings and roll into a sausage shape. Then roll out until you have a long flat strip. Dampen the edge of the casserole dishes and press a strip of pastry all the way around the edge of the dishes to form a lip. Then brush the strips of pastry with a little beaten egg. Add a pastry lid to each and brush the top with a little beaten egg. Place the pies on a baking sheet and bake in the top of the oven for about 20 minutes until the pastry is risen and golden.

To serve

Nice served straight from the dish with some mashed sweet potato and a green vegetable such as broccoli.

Quick tip

Use a carton of fresh white sauce or cheese sauce to save time.

Roast chicken dinner/Mum's Sunday veggie roast

TIME TO PREPARE: 30 MINUTES
TIME TO COOK: 30 MINUTES
SERVES 4 (2 CHICKEN AND 2 VEGGIE)

This recipe is for two chicken and two vegetarian dinners, but you can alter the number of chicken breasts/Quorn fillets to suit your requirements, or, if you prefer, you can roast a whole chicken or turkey – just adjust the cooking time accordingly. The process looks long and complicated, but if you follow the step by step instructions you can have an appetizing and healthy roast dinner on the table in one hour from start to finish.

Health note

High in protein, fibre, vitamins and minerals – plus huge comfort food factor!

Countdown

Begin by preheating the oven to 200C/400F/gas mark 6. Prepare the root vegetables (see below). Make the gravy, the stuffing and the batter mixture as shown below. Prepare a green vegetable such as broccoli, Savoy cabbage or Brussels sprouts.

Set the oven timer to 30 minutes
30 minutes from serving:
Put the prepared root vegetables into the pre-heated oven. Prepare the chicken and Quorn as shown below.
20 minutes to go:
Put the prepared chicken and the Quorn into the oven. Put the stuffing balls in the tray with the root vegetables, baste the vegetables with a little oil. Put the oiled Yorkshire pudding tin in the oven to heat up.
15 minutes to go:
Add the Yorkshire pudding batter to the hot tin and put into the oven. Put a pan of water on to boil for the green vegetables. Lay the table.
5 minutes to go:
Warm the chicken gravy and the remainder of the vegetable gravy in a saucepan or in the microwave. Remove the foil from the chicken and check that it is cooked by piercing with a skewer or fork, if the juice runs clear it is cooked. Remove from the oven and keep warm. Add the green vegetables to the boiling water

ROAST CHICKEN/QUORN

Ingredients

2 large chicken breasts with skin removed
4 Quorn chicken-style fillets
1 tablespoon (15 ml) olive oil
¼ pint (150 ml) vegetarian gravy
Salt and pepper
4 tablespoons (60 ml) fresh mixed herbs including parsley, sage, rosemary and thyme
(or 2 teaspoons [10 ml] dried mixed herbs)

Method

The Chicken
Step one:
Brush each chicken breast with olive oil and sprinkle on 2 tablespoons (30 ml) fresh herbs (or 1 teaspoon [5 ml] of dried) and season with salt and pepper. Put in a non-stick roasting dish, cover with foil and cook in the pre-heated oven for 20–25 minutes until the chicken is cooked but still moist.

Step two:
Remove the foil for the last 10 minutes of cooking to allow the chicken to brown.

The Quorn
Put the Quorn fillets into a shallow roasting dish and add 2 tablespoons (30 ml) fresh herbs (or 1 teaspoon [5 ml] dried herbs) and ¼ pint (150 ml) of vegetarian gravy. Cover with foil and cook in the oven for 20 minutes.

VEGETABLE GRAVY

Ingredients

1 tablespoon (15 ml) olive oil
1 medium onion chopped finely
2 sticks celery chopped finely
1 tablespoon (15 ml) cornflour made to a paste with cold water
1 bay leaf
½ pint (300 ml) vegetable stock
1 tablespoon (15 ml) yeast extract
1 tablespoon (15 ml) dry sherry (optional)
Salt and pepper to taste

Continued on next page

Method

Step one:
Pour the oil into a small saucepan and warm over a medium heat. Add the chopped onion and celery to the oil and cook for 5 minutes until the vegetables are soft.

Step two:
Add the cornflour paste to the pan and stir to mix. Stir in the vegetable stock a little at a time until the gravy thickens and then add the sherry and the yeast extract. Add the bay leaf, and salt and pepper to taste.

Step three:
Cook for five minutes, remove from heat, discard the bay leaf, and sieve or blend with a hand blender.

CHICKEN GRAVY

Ingredients

1 tablespoon (15 ml) fat and the juices from the dish in which the chicken has been cooked
½ pint (300 ml) chicken or vegetable stock
1 tablespoon (15 ml) cornflour made to a paste with cold water
1 bay leaf
1 tablespoon (15 ml) dry sherry (optional)
Salt and pepper to taste

Method

Step one:
Pour the fat and juices from the chicken into a small saucepan and heat through on a medium heat.

Step two:
Add the cornflour and stir rapidly, then add the stock a little at a time until the gravy thickens, then add the bay leaf and the sherry. Season with salt and pepper to taste.

Step three:
Cook over a low heat for 5 minutes, remove the bay leaf and sieve or blend with a hand blender.

ROASTED ROOT VEGETABLES

Ingredients

4 tablespoons (60 ml) olive oil
1 tablespoon (15 ml) each chopped fresh rosemary, flat leaf parsley and thyme
 (use ½ teaspoon each of dried herbs if fresh is unavailable)
Salt and pepper to taste
4 large Maris Piper or roasting potatoes
2 large sweet potatoes
2 large parsnips
4 carrots

Method

Step one:
Put a large pan of salted water on to boil. Pre-heat the oven to
200C/400F/gas mark 6. Put a large non-stick roasting dish into the oven.

Step two:
Peel the root vegetables and cut into large chunks. Place the vegetables in
the boiling water, turn down the heat and cook for 5 minutes.

Step three:
Put the olive oil in the baking dish and heat until smoking hot. Drain the root
vegetables and add the herbs and seasoning. Put the lid back on the pan and
shake the potatoes vigorously. Put the root vegetables into the roasting tin
and cook on the same high heat for 20–30 minutes, turning halfway through
cooking, until crispy and browned.

HERB and APPLE STUFFING

Ingredients

4 oz (110 grams) wholemeal breadcrumbs
1 oz (25 grams) butter
1 medium free range egg, beaten
1 medium onion chopped finely
1 large Bramley cooking apple, peeled, cored and coarsely grated
Zest of 1 lemon and 1 tablespoon (15 ml) of the juice
1 tablespoon (15 ml) each fresh chopped parsley, thyme and rosemary
   (use ½ teaspoon each of dried herbs if fresh are unavailable)
Salt and black pepper to taste

Method

Step one:
Put the butter into a medium sized saucepan and melt over a low heat.

Step two:
 Add the onion and cook for about 5 minutes until it is soft but not browned. Remove from the heat.

Step three:
Add the breadcrumbs and stir thoroughly to ensure they are all coated with the butter.

Step four:
Add the remaining ingredients, stir thoroughly and allow the mixture to cool.

Step five:
When cool, form the stuffing into eight even-sized balls. Cook in the same roasting tray with the roasted vegetables for about 20 minutes on 200C/400F/gas mark 6 until a golden, crispy brown.

YORKSHIRE PUDDING

This recipe makes eight individual Yorkshire puddings using a minced pie tin, or four individual puddings using a Yorkshire pudding tin.

3 oz (75 grams) plain white flour
1 medium free range egg
5 fl oz (150 ml) skimmed milk
Salt and white pepper
2 tablespoons (30 ml) sunflower oil

Method

Step one:
Spoon the sunflower oil into the tin and put it on the top shelf of the hot oven.

Step two:
Sieve the flour, salt and pepper into a mixing bowl. Make a well in the centre of the flour and add the egg. Mix with the flour until absorbed and gradually add the milk until a thin batter is formed.

Step three:
When the oiled tin is smoking hot, remove it from the oven and add the batter mixture. Cook at the top of the oven for 10–15 minutes until the puddings are fully risen and golden brown.

To serve

Dish up the roasted root vegetables, the stuffing and the Yorkshire puddings onto warmed plates. Add a chicken breast or two Quorn fillets to each plate and serve with the green vegetable and the remainder of the gravy.

Spanish style chicken/tofu

TIME TO PREPARE: 15 MINUTES
TIME TO COOK: 30 MINUTES
SERVES: 8 (4 CHICKEN AND 4 VEGGIE)

This is a quick, one-pot dish that combines meat/tofu and vegetables in a classic Mediterranean tomato sauce.

Ingredients

4 free range, boneless and skinless
   chicken breasts
8 oz (225 grams) tofu
4 tablespoons (60 ml) olive oil
1 large Spanish onion
2 lbs (900 grams) new potatoes
1 lb (450 grams) green beans
4 cloves garlic
2 red peppers
2 yellow peppers
2 x 14 oz (400 grams) tins chopped tomatoes
10 fl oz (300 ml) white wine or vegetable stock
2 teaspoons (10 ml) paprika
2 tablespoons (30 ml) chopped fresh basil
2 teaspoons (10 ml) dried oregano
2 oz (50 grams) black olives (stone removed)
Salt and freshly ground black pepper to taste

Health note

Both the chicken and the tofu are high in protein and low in fat. This dish is also a good source of vitamins A, B, C and E.

Method

Step one:
Cut the tofu into 1" (2.5 cm) chunks. Peel and chop a garlic clove and place it in a bowl with 2 tablespoons (30 ml) of the olive oil. Add the tofu chunks and season well with salt and black pepper. Cover and chill in the refrigerator.

Step two:
Scrub the potatoes and cut in half. Top and tail the green beans. Peel and chop the onion and the garlic finely. De-seed the peppers then slice into ½" (1.25 cm) strips. Finely chop the basil. Chop the chicken into 2" (5cm) cubes.

Step three:
Place two large heavy based saucepans on the hob over a medium heat. Add 2 tablespoons (30 ml) oil, half the onion and half the garlic to one saucepan and cook over a low heat for about 5 minutes until the onions and garlic are softened.

Step four:
Add the chicken and 1 teaspoon (5 ml) paprika to the cooked onions and garlic and stir to coat. Cook over a medium heat, turning frequently until the chicken is sealed and golden.

Step five:
Remove the tofu from the fridge and pour it into the empty pan with the oil and garlic. Add another tablespoon (15 ml) olive oil, the remainder of the onions and garlic and 1 teaspoon (5 ml) paprika. Cook over a low heat for about five minutes, turning frequently until the onions and garlic are softened and the tofu is golden.

Step six:
Add a tin of tomatoes, half the white wine or vegetable stock, 1 tablespoon (15 ml) fresh basil and 1 teaspoon (5 ml) oregano to each pan, and season with salt and freshly ground black pepper. Bring both pans to the boil, stirring frequently.

Step seven:
Add half the potatoes, the peppers, the olives and the green beans to each pan, lower the heat to medium and cook for 30 minutes until the vegetables are tender. Check from time to time that there is sufficient liquid and top up with more water/wine if necessary.

To serve

Sprinkle with a little chopped basil and serve with fresh crusty bread or a crisp green salad.

Quick tip

If you make more than you need, this dish will freeze well. To use simply defrost thoroughly and reheat in a saucepan or the oven for 30 minutes until piping hot.

Chicken breasts/Chicken-style fillets with warm tomato salsa

TIME TO PREPARE: 10 MINUTES
TIME TO COOK: 20 MINUTES
SERVES: 4 (2 CHICKEN AND 2 VEGGIE)

This dish can be prepared and on the table in about half an hour. I use salsa a lot in cooking to replace traditional rich, fatty sauces. The salsa can be made in advance and simply warmed through when needed.

Ingredients

2 free range boneless and skinless
  chicken breasts
4 Quorn chicken-style fillets
4 fl oz (120 ml) white wine
  or vegetable stock
2 cloves garlic
2 tablespoons (30 ml) chopped, fresh coriander
2 tablespoons (30 ml) olive oil
Juice and zest of a lime
Salt and pepper
For the salsa (see recipe on p. 274)

Health note

The chicken and Quorn are both high in protein and low in fat. This dish is also a good source of vitamins A, B, C and E.

Method

Step one:
Peel and thinly slice 2 cloves garlic. Cut three diagonal slits in each chicken breast and rub a little olive oil over the chicken and into the cuts. Then add a sliver of garlic and a little chopped coriander into each cut, and season well with salt and pepper.

Step two:
Mix the remainder of the garlic slivers and 1 tablespoon chopped coriander with a tablespoon (15 ml) olive oil. Rub this mixture all over the Quorn fillets and season well with salt and pepper.

Step three:
Place the chicken and the Quorn in separate ovenproof dishes, pour half the lime juice and half the wine or stock over each dish and sprinkle with the lime zest. Cover the dishes with foil and cook in the oven for 20 minutes on 200C/400F/gas mark 6. Test that the chicken is thoroughly cooked by piercing with a skewer, if the juices run clear it is cooked.

To serve

Spoon the salsa over the cooked chicken/Quorn and serve with brown rice, pasta or wedge potatoes and a mixed salad.

Quick tip

If you are really short of time use commercially prepared salsa and chop some fresh tomatoes and peppers into it.

Creamy chicken/Quorn and spinach curry

TIME TO PREPARE: 10 MINUTES
TIME TO COOK: 20 MINUTES
SERVES: 4 (2 CHICKEN AND 2 VEGGIE)

This is a mild, delicately spiced curry which can be made in one pot, on the hob, in half an hour. Using a curry paste may seem like cheating but it produces a mellow flavour, unlike fresh spices which can be harsh and too hot when used in quick cook curries.

Ingredients

2 free range, skinless and boneless
    chicken breasts
8 oz (225 grams) Quorn chicken-style pieces
2 tablespoons (30 ml) sunflower oil
1 large onion
4 cloves garlic
4 large tomatoes
1 small bunch of fresh coriander
8 oz (225 grams) fresh spinach
4 tablespoons (60 ml) green curry paste
6 fl oz (175 ml) natural yoghurt
2 x14 oz (400 grams) tins chopped tomatoes
Salt and pepper

Health note

The chicken and the Quorn are high in protein and low in fat. This dish is also a good source of vitamins A, B and E.

Method

Step one:
Pour the oil into a large, heavy based saucepan and warm through on a medium heat.

Step two:
Peel and chop the onions and the garlic and add to the oil. Cook over a low heat for 5 minutes until softened.

Step three:
Peel and quarter the fresh tomatoes and add to the pan with the tinned tomatoes and the curry paste. Chop the coriander finely and add to the pan. Stir well and season with salt and black pepper to taste. Bring to the boil gently.

Step four:
Remove the pan from the heat and pour half the sauce into another heavy based saucepan.

Step five:
Chop the chicken into 2" (5 cm) chunks and add to one saucepan. Stir thoroughly, cover and simmer over a medium heat for 25 minutes.

Step six:
Add the Quorn to the other pan and cover and simmer over a medium heat for 25 minutes.

Step seven:
Wash and dry the spinach and add half to each pan 5 minutes before serving.

Step eight:
Remove both pans from the heat. Stir half the yoghurt into each pan.

To serve

Serve with some plain boiled rice or naan breads and some mango chutney.

Quick tip

If you wish to freeze this dish you should cook to Step six and freeze before adding the spinach and the yoghurt. To use, simply defrost thoroughly and cook on the hob or in the oven for 20–30 minutes until piping hot. Then add the spinach and the yoghurt just before serving.

Chicken breast/hummus in ciabatta bread with roasted vegetable salad

TIME TO PREPARE: 10 MINUTES
TIME TO COOK: 20 MINUTES
SERVES: 4 (2 CHICKEN AND 2 VEGGIE)

This dish is popular with adults and children alike and is so quick and easy to prepare.

Ingredients

2 tablespoons (30 ml) olive oil
2 free range, boneless and skinless
  chicken breasts
4 oz (110 grams) hummus
  (see recipe p. 275)
4 tablespoons (60 ml) tofu mayonnaise
  (see recipe p. 91) or use low fat mayonnaise
2 long ciabatta loaves
  (or 4 large ciabatta rolls)
4 oz (110 grams) tomato salsa
  (see recipe p. 272)
4 oz (110 grams) bag of fresh rocket or spinach
1 red, 1 green and 1 yellow pepper
1 red onion
Salt and freshly ground black pepper to taste

Health note

The chicken and hummus are high in protein and low in fat. The chickpeas contain protein and fibre, iron and zinc.

Method

Step one:
Brush each chicken breast with a little olive oil and season with salt and black pepper. Put the chicken into an ovenproof dish, cover with foil and cook in the oven on 200C/400F/gas mark 6 for 20 minutes.

Step two:
De-seed the peppers and cut them into quarters. Peel the onion and slice into eight segments lengthways. Place the vegetables into an ovenproof dish and drizzle over the remainder of the olive oil. Season the vegetables with salt and pepper and place in the oven for 15 minutes.

Step three:
Cut the ciabatta loaves in two lengthways and cut each almost, but not quite, in half widthways. Place the four rolls on four dinner plates. Spread the inside bottom half of each roll with a heaped tablespoon (15 ml) of hummus and the inside, top half of each roll with a heaped tablespoon (15 ml) of mayonnaise. Add a layer of rocket or spinach to the bottom half of each roll.

Step four:
When the chicken and the peppers are cooked, remove them from the oven and allow them to cool slightly. Slice each chicken breast in two lengthways.

Step five:
Place a layer of the roasted vegetables onto each roll, top two of the rolls with a chicken breast. Top the remaining two rolls with another tablespoon (15 ml) of the hummus.

Step six:
Spoon the salsa over the rolls, and season well with salt and pepper.

To serve

Cut each roll in half and serve with a mixed salad and some thin French fries.

Quick tip

You can use commercially prepared salsa, hummus and mayonnaise to save time.

Caribbean chicken/chicken-style Quorn

TIME TO PREPARE: 10 MINUTES
TIME TO COOK: 20 MINUTES
SERVES: 4 (2 CHICKEN AND 2 VEGGIE)

This dish is an exciting mix of sweetness and spice, tender chunks of chicken or Quorn, chunky mixed vegetables and succulent fruit.

Ingredients

2 skinless and boneless chicken breasts
8 oz (225 grams) Quorn chicken-style pieces
1 red, 1 green and 1 yellow pepper
4 oz (110 grams) fresh pineapple chunks
　　or small tin pineapple
¼ pint (150 ml) pineapple juice
　　(you can use the juice from the tinned
　　pineapple or, if using fresh, buy a small
　　carton pineapple juice)
¼ pint (150 ml) water
2 tablespoons (30 ml) cornflour
2 tablespoons (30 ml) sunflower oil
2 tablespoons (30 ml) white wine vinegar
2 tablespoons (30 ml) brown sugar
1" (2.5 cm) piece fresh ginger, peeled and grated
2 cloves garlic
3 oz (75 grams) cashew nuts
1 oz (25 grams) dried coconut
2 limes
Salt and pepper to taste

Health note

High in protein, low in fat and a good source of iron, vitamins B and C.

Method

Step one:
You will need two woks or large frying pans. Put 1 tablespoon of the oil in each and place on the hob over a low heat.

Step two:
Chop the chicken into 2" (5 cm) chunks and add to one pan. Cook for 5 minutes over a medium heat, turning frequently until the chicken is white on all sides.

Step three:
Place the Quorn chicken-style pieces in the other pan and cook over a low heat for 5 minutes.

Step four:
Peel and chop the garlic and add 1 clove together with half the ginger to each pan. De-seed and chop the peppers and add half to each pan. Cook over a medium heat for a further 5 minutes, stirring occasionally to prevent sticking.

Step five:
Add the cornflour to a jug or mixing bowl and mix in the water slowly to avoid lumps. Add the pineapple juice, the white wine vinegar, brown sugar, coconut and juice of one lime. Stir vigorously to mix.

Step six:
Add half the cashews, pineapple and half the pineapple sauce to each pan, season with salt and pepper. Stir vigorously and increase the heat to bring the mixture to the boil. Stir until the sauce begins to thicken then turn the heat to low and leave to simmer for 10 minutes until the chicken, Quorn and vegetables are cooked through.

To serve

Serve garnished with a wedge of lime and some brown rice to which you have added peas and sweetcorn.

Mexican fajitas

TIME TO PREPARE: 15 MINUTES
TIME TO COOK: 20 MINUTES
MAKES 8 (4 CHICKEN AND 4 VEGGIE)

Fajitas can be made using steak, chicken, seafood, tofu, Quorn and vegetables. This recipe is for chicken and tofu fajitas, and includes recipes for the pico de gallo and the guacamole that are served with the fajitas.

Ingredients

2 free range, skinless and boneless
   chicken breasts
4 oz (110 grams) tofu
2 tablespoons (30 ml) olive oil
8 wheat flour tortillas
2 red, 2 green and 2 yellow peppers
2 large carrots
2 tomatoes
8 baby sweetcorn
2 red onions
2 cloves garlic
For the sauce:
2 small birds eye green or red chillies de-seeded and finely chopped
2 cloves garlic peeled and finely chopped
1 tablespoon (15 ml) white wine vinegar
1 tablespoon (15 ml) olive oil
1 tablespoon (15 ml) brown sugar
2 tablespoons (30 ml) fresh lime juice
1 teaspoon (5 ml) dried oregano
1 teaspoon (5 ml) cumin powder
½ bottle Mexican beer or lager (use ordinary if you can't find Mexican)
For the Guacamole: (see recipe on p. 276)
For the Pico de Gallo: (see recipe on p. 277)

Health note

The chicken and tofu are high in protein and fibre and low in fat. Also provide iron, vitamins B, C and D and folate.

Method

If making the pico de gallo and the guacamole, start by making those first and store in the fridge until needed:
For the fajitas:

Step one:
Put all of the sauce ingredients into a screw top jar or blender and shake vigorously or blend for about 30 seconds.

Step two:
Cut the chicken and the tofu into ½" (1.25 cm) wide finger-length strips.

Step three:
De-seed the peppers and cut into ½" (1.25 cm) wide, finger-length strips. Peel the carrots and slice into ½" (1.25 cm) wide, finger-length strips. Slice the tomatoes thinly. Slice the sweetcorn in half lengthways. Peel the onion and slice thinly.

Step four:
Use two separate heavy based frying pans or woks (if you do not have two, cook the tofu mixture first and keep it warm while you cook the chicken mixture).

Step five:
Place 1 tablespoon (15 ml) oil into each pan and warm through over a low heat. When warm, add half the onions and half the garlic to each pan. Add the chicken to one pan and the tofu to the other. Cook over a medium to high heat for 5 minutes, turning frequently to prevent burning.

Step six:
Pre-heat the oven to 190C/375F/gas mark 5. Wrap the tortillas in foil and warm through in the oven for 5 minutes.

Step seven:
Add half the remaining vegetables to each pan and half the sauce to each pan. Cook over a medium to high heat for a further 10 minutes until the meat and tofu are well cooked and the vegetables are tender but still crunchy.

To serve

For each person wrap two tortillas in a dinner napkin, place half the chicken or tofu mixture in a bowl and set the bowl and the tortillas on a large dinner plate. Serve the pico de gallo and the guacamole in separate bowls for diners to help themselves. Serve with extra bowls of shredded lettuce, sour cream and grated cheese.

Quick tip

To save time you can buy the guacamole and replace the pico de gallo with bought spicy salsa dip.

Coq au vin/Burgundy-style casserole

TIME TO PREPARE: 20 MINUTES
TIME TO COOK: 1 HOUR
SERVES 6 (3 CHICKEN AND 3 VEGGIE)

This classic French dish remains a popular dinner party favourite. The vegetarian recipe uses vegetables with a firm texture and rustic flavour that can withstand the long, slow cooking required.

Ingredients

2 free range chicken breasts with bone in and skin on

2 free range chicken thighs with bone in and skin on

14 oz (400 grams) tin chickpeas

4 rashers unsmoked, streaky bacon

16 small shallots or button onions

10 oz (275 grams) fresh chestnut mushrooms

2 oz (50 grams) dried mushrooms

2 medium aubergines

3 carrots

1 lb (450 grams) new potatoes

4 cloves garlic

2 bay leaves

2 sprigs thyme

1 teaspoon (5 ml) oregano

1 bottle (750 ml) burgundy red wine

½ pint (275 ml) vegetable stock

2 tablespoons (30 ml) olive oil

2 tablespoons (30 ml) cornflour

1 oz (25 grams) plain flour

1 French baguette

Salt and pepper to taste

2 tablespoons (30 ml) butter

Health note

The chicken is high in protein and low in fat. The chickpeas are also high in protein and fibre, antioxidants, iron and zinc.

Method

Step one:
Place 1 oz (25 grams) plain flour in a bowl and season with salt and pepper. Dip each chicken portion in the flour ensuring that all of the chicken is covered.

Step two:
Peel the shallots or button onions and leave whole. Peel and finely chop the garlic. Roll each bacon rasher up and cut each roll in two. Reconstitute the dried mushrooms according to the pack instructions. Cut the aubergines into 2" (5 cm) thick slices and spread them out on a plate, sprinkle each slice with a little salt. Peel the carrots and cut into 2" (5cm) chunks. Cut the potatoes in half. Mix the cornflour with water until it forms a thin paste. Drain the chickpeas.

Step three:
You will need two large, heavy based saucepans. Add 1 tablespoon (15 ml) oil to each pan and heat through gently. Remove from the heat and add a chopped clove of garlic to each pan.

Step four:
Add the chicken pieces to one pan and return to the hob. Cook over a low heat until the chicken is sealed and golden on all sides. Add the bacon, 1 bay leaf, ½ teaspoon (1.25 ml) oregano, and a sprig of thyme, cook for a couple of minutes until the bacon is crispy. Add half the potatoes, half the reconstituted dried mushrooms, one sliced carrot, half the onions and half the wine, season with salt and freshly ground black pepper. Bring the pan to a gentle boil, then cover and reduce the heat to a low simmer. Simmer for 45 minutes, stirring from time to time and adding more wine if necessary.

Step five:
Add to the veggie pan: 1 clove of garlic, the remainder of the aubergine, onions, potatoes and carrots. Put back on the hob and cook the vegetables over a medium heat, turning frequently, for five minutes. Add the bay leaf, ½ teaspoon (1.25 ml) oregano, the thyme, the remainder of the reconstituted dried mushrooms, the red wine and the chickpeas, and season with salt and pepper. Bring to a gentle boil then reduce the heat, cover and simmer for 35 minutes.

Step six:
15 minutes before the end of the cooking time add half the fresh mushrooms and half the cornflour paste to each pan and turn the heat up to medium. Add a little vegetable stock or wine if needed. Stir thoroughly and cook for the remaining 15 minutes uncovered.

Continued on next page

Step seven:
5 minutes before serving mix the remaining 2 cloves of garlic into 2 tablespoons (30 ml) butter. Cut 16 diagonal slices of French baguette and butter one side with the garlic butter. Place the bread on an oiled baking sheet and bake at the top of a hot oven 200C/400F/gas mark 6 for 3–5 minutes until the bread is golden and crispy.

Step eight:
Transfer the casseroles into two serving dishes. Overlap the garlic bread slices in a circle around the top of each casserole and serve.

To serve

This is a very rich dish and is best served with some plain, buttered tagliatelli or some brown rice.

Quick turkey/vegetable and cashew stir fry

TIME TO PREPARE: 10 MINUTES
TIME TO COOK: 10 MINUTES
SERVES: 4 (2 TURKEY AND 2 VEGGIE)

This is a really light, healthy dish that can be prepared and cooked in minutes.

Ingredients

2 thinly sliced turkey breast steaks
   with all skin and fat removed
1 large onion
½ small white cabbage
3 carrots
4 oz (110 grams) tin water chestnuts
1 green and 1 red pepper
8 baby corn cobs
4 oz (110 grams) fine green beans
4 oz (110 grams) unsalted cashew nuts
1 small bag bean sprouts
2 cloves garlic
2 teaspoons (10 ml) grated fresh ginger
Juice and zest of 1 lemon
Juice and zest of 1 lime
3 tablespoons (45 ml) dark soy sauce
3 tablespoons (45 ml) sunflower oil
Salt and pepper

Health note

The turkey and the cashews are high in protein and the fast cooking method preserves the vitamins and minerals in the vegetables. If served with rice, the cashews and the rice combined make a perfect protein.

Method

Step one:
You will need a large wok or frying pan and a small frying pan. Slice the turkey into ½" (1.25 cm) wide, finger-length strips. Peel the onion, cut it in half and slice thinly. Cut the cabbage in half and slice thinly. Top and tail the carrots and cut into thin, finger-length strips. Drain the water chestnuts. De-seed the peppers and slice them into ½" (1.25 cm) strips. Cut the corn cobs in half lengthways. Top and tail the green beans, then cut them in half. Wash and drain the bean sprouts. Peel the garlic and chop finely.

Step two:
Add a tablespoon of oil to the small frying pan and place on the hob over a

Continued on next page

high heat until the oil is hot. Add the turkey strips and stir quickly for 2 minutes, then turn and stir quickly for a further 2 minutes. Add 1 tablespoon of the soy sauce to the turkey and cook for a further minute, stirring frequently. Remove from the heat and keep warm.

Step three:
Pre-heat the grill and line the grill pan with lightly greased foil. Spread the cashew nuts over the grill pan and place under the hot grill, turn when the cashews are golden and allow the other side to turn golden. Remove the cashews from the heat, sprinkle with a little salt and some soy sauce and allow them to cool.

Step four:
You will probably need to cook the vegetables in two batches depending on the size of your wok. Add 1 tablespoon (15 ml) oil to the wok and place on the hob over a high heat until smoking, add half the garlic and half the onion and stir very quickly until the onion begins to brown. Push the onion up the sides of the pan and then add half each of the ginger, carrots and the sweetcorn, stir quickly for about half a minute, then push the carrots and sweetcorn to one side and add half each of the peppers, the green beans and the water chestnuts, stir very quickly for another minute, then stir all the ingredients into each other, moving them about from the middle to the outside of the pan. Add half each of the cashew nuts, cabbage and the bean sprouts, the soy sauce, the lemon and lime juice. Season well with salt and pepper and stir fry for a further 2 minutes. Remove from the heat and transfer to a serving dish to keep warm.

Step five:
Put the remaining tablespoon of oil into the wok and return it to the hob. Heat the oil over a high heat until smoking then add the turkey and repeat step four for the vegetables.

To serve

Serve with some steamed, wholegrain brown rice.

Quick tip

If you prefer a spicier dish add some chilli sauce at Step four. You can use virtually any mix of vegetables in this stir fry, the simple rule is to start cooking the harder vegetables first and finish with the softer vegetables.

Mediterranean vegetable and turkey/spicy veggie sausage kebabs

TIME TO PREPARE: 10 MINUTES + MARINATING
TIME TO COOK: 20 MINUTES
SERVES: 4

These kebabs are quick to prepare and produce a mouth-watering aroma as they cook. Perfect for the barbeque, or cook quickly under a hot grill. The recipe given will make four turkey kebabs and four vegetarian kebabs simply increase or reduce the ingredients to suit your needs.

Ingredients

4 lean turkey breast steaks
4 spicy vegetarian sausages
4 large red and 4 large green peppers
16 cherry tomatoes
8 courgettes
4 small red onions
For the marinade:
6 tablespoons (90 ml) olive oil
4 tablespoons (60 ml) white wine vinegar
Juice of a lemon
1 tablespoon (15ml) each chopped fresh flat leaf parsley, thyme and coriander
　 (if you don't have fresh herbs use a teaspoon [5ml] of dried mixed herbs)
Salt and pepper to taste

Health note

The turkey and the veggie sausages are high in protein and low in fat. The vegetables are a good source of antioxidants, betacarotene and vitamin C.

Method

Step one:
Cut the tops off the peppers, then cut in half lengthwise and remove the core and seeds. Cut the peppers in half again widthwise so that each pepper provides four chunky slices. Slice the courgettes into 1" (2.5cm) slices. Peel the onions and cut into quarters lengthwise.

Step two:
Place all of the marinade ingredients into a screw top jar or blender and shake or blend well to mix. Add the vegetables to the marinade and mix thoroughly.

Continued on next page

Step three:
Cut the turkey steaks into 2" (5 cm) cubes. On a separate chopping board
and with a different knife cut the vegetarian sausages into 2" (5 cm) slices.

Step four:
Take four metal skewers and starting with a cherry tomato, thread as follows:
tomato, turkey cube, green pepper, turkey, red pepper, turkey, courgette,
onion, turkey and so on until all the turkey and one half of the vegetables
have been used.

Step five:
Take the remaining four metal skewers and thread the vegetables and
vegetarian sausages onto the skewers in the same way. The aim is to create a
pleasing mix of colours, flavours and textures.

Step six:
Put the turkey kebabs on a large plate and the vegetarian kebabs on a
separate plate. Reserve a couple of tablespoons of the marinade for basting
and pour half the remaining marinade over the turkey kebabs and the
remaining half over the vegetarian kebabs.

Step seven:
Cook the kebabs under the pre-heated grill or on the barbeque for 20
minutes, turning frequently. If serving a mixture of turkey and vegetarian
kebabs at the same meal, the vegetarian kebabs should be cooked first
(otherwise you will have to wash the grill in between). Baste with a little of
the marinade from time to time. When cooked transfer to a warmed plate,
cover with foil and keep warm in the oven. Once the vegetable kebabs are
cooked, add the turkey kebabs to the grill or barbeque and cook, turning
frequently, over a high heat for about 20 minutes until the meat juices run
clear.

To serve

Serve as a main course with the Jewelled Summer tabbouleh (recipe on p. 98) or
with nutty brown rice, peas and sweetcorn. If serving at a barbeque serve with
warm, wholemeal pitta breads and some spicy tomato salsa (recipe on p. 272).

Beef dishes

Beef stroganoff / Mixed mushroom stroganoff

TIME TO PREPARE: 15 MINUTES
TIME TO COOK: 20 MINUTES
SERVES: 4 (2 MEAT AND 2 VEGGIE)

A classic dish that is quick and easy to prepare yet impressive enough for entertaining. The shiitake mushrooms give a wonderful depth of flavour.

Ingredients

8 oz (225 grams) fillet steak
4 tablespoons (60 ml) sunflower oil
2 onions
8 oz (225 grams) chestnut mushrooms
8 oz (225 grams) shiitake mushrooms
2 tablespoons (30 ml) cognac
Juice and zest of 1 lemon
8 oz (225 grams) carton of low fat crème fraiche
2 tablespoons (30 ml) tomato purée
2 tablespoons (30 ml) paprika
2 tablespoons (30 ml) caraway seeds
2 cloves garlic
½ pint (300 ml) vegetable stock
2 tablespoons (30 ml) chopped, fresh parsley

Health note

The steak is high in protein and I have decreased the amount of overall fat in the dish by using low fat crème fraiche instead of the traditional sour cream and by replacing the butter with sunflower oil.

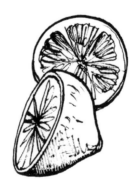

Method

Step one:
Put the caraway seeds into a cup and pour on 1 fl oz (30ml) of boiling water. Cut the steak into 1″ (2.5cm) thick, finger-length strips. Peel the onions and slice thinly. Peel the garlic and chop finely.

Step two:
You will need two heavy based frying pans or woks. To one pan, add 2 tablespoons (30 ml) sunflower oil and warm over a medium heat. When the oil is hot add half the onions and garlic and the steak and stir, turning frequently until browned on all sides. Add a quarter of the mushrooms, cook for a further 2 minutes and remove from the heat.

Step three:
To the empty frying pan add 2 tablespoons (30 ml) sunflower oil and heat gently over a medium heat. When the oil is hot add the remainder of the onions and the garlic and fry gently over a low heat until the onion is softened but not brown.

Step four:
Add three-quarters of the mushrooms to the onions in the vegetarian pan and fry over a medium heat for about 5 minutes until tender.

Step five:
Add half the paprika and the tomato purée to each pan and stir well. Drain the liquid from the caraway seeds and add half the liquid with half the vegetable stock to each pan and stir well.

Step six:
Bring both pans up to a gentle boil and add half the cognac to each. Lower the heat and simmer for 10 minutes.

Step seven:
Just before serving, remove from the pans from the heat and stir half the crème fraiche, the lemon juice and zest into each pan, then season well with salt and pepper to taste. Sprinkle with the chopped parsley and a little paprika.

To serve

This is delicious served on a bed of pasta with a crisp green salad.

Beef Bourguignon/Tofu à la Bourguignon

TIME TO PREPARE: 20 MINUTES
TIME TO COOK: 3 HOURS
SERVES 8 (4 MEAT AND 4 VEGGIE)

This classic French dish benefits from being made the day before it is needed to allow the flavours to develop. Allow it to cool and refrigerate overnight, then place in a casserole dish, cover with a lid or foil and heat through in a hot oven for 30 minutes until piping hot.

Ingredients

1lb (450 grams) braising steak, fat removed and cut into 2" (5 cm) cubes
4 oz (110 grams) piece unsmoked streaky bacon cut into cubes
1lb (450 grams) firm tofu cut into 2" (5 cm) cubes
1 lb (450 grams) shallots or button onions
Large onion
4 cloves garlic
8 oz (225 grams) chestnut mushrooms
2 x bouquet garnis each made with a sprig of thyme, a bay leaf and a sprig of curly parsley
2 bay leaves
2 tablespoons (30 ml) plain flour
4 tablespoons (60 ml) olive oil
1 bottle (750 ml) burgundy red wine
½ pint (300 ml) beef stock
½ pint (300 ml) vegetable stock
2 tablespoons (30 ml) tomato purée
1 large tomato
1 tablespoon (15 ml) soy sauce
Salt and freshly ground black pepper

Health note

The flavour of the meat dish relies on the fat in the meat and the long slow cooking. However, if you make it the day before you need it and skim the fat from the surface you can reduce the overall fat content.

Method

Step one:
Peel the shallots or button onions and leave whole. Peel and finely chop the garlic. Peel the large onion and slice it thinly. Thinly slice the mushrooms and roughly chop the tomato.

To make the beef casserole
Step two:
Pre-heat the oven to 150C/300F/gas mark 2. You will need a large, heavy based saucepan. Put the pan on the hob over a medium heat and add 1 tablespoon olive oil, heat until hot then add the beef a few chunks at a time and fry over a medium heat turning it frequently until sealed and brown on all sides. When nicely browned remove the beef from the pan, using a slotted spoon, and keep warm on a plate. Add half the sliced onion to the pan and cook for a further 2 minutes or so until the onion is beginning to brown then return the beef to the pan. Sprinkle 1 tablespoon (15 ml) seasoned flour over the beef and stir well, cook for a further minute, gradually add half a bottle of red wine and half the beef stock, stirring constantly. Add a bouquet garni, a bay leaf, half the garlic and a tablespoon of tomato purée and season with salt and pepper. If your saucepan is suitable for the oven put the lid on and transfer to the oven to cook for 2 hours (if not transfer to a casserole dish and cover with a lid or a double layer of foil), check from time to time and top up with extra wine or beef stock if the dish requires it.

To make the tofu casserole
Step three:
You will need a heavy based saucepan. Put the pan on the hob over a low heat and add 1 tablespoon (15 ml) olive oil, heat until just hot. Add the remainder of the sliced onions and chopped garlic and cook over a low heat for 5 minutes until softened. Stir in 1 tablespoon (15 ml) tomato purée, half the vegetable stock and half a bottle of red wine, stirring constantly, bring to the boil and simmer for one minute. Next add the soy sauce, bouquet garni and the bay leaf. Reduce the heat to a low simmer, add the tofu and the tomato, season with salt and pepper then cover and simmer for 25 minutes. Check from time to time and top up with the extra vegetable stock or some more wine if required.

Both dishes
Step four:
When the beef has cooked for 2 hours and the tofu for 25 minutes place 1 tablespoon (15 ml) oil in a frying pan and fry the button onions and mushrooms for 1 minute. Add half the onions and mushrooms to each pan. Fry the bacon lightly and add the bacon to the beef pan. Cook the beef for a further hour and the tofu for a further 15 minutes. The tofu dish will cook faster than the beef, but once cooked you can allow it to cool and simply reheat once the beef is ready.

To serve

This is lovely served with mashed sweet potato or spinach tagliatelli and a dark green vegetable such as broccoli.

Steak and chips/peppered vegetable 'steak' and chips

TIME TO PREPARE: 10 MINUTES
TIME TO COOK: 30 MINUTES
SERVES: 4 (2 MEAT AND 2 VEGGIE)

Steak and chips probably seems like an odd recipe to include in a healthy cookery book, but you can reduce the fat by choosing lean cuts of meat and making the reduced fat oven chips to the recipe below.

Ingredients

2 medium size sirloin or fillet steaks
2 Quorn peppered steaks
1 large onion
4 tablespoons (60 ml) olive oil
4 large ripened on the vine tomatoes
4 large flat mushrooms
8 oz (225 grams) frozen peas
2 lb (900 grams) potatoes
Salt and pepper

Health note

Steak and Quorn are both high in protein. Provides fibre, carbohydrate, iron, vitamins B, C and D.

Method

Step one:
Put a large pan of salted water on to boil. Peel the potatoes and cut them into chips. Put the chips into a blanching basket, or metal steamer, and place them in the pan of boiling water for 2 minutes. Remove from the heat, drain and allow them to cool. When cool, pat dry with some kitchen towel and, using a pastry brush, brush them all over with some olive oil.

Step two:
Pre-heat the oven to 200C/400F/gas mark 6. Place the chips on a baking sheet and cook in the oven for 10 minutes.

Step three:
While the chips are cooking pre-heat the grill, wash the steaks and pat them dry then season with salt and pepper. Rub a little olive oil into each steak and place under the hot grill. Grill each side for 5–10 minutes depending upon how well you like your steak cooked. After the chips have cooked for 10 minutes, gently turn them over with a spatula, and cook for a further 10–15 minutes until crispy and golden outside and tender inside.

Step four:
While the steak and chips are cooking brush the Quorn steaks with a little olive oil and place on a baking tray. Cook in the oven for 7 minutes and then turn, brush with a little more oil and cook for a further 7 minutes.

Step five:
Peel the onions and slice them thinly. Pour 1 tablespoon (15 ml) olive oil into a frying pan and fry the sliced onions gently for about 5 minutes, until softened, then turn the heat down to the lowest setting to keep the onions warm.

Step six:
Cut the tomatoes in half. Place the tomatoes and mushrooms on a baking tray and brush with a little olive oil, season with salt and freshly ground black pepper and cook in the oven for 5 minutes.

Step seven:
Put the peas in a pan with some boiling water and a pinch of salt. Bring to the boil and cook for 5 minutes.

To serve

Serve the steak/Quorn steak with the chips, peas, mushrooms, onions and tomatoes.

Quick tip

You can use frozen, low fat oven chips to save time.

Roast beef/savoury loaf with roast potatoes and Yorkshire pudding

TIME TO PREPARE: 30 MINUTES
COOKING/RESTING TIME: 1½ TO 2 HOURS
SERVES: 8 TO 10 (4 TO 5 MEAT AND 4 TO 5 VEGGIE)

The traditional British Sunday lunch can easily be adapted to cater for vegetarians. The key points to remember are that the potatoes for vegetarians should not be cooked around the meat, you will need to make separate vegetable gravy and you cannot cook the Yorkshires for the vegetarians in the beef fat or lard. You could cook your roast as usual and simply cook a few additional potatoes and Yorkshires for the vegetarians in separate trays. The savoury loaf can be prepared the day before and simply warmed through in a hot oven before serving.

Ingredients

3 lb (1350 grams) joint of sirloin beef
4 tablespoons (60 ml) sunflower oil
   for basting
For the savoury loaf:
1 lb (450 grams) vegetarian soya mince
1 medium onion
2 oz (50 grams) breadcrumbs
2 tablespoons (30 ml) olive oil
1 tablespoon (15 ml) fresh rosemary
   (or 1 tsp [5 ml] dried)
1 tablespoon (15 ml) fresh thyme
   (or 1 tsp [5 ml] dried)
2 large free range eggs
3 tablespoons (45 ml) natural yoghurt
2 tablespoons (30 ml) dark soy sauce
Salt and freshly ground black pepper to taste
For the roast potatoes:
4 lb (1800 grams) roasting potatoes
   such as Maris Piper
8 tablespoons (120 ml) sunflower oil
Salt
For the Yorkshire puddings: (see recipe on p. 141)
For the vegetarian gravy: (see recipe on p. 137)

Health note

Although high in saturated fat, the beef is a good source of protein, iron and vitamin D. The savoury loaf contains soya which is high in protein, calcium and isoflavones (which are thought to combat cancer), the potatoes and the vegetables provide fibre, carbohydrates, vitamin C and folic acid.

For the beef gravy:
Juices and some fat from the roasting tin
1 tablespoon (15 ml) cornflour
¾ pint (450 ml) beef stock (either fresh or made using a stock cube)
For the vegetables:
2 lb (900 grams) broccoli or cauliflower
1 lb (450 grams) carrots

Method

Step one:
Pre-heat the oven to 240C/475F/gas mark 9. Wash the beef and pat it dry, season with some freshly ground black pepper and rub all over with 2 tablespoons (30 ml) sunflower oil. Take a large, heavy based roasting tin and add 2 tablespoons (30 ml) of sunflower oil. Put the joint of beef in the roasting tin and cook in the hot oven for 20 minutes, basting frequently.

Step two:
Peel the potatoes, cut them into large chunks and place in a pan of cold water. Cut the broccoli/cauliflower into florets. Peel the carrots and slice finely. Make the Yorkshire pudding batter. Make the vegetable gravy.

Step three:
When the joint has been in the oven for 20 minutes turn the heat down to 190C/375F/gas mark 5 and cook for a further 45 minutes if you like your beef rare, 60 minutes if medium and 75 minutes if well done. Remember to baste the joint frequently as this improves the flavour.

Step four:
To make the savoury loaf you will need a large frying pan and a well greased 1 lb loaf tin. Put 2 tablespoons (30 ml) olive oil in the pan and heat gently over a low heat. Peel and chop the onion finely, add it to the pan and cook gently for about 5 minutes until softened. Add the vegetarian mince and the herbs to the onion and cook for a further 5 minutes, stirring frequently. Remove the pan from the heat. Place the mixture in a large bowl. Beat the eggs with the yoghurt and the soya sauce and add to the mince mixture with the breadcrumbs. Mix well and season with salt and freshly ground black pepper. Pour the mixture into the loaf tin and flatten the top with a wooden spoon or palette knife. Bake in the oven above the beef joint for 45 minutes. At the end of the cooking time remove the loaf from the oven and allow it to cool in the tin for at least 15 minutes. Slide a palette knife around the sides of the tin to loosen it and invert the loaf onto a serving dish. Cover with foil to keep warm until needed.

Continued on next page

Step five:
Boil the potatoes for 5 minutes, then drain. While the potatoes are still in the pan sprinkle them with salt and pepper. Put the lid back on and shake the pan vigorously.

Step six:
When the beef is cooked, remove it from the oven and place it on a warmed serving dish and cover with foil. Turn the heat in the oven up to 220C/425F/gas mark 7. Pour the remaining 6 tablespoons (90 ml) of sunflower oil into a shallow, heavy based roasting tray and place in the oven until the oil is smoking hot. Remove the tray from the oven and add the potatoes. Put back in the oven, reduce the heat to 200C/400F/gas mark 6 and cook for 30–40 minutes, turning the potatoes halfway through the cooking time. The potatoes should be golden brown and crispy on the outside and tender on the inside.

Step seven:
15 minutes before the potatoes are cooked, brush the Yorkshire pudding tin with a little sunflower oil and place on the top shelf of the oven. When the oil is smoking, remove the tin from the oven and pour in the Yorkshire pudding batter. Return the tin to the oven and cook for 10–15 minutes until the Yorkshire puddings are risen and golden.

Step eight:
10 minutes before serving put a large pan of salted water on to boil. When the water is boiling add the green vegetable, place a steamer over the vegetables and put the carrots in the steamer (if you haven't got a steamer cook the carrots in a separate pan). Cover and cook for 10 minutes.

Step nine:
To make the beef gravy spoon the meat juices and 1 tablespoon meat fat into a frying pan, heat through and stir in the cornflour until it is all mixed in with the fat and the meat juices, then gradually add the beef stock until the gravy is the thickness you prefer. Season the gravy with salt and pepper and cook over a low heat for 5 minutes.

Countdown

Correct timing is the key to producing a perfect Sunday roast and the timing will depend upon the size of your joint and how you like it cooked. Calculate the cooking time of the meat (see Step three). Once the meat is cooked it needs 45 minutes to relax so that the flavours can develop, this also makes it much easier to carve.

- Calculate the cooking time for beef and cook.
- 45 minutes before the end of the cooking time for the beef put the savoury loaf in the oven.
- Remove the beef and the savoury loaf from the oven and cover with foil. Keep the loaf warm. The beef will retain its heat.
- **45 minutes from serving:**
As soon as you remove the meat from the oven put the potatoes in to cook for 45 minutes.
- **15 minutes from serving:**
Put the Yorkshire puddings in the oven.
- **10 minutes from serving:**
Put the vegetables on to cook.
- **5 minutes from serving:**
Warm through the beef and the vegetable gravy.

To serve

Carve the beef and the savoury loaf and serve with the roast potatoes, Yorkshire puddings, vegetables and gravy.

Beef balti/chickpea and vegetable balti with naan bread and cucumber raita

TIME TO PREPARE: 10 MINUTES
TIME TO COOK: 20 MINUTES
SERVES: 4 (2 BEEF AND 2 VEGGIE)

Balti dishes are medium spiced curries that are quick to prepare and cook, as they are stir fried in a wok. Traditionally the curry is served in a metal balti dish with naan bread and some cucumber raita for dipping.

Ingredients

3 tablespoons (45 ml) sunflower oil
1 medium onion
2 cloves garlic
8 oz (225 grams) lean frying steak
14 oz (400 grams) tin chickpeas
2" (5cm) piece fresh root ginger
1 small red or green chilli
1 green and 1 red pepper
2 x 14 oz (400 grams) tins chopped tomatoes
Juice and zest of 1 lemon
1 tablespoon (15 ml) garam masala
2 tablespoons (30 ml) tomato purée
2 teaspoons (10 ml) ground cumin
1 small bunch fresh coriander
2 tablespoons (30 ml) white wine vinegar
2 teaspoons (10 ml) brown sugar
4 large naan breads
Salt and pepper to taste
For the cucumber raita: (see recipe on p. 347)

Health note

Buy lean frying steak to reduce the fat. The beef contains protein and iron. The chickpeas and the naan bread combined create a perfect protein.

Method

Step one:
Pre-heat the oven to 150C/300F/gas mark 2. Wrap the naan breads in foil and place on a baking tray. Put in the oven on the bottom shelf.

Step two:
Peel and thinly slice the onion, de-seed the peppers and slice into strips. Peel and grate the root ginger. Peel and chop the garlic. Slice the chilli in half and remove the seeds (best done under cold running water) then chop finely. Slice the steak into 1" (2.5 cm) wide finger-length strips. Drain the chickpeas. Chop the coriander finely.

Step three:
Put the tomato purée in a small bowl and add the chilli, the garam masala and the cumin and stir.

Step four:
Put the oil into a large wok and heat gently over a medium heat. Add the onions, garlic and ginger and cook for about 5 minutes, stirring frequently, until the onion is softened. Add the tomato purée mixture, vinegar, lemon juice and zest, sugar and stir. Cook for a further 5 minutes. Add the tinned tomatoes, coriander and some salt and black pepper, stir and cook for a further 5 minutes.

Step five:
Pour half the sauce into a casserole dish and add half the peppers and all of the chickpeas, stir well then cover and cook in the oven on 190C/375/gas mark 5 for 20 minutes. Remove the naan breads from the oven and keep wrapped in foil to keep warm.

Step six:
Pour the remainder of the sauce into a bowl. Wash the wok and pour in 1 tablespoon (15 ml) sunflower oil. Heat gently over a medium heat and add the steak and fry for 5 minutes, stirring frequently. Add the peppers and the balti sauce and cook on the hob for 15 minutes.

To serve

Serve the curry in bowls or balti dishes with the naan bread and the cucumber raita.

Pot roast beef/butterbean and spring vegetable casserole

TIME TO PREPARE: 15 MINUTES
TIME TO COOK: 3 HOURS
SERVES: 8 (4 MEAT AND 4 VEGGIE)

Pot roasts are cooked long and slow in the oven and are ideal for when you are going out for the day but want a roast to come home to. You can roast all the vegetables and the meat together, so all you need to do when you return home is dish up and enjoy.

Ingredients

For the beef pot roast:
2lb (900 grams) joint of silverside,
    top rump or rolled brisket
4 small shallots or button onions
4 baby carrots
4 stalks celery
4 oz (110 grams) chestnut mushrooms
2lb (900 grams) mixed root vegetables
    (potatoes, parsnips, turnips, swede)
2 tablespoons (30 ml) olive oil
1 bouquet garni made from a sprig of parsley,
    thyme, sage and a bay leaf
8 fl oz (250 ml) hot beef stock
1 tablespoon (15 ml) cornflour
Salt and freshly ground black pepper
For the butterbean casserole:
1 medium onion
2 tablespoons (30 ml) olive oil
4 baby carrots
4 oz (110 grams) fine green beans
1 bulb fennel
2lb (900 grams) mixed root vegetables
    (potatoes, parsnips, turnips, swede)
4 stalks celery
2 x 14 oz (400 grams) tins butter beans
1 oz (25 grams) dried barley
½ pint (300 ml) hot vegetable stock (see recipe on p. 64)

Health note

Pot roasts rely on the cheaper, fattier meats, but do trim off as much excess fat as possible before cooking. This dish is high in protein, fibre, complex carbohydrates, and the chickpeas and the barley combine to form a perfect protein.

½ pint (300 ml) dry cider
1 tablespoon (15 ml) cornflour
1 bouquet garni made from a sprig of parsley, thyme, sage
1 bay leaf
Salt and freshly ground black pepper to taste

Method

FOR THE POT ROAST:
Step one:
You will need a large casserole dish or pan that can be heated on the hob and put in the oven, or a large, heavy based pan and a separate casserole dish. Heat the olive oil in the pan, add the beef and fry gently, turning it until it is browned all over. Using a slotted spoon remove the meat from the pan onto a plate.

Step two:
Peel the shallots or onions and the root vegetables. Leave the carrots and onions whole and chop the remaining vegetables into 1″ (2.5 cm) dice. Add the vegetables to the oil in the pan and fry gently until browned.

Step three:
Return the meat to the pan and add the hot beef stock, the bay leaf and bouquet garni, and season with salt and black pepper. Cover the dish with foil and, if you have one, put the lid on over this. Place in the oven or transfer to a casserole dish and cover. Cook on 150C/300F/gas mark 2 for 3 hours.

Step four:
At the end of the cooking time remove the dish from the oven and place the meat and vegetables in a warmed serving dish. Put the cooking dish with the liquid in on the hob, or if your dish is unsuitable for the hob transfer the liquid into a saucepan. Bring the liquid to the boil. Mix the cornflour with a little water to make a paste and stir this into the boiling liquid. Cook for 3–5 minutes until the sauce is thickened.

To serve

Carve the beef into thick slices and serve with the vegetables and the gravy.

Method

FOR THE BUTTERBEAN CASSEROLE:
Step one:
As before you will need a large casserole that can do duty on both the hob and in the oven, or a separate pan and oven dish. Thinly slice the onion. Scrub the carrots and leave whole. Top and tail the green beans and cut in half. Cut the fennel into eight. Peel the root vegetables and cut into chunks. Cut the celery into 3″ (7.5 cm) lengths.

Step two:
Pour 2 tablespoons (30 ml) olive oil into the pan and heat gently over a medium heat. Add the sliced onion and cook gently for 5 minutes until softened. Add the root vegetables, the fennel and carrots and cook for a further 5 minutes. Mix the cornflour with a little water to form a paste and stir this into the vegetables.

Step three:
Add the stock, cider, celery, green beans, butter beans, barley, bay leaf and bouquet garni, season with salt and pepper and bring to a gentle boil. Cover the pan with foil or a lid and place in the oven or transfer to an oven dish and cover. Cook in the oven with the beef pot roast. If your oven is not large enough to take two casseroles you can cook the butterbean casserole very gently on the hob using the lowest heat setting. The dish will be cooked in about an hour, but can be allowed to cook longer if needed. Check the liquid from time to time and top up with some more stock or cider if necessary.

To serve

Serve in deep bowls with some crusty bread to mop up the juices.

Steak and kidney pudding/savoury vegetable pudding

TIME TO PREPARE: 20 MINUTES
TIME TO COOK: 5 HOURS
SERVES: 8 (4 MEAT AND 4 VEGGIE)

A classic British dish and the ultimate in comfort food. The savoury vegetable pudding has become just as popular as its steak and kidney counterpart.

Ingredients

For the steak and kidney:
1 lb (450 grams) lean shoulder of beef
6 oz (175 grams) ox kidney
1 medium onion
2 tablespoons (30 ml) plain flour
   seasoned with salt and pepper
4 fl oz (120 ml) beef stock
Worcester sauce
Salt and pepper
For the savoury mix:
6 oz (175 grams) soya mince
1 medium onion
14 oz (400 grams) tin chopped tomatoes
2 tablespoons (30 ml) olive oil
1 tablespoon (15 ml) cornflour
1 teaspoon (5 ml) yeast extract
4 fl oz (120 ml) vegetable stock
1 medium free range egg
2 oz (50 grams) fresh wholemeal
   breadcrumbs
Salt and pepper
For the pastry:
16 oz (450 grams) self raising flour
8 oz (350 grams) vegetable suet
Cold water
Salt and pepper

Health note

This dish is high in saturated fat because of the suet and the beef. There isn't a substitute for suet, which is necessary as it melds with the other ingredients and cooks slowly to produce the light, airy texture required. On a positive note, the beef, soya and kidney are high in protein, and the dish is high in fibre and carbohydrates. Save for a once-in-a-while treat.

Continued on next page

Method

Step one:
You will need two 1 litre (1¾ pint) pudding basins that have been well greased, two metal steamers and two large saucepans. If you do not have a metal steamer then use a large saucepan and place an upturned saucer in the bottom. Fill the saucepan with enough water to reach ⅔ of the way up the pudding. Bring the water to the boil.

Step two:
Begin by making the savoury mixture. Peel and chop the onion. Put the olive oil into a medium saucepan and heat gently, add the onion and fry gently for about 5 minutes until softened. Add the tinned tomatoes and stir in the veggie mince, the yeast extract, and the stock. Bring to a gentle boil. Mix the cornflour with a little water to make a paste and add this to the mixture to thicken it. Cook gently for a further 5 minutes then remove from the heat. Beat the egg and stir into the mixture, then add the breadcrumbs and season with salt and pepper.

Step three:
Make the pastry. Put the flour and the suet into a mixing bowl and season well with salt and pepper. Stir to mix, then gradually add a little cold water until the mixture forms a stiff, elastic dough. Divide the dough into three equal balls. Roll out two of the dough balls on a lightly floured board and use to line the pudding basins.

Step four:
Chop the steak and the kidney into 1″ (2.5 cm) cubes, coat with the seasoned flour then add to one of the pastry lined basins. Next add the sliced onions, pushing them under and around the meat, then add the beef stock and enough cold water to just cover the meat, add a dash of Worcester sauce and season well with salt and black pepper.

Step five:
Add the savoury mix to the other pudding basin and top up with a little stock if necessary to ensure the liquid just covers the filling.

Step six:
Roll out the remaining pastry and cut out two circles big enough to cover each basin. Dampen the underneath edges of the pastry and place on top of the puddings. Seal the edges by pinching with your fingers or a fork. Cut out two foil circles 4″ (10 cm) larger than the top of the basins. Grease the

underside of the foil and make a 2″ (5 cm) pleat in the centre of each. Put the foil over the basins and tie securely with string.

Step seven:
Put the puddings into the boiling water and cover. Steam for 5 hours, checking from time to time to ensure that the water has not boiled away. Always use boiling water if you need to top up the water in the pan.

To serve

This dish is very filling so you will need to add only some lightly steamed vegetables and some extra gravy.

Crispy beef/marinated tofu stir fry

TIME TO PREPARE: 2 HOURS MARINATING OR OVERNIGHT + 15 MINUTES
TIME TO COOK: 10 MINUTES
SERVES: 4 (2 MEAT AND 2 VEGGIE)

This appetising supper dish can be prepared and cooked in less than 30 minutes. The beef and tofu need to be marinated for at least 2 hours, but preferably overnight.

Ingredients

8 oz (225 grams) lean sirloin steak
8 oz (225 grams) firm tofu
2 stems lemon grass
1 tablespoon (15 ml) yellow bean sauce
1 tablespoon (15 ml) hot chilli sauce
3 cloves garlic
2″ (5 cm) piece fresh ginger
3 teaspoons (15 ml) Chinese five
   spice powder
2 tablespoons (30 ml) cornflour
6 tablespoons (90 ml) sunflower oil
6 tablespoons (90 ml) dark soy sauce
6 tablespoons (90 ml) rice wine
   or dry sherry
Large bunch spring onions
2 leeks
2 carrots

Health note

High in protein and low in fat, the fast cooking retains the vitamins and minerals in the vegetables.

Method

Step one:
Make the marinade. Put 2 tablespoons (30 ml) each of sunflower oil, soy sauce and rice wine or dry sherry into a bowl with 1 clove garlic and 1 teaspoon (5 ml) of Chinese five spice powder.

Step two:
Slice the beef and the tofu into ½″(1.25 cm) wide, finger-length strips. Put the beef and the tofu into separate bowls and pour half the marinade over each. Cover and refrigerate for at least 2 hours or preferably overnight.

Step three:
Remove the outer leaves of the lemon grass, trim off the top and slice the remainder very finely. Peel and chop the garlic finely. Top and tail the spring onions and the leeks, cut them into matchstick-size lengths, then slice them very finely. Peel the carrots and cut them into thin matchstick-size strips. Peel the ginger and grate finely.

Step four:
Mix the cornflour with the remaining five spice powder and divide between two polythene bags or sprinkle onto two plates. Remove the beef and the tofu from the marinade. Put the beef into one bag or onto one plate and shake or turn in the flour to ensure it is fully coated. Do likewise with the tofu in the other bag/plate.

Step five:
You will need two large frying pans or woks. Place the wok/frying pans on a high heat until very hot. Add 1 tablespoon (15 ml) of sunflower oil to each pan and heat until sizzling. Quickly add the beef to one pan and tofu to the other. Stir fry quickly, moving the meat/tofu around the pan, turning frequently until golden. Using a slotted spoon remove the meat/tofu from the pans and put on separate plates, cover with foil to keep warm.

Step six:
Put the pans back on the hob. Add another tablespoon (15 ml) of oil to each pan and when sizzling quickly add the vegetables in this order, stirring quickly for 30 seconds between each vegetable: garlic, lemon grass, ginger, carrots, leeks, onions. Next add the bean sauce, chilli sauce, soy sauce and rice wine/dry sherry and stir.

Step seven:
Return the meat and the tofu to their respective pans and stir fry for a further minute until piping hot.

To serve

Serve with plain boiled rice or Chinese noodles.

Lamb dishes

Lamb kebabs/vegetable kebabs with minted couscous

TIME TO PREPARE: 15 MINUTES
TIME TO COOK: 10 TO 15 MINUTES
SERVES: 4 (2 LAMB AND 2 VEGGIE)

A lovely dish for an early summer barbeque, the sweet aromatic lamb and vegetable kebabs are served with a refreshing mint couscous and topped with creamy Greek yoghurt.

Ingredients

For the kebabs:
1lb (450 grams) lean lamb fillet or leg steak
4 large red and 4 large green peppers
4 courgettes
2 medium red onions
16 cherry tomatoes
2 tablespoons (30 ml) olive oil
2 cloves garlic
2 sprigs rosemary
For the couscous:
Large bunch of mint
8 oz (225 grams) couscous
14 fl oz (400 ml) vegetable stock
   (see recipe on p. 64)
   or use stock cubes or powder
4 spring onions
1 clove garlic
1 tablespoon olive oil
8 fl oz (250 ml) carton Greek yoghurt

Health note

Buy lean fillet or leg steak to reduce the fat. This dish is high in protein, vitamins A, B, C, E, folate, iron and calcium.

Method

Step one:
You will need eight metal kebab skewers. To make the kebabs pour 2 tablespoons (30 ml) oil into a small bowl. Peel and chop the garlic finely and add to the bowl. Remove the stalks from the mint and rosemary and chop the leaves very finely. Add 2 tablespoons (30 ml) of the chopped herbs to the bowl and reserve the rest for later, season well with salt and freshly ground black pepper.

Step two:
Chop the lamb into 2" (5cm) cubes and place in a bowl. Pour half the marinade over the lamb and mix to ensure it is completely covered. Cover with cling film and chill in the fridge.

Step three:
De-seed the peppers, cut in half widthways then cut each half into four. Slice the courgettes into 2" (5 cm) slices. Cut each onion into four lengthways. Put all the vegetables into a bowl and pour the remaining marinade over them. Mix thoroughly to ensure all the vegetables are coated.

Step four:
While the lamb and the vegetables are marinating make the couscous. Put the stock into a saucepan and bring to the boil. Top and tail the onions and chop finely. Peel the garlic and chop finely. Put 1 tablespoon (15 ml) olive oil into a large saucepan and heat gently. When the oil is hot, add the onions and garlic, and cook for 2 minutes stirring constantly. Add the boiling stock then stir in the couscous. Remove from the heat immediately, cover and leave to stand for 10 minutes.

Step five:
While the couscous is standing, finish the kebabs. Remove the meat and vegetables from the fridge. Start by threading a cherry tomato onto each skewer. Then make up four lamb kebabs by adding a cube of lamb then a piece of vegetable, finishing with another cherry tomato. Make up the vegetable kebabs by threading the vegetables onto the skewers; alternate the vegetables so that you get a pleasing mix of textures and colours. Grill the vegetable kebabs first. They will take 5–7 minutes under a hot grill or on the barbeque. Put them on a plate and keep warm. Grill the lamb kebabs which will also take 5–7 minutes depending how well you like your lamb cooked.

Step six:
Finish the couscous by stirring in the remainder of the chopped herbs and seasoning well with salt and pepper.

To serve

Spoon a quarter of the couscous onto each plate. Add two lamb kebabs to two of the plates and two vegetable kebabs to the remaining two. Spoon the Greek yoghurt over the kebabs and garnish with a little chopped mint.

Lamb/vegetable pittas with cucumber dip and roasted vegetables

TIME TO PREPARE: 15 MINUTES
TIME TO COOK: 15 MINUTES
SERVES: 4 (2 LAMB AND 2 VEGGIE)

This dish can be prepared and cooked in less than 30 minutes. The tender, spicy lamb and vegetables are served in warmed pitta breads with aromatic roasted vegetables and a cooling cucumber dip.

Ingredients

4 wholemeal pitta breads
1lb (450 grams) lean lamb fillet or leg steak
4 Quorn lamb-style grills
3 tablespoons (45 ml) olive oil
2 tablespoons (30 ml) tomato purée
2 cloves garlic
2 teaspoons (10 ml) ground cumin
1 teaspoon (5 ml) each of mild chilli
   powder and ground ginger
2 tablespoons (30 ml) fresh chopped mint
   and rosemary (or 2 teaspoons
   [10 ml] each of dried)
1 tablespoon (15 ml) fresh chopped coriander
   (or a teaspoon [5ml] of dried)
3 large peppers
2 medium red onions
4 large tomatoes
Cucumber raita (see recipe p. 347)

Health note

Trim the fat from the meat to reduce the fat content. This dish is high in protein, and a good source of vitamins A, B, C and folate, calcium, iron selenium and zinc.

Method

Step one:
Pre-heat the oven to 200C/400F/gas mark 6. Prepare the roasted vegetables. De-seed the peppers and cut them and the tomatoes into quarters. Peel the red onions and cut into quarters. Place the vegetables in an oven dish with 1 tablespoon (15 ml) olive oil, and 1 tablespoon (15 ml) fresh rosemary (or 1 teaspoon [5ml] dried rosemary), season well with salt and black pepper and cover with foil. Place the vegetables into the hot oven and cook for 20 minutes.

Step two:
Cut the lamb and the Quorn grills into 2″ (5cm) cubes and put into separate bowls. Mix 2 tablespoons (30 ml) olive oil with the tomato purée, the cumin, chilli powder, ginger, coriander and mint and stir well. Peel and chop the garlic finely and stir into the mixture. Put half the mixture into the lamb, the other half into the Quorn and stir well to ensure that the meat and Quorn are covered with the mixture.

Step three:
Line two baking trays with foil and grease lightly to prevent sticking. Spread the lamb out on one tray and the Quorn on the other. Cook in the hot oven for 10–15 minutes turning once until the lamb is tender and the Quorn is cooked.

Step four:
Toast the pitta breads under the grill until they puff up. Remove and allow them to cool for a moment. Carefully slice each pitta open with a sharp knife and fill two pittas with the lamb mixture and two with the Quorn mixture.

To serve

Dish up the roasted vegetables onto four dinner plates. Place a stuffed pitta onto each plate and spoon over the cucumber raita. Garnish with some mint leaves.

Lamb/vegetable rogan josh with coriander and lemon rice

TIME TO PREPARE: 20 MINUTES
TIME TO COOK: 30 MINUTES
SERVES: 8 (4 LAMB AND 4 VEGGIE)

This curry is quite spicy, if you prefer it less hot reduce the amount of rogan josh paste. As with all curries this benefits from being cooked a day or two before it is eaten.

Ingredients

1lb (450 grams) lean lamb fillet or leg steak
1lb (450 grams) firm tofu
4 tablespoons (60 ml) sunflower oil
2 medium onions
2" (5 cm) piece fresh root ginger
2 cloves garlic
4 tablespoons (60 ml) rogan josh curry paste
1 teaspoon (5 ml) chilli powder
2 teaspoons (10 ml) turmeric
2 x 14 fl oz (400 grams) tins chopped tomatoes
5 fl oz (150 ml) plain yoghurt
2 tablespoons (10 ml) almond flakes
Salt and pepper
For the rice:
16 oz (450 grams) basmati rice
24 fl oz (700 ml) cold water
2 tablespoons (30 ml) fresh coriander
Juice and zest of 1 lemon
4 tablespoons (60 ml) sunflower oil
1 onion
1 teaspoon (5 ml) salt
Freshly ground black pepper

Health note

This dish is high in protein and relatively low in fat; provides carbohydrates, calcium, iron, zinc, folate and vitamins A, B, C, D E and K.

Method

Step one:
Begin by making the rogan josh. Place the sunflower oil in a large saucepan and heat gently over a medium heat. Peel the onion, garlic and ginger and

chop finely, add to the pan and cook over a low heat for 5 minutes until the onion has softened. Add the chilli powder and turmeric and cook very gently for a further 2 minutes. Add the tinned tomatoes and the rogan josh paste, stir well and cook for a further 5 minutes, season well with salt and pepper.

Step two:
Cut the lamb and the tofu into 2″ (5 cm) cubes and put into two saucepans. Add half the curry sauce to the lamb and the other half to the tofu. Cook over a medium heat for 10 minutes.

Step three:
Remove the pans from the heat and allow them to cool for a couple of minutes. Add half the yoghurt to each pan, a tablespoon at a time, stirring well to prevent curdling, add the almonds and season well with salt and freshly ground black pepper. Return to hob and cook on a low heat for a further 20 minutes until the sauce has thickened.

Step four:
While the curry is cooking begin the rice, which will take 30 minutes. Place the oil in a large, heavy based saucepan and heat gently. Peel the onions, chop finely and add to the pan, fry gently over a low heat for 5 minutes. Add the rice and stir well, then add the cold water, salt and freshly ground black pepper. Bring to the boil, stirring frequently, then turn the heat to the lowest setting, put the lid on and cook for 20–25 minutes until all the liquid has been absorbed.

Step five:
When the rice is cooked remove from the heat and stir in the chopped coriander, lemon juice and zest, the put the lid back on and leave for five minutes.

To serve

Serve the rogan josh with the rice and some lime pickle or mango chutney. This is also nice with the cucumber raita (see recipe on p. 347).

Quick tip

The curry can be made in advance and refrigerated for a day or two. To serve, reheat in a saucepan over a low/medium heat for about 20–30 minutes until piping hot. Any left over rice makes a tasty filling for stuffed peppers.

Lamb chops/vegetable grills Provençal

TIME TO PREPARE: 10 MINUTES
TIME TO COOK: 15 MINUTES
SERVES: 4 (2 LAMB AND 2 VEGGIE)

Lamb chops are so quick and easy to prepare and delicious served with this herby tomato sauce, green beans and olives.

Ingredients

4 lean lamb chops
4 Quorn lamb-style grills
1 large onion
3 tablespoons (45 ml) olive oil
2 cloves garlic
2 tablespoons (30 ml) fresh basil
Teaspoon (5 ml) each dried oregano and rosemary
8 oz (225 grams) fine green beans
4 oz (110 grams) pitted black olives
2 x 14 oz (400 grams) tins chopped tomatoes
2 tablespoons sun dried tomato purée
Salt and pepper

Health note

Trim the fat from the lamb chops to reduce the level of saturated fat. This dish is high in protein, and provides vitamins B, C, E, folate and zinc.

Method

Step one:
Prepare the Provençal sauce. Pour 2 tablespoons (30 ml) olive oil into a medium-sized saucepan and heat gently. Peel the onions and garlic and chop finely, add to pan and fry gently for 5 minutes until softened. Add the tinned tomatoes, green beans, basil, oregano and tomato purée, season with salt and pepper, stir well and cook, uncovered, over a medium heat for 20 minutes.

Step two:
Brush the lamb chops and Quorn grills with a little olive oil, season with salt and pepper and sprinkle with a little rosemary. Put the Quorn grills on an oven tray and cook in the oven on 190C/375F/gas mark 5 for 14 minutes, turning halfway through cooking. Grill the lamb chops for 5–7 minutes each side under a hot grill.

To serve

Spoon the Provençal sauce over the lamb and the Quorn. Delicious served with mashed potato and a dark green vegetable such as broccoli, Savoy cabbage or spring greens.

Lamb chops/veggie lamb steaks with redcurrant sauce

TIME TO PREPARE: 10 MINUTES
TIME TO COOK: 20 MINUTES
SERVES 4 (2 LAMB AND 2 VEGGIE)

Although quick and easy to prepare and cook, this dish is elegant enough to serve at a dinner party.

Ingredients

4 lean lamb cutlets
4 Quorn lamb-style steaks
1 tablespoon (15 ml) olive oil
8 oz (225 grams) fresh redcurrants
Juice and zest of medium orange
1 teaspoon (5 ml) paprika
4 fl oz (120 ml) red wine
2 oz (50 grams) sugar
Salt and black pepper

Health note

Trim the fat from the meat to reduce the level of saturated fat. High in protein and an excellent source of vitamins B, C and E, iron and zinc.

Method

Step one:
Brush the lamb cutlets and the Quorn steaks with olive oil and season well with salt and pepper. Place the Quorn steaks on an oven tray and cook in the oven on 190C/375F/gas mark 5 for 15 minutes, turning halfway through cooking. Grill the lamb cutlets under a hot grill for 5–7 minutes each side.

Step two:
Place 6 oz (175 grams) of redcurrants, the orange juice and zest, the wine, the paprika and the sugar in a small pan, stir to mix and heat gently over a low heat for 15–20 minutes until the sauce has thickened.

To serve

Spoon the sauce over the lamb/Quorn and garnish with the reserved redcurrants. Serve with some sauté potatoes and green beans.

Quick tip

If redcurrants are not in season, use a jar of redcurrant sauce instead, simply tip the sauce into the pan with the other ingredients and heat through gently.

Irish/savoury stew with dumplings

TIME TO PREPARE: 20 MINUTES
TIME TO COOK: 2 TO 3 HOURS
SERVES: 12 (6 MEAT AND 6 VEGGIE)

There are as many recipes for traditional Irish stew as there are Irish cooks. The vegetarian version uses a mix of beans and pulses to produce a tasty and nutritious alternative.

Ingredients

2 lb (900 grams) lean middle neck or
    scrag end of lamb
1 oz (25 grams) flour seasoned with
    salt and pepper
14 oz (400 grams) tin haricot beans
2 tablespoons (30 ml) sunflower oil
14 oz (400 grams) tin flageolet beans
3 oz (75 grams) dried red lentils
4 oz (110 grams) pearl barley
2 large onions
4 carrots
4 leeks
2 lb (900 grams) old potatoes
2 tablespoons (30 ml) fresh flat leaf parsley
    (or 2 teaspoons [10 ml] of dried)
2 teaspoons (10 ml) fresh sage
    (or 1 teaspoon [5 ml] of dried)
2 sprigs thyme
    (or one teaspoon [5 ml] of dried)
4 fl oz (120 ml) Guinness
1½ pints (900 ml) hot water
1½ pints (900 ml) vegetable stock
Salt and freshly ground black pepper
For the dumplings:
8 oz (225 grams) self raising flour
4 oz (110 grams) vegetarian suet
Salt and pepper

Health note

Trim as much fat as possible from the lamb to reduce the saturated fat. If you cook this the day before, you can skim further fat from the surface when the dish cools. This dish is a good source of protein, iron, calcium, carbohydrates and vitamins A, B, E, selenium and zinc. The pulses and barley combine to make a perfect protein.

Continued on next page

Method

Step one:
Make the lamb casserole. Cut the lamb into 2" (5cm) cubes. Dip the lamb in
the seasoned flour and ensure it is coated on all sides.

Step two:
Peel and slice the potatoes into 1" (2.5 cm) slices. Peel and slice the onions
into ½" (1.25 cm) slices. Peel the carrots and cut into 2" (5 cm) chunks. Wash
the leeks and cut into 1" (2.5 cm) pieces. Wash the parsley and sage (if using
fresh) and chop finely.

Step three:
Set aside half the potatoes, onions, carrots, leeks and herbs. Layer the
remaining herbs and vegetables alternately with the lamb until you have used
up all the meat, vegetables and herbs, season well with salt and black pepper.
Pour on the Guinness and top up with hot water until the lamb and
vegetables are completely covered. Add 2 oz (50 grams) pearl barley and stir
well.

Step four:
Place on the hob over a medium heat and bring to the boil. Some grey scum
may appear on the surface, spoon this off then put the lid on or cover with
foil, turn down the heat to the lowest setting and simmer gently for 2 hours.

Step five:
Make the vegetable stew. Place 2 tablespoons (30 ml) sunflower oil in a large
pan and heat gently on the hob. Add the remainder of the onions and cook
for 5 minutes until softened. Add the remainder of the vegetables, and the
lentils and cook for a further 5 minutes, stirring frequently to ensure that the
lentils do not stick.

Step six:
Drain the haricot and flageolet beans, add to the pan with the herbs and
enough vegetable stock to cover the vegetables. Sprinkle in the remainder of
the barley and season well with salt and pepper. Bring to the boil and stir
well, turn the heat to the lowest setting and simmer for 1 hour (you can leave
this to cook for longer if you want to make and serve it at the same time as
the Irish stew). Check the level of the liquid from time to time and top up
with vegetable stock if necessary.

Step seven:
To make the dumplings put the flour and suet into a mixing bowl with a large pinch of salt and some freshly ground black pepper. Stir well and mix in a little cold water until you have a stiff, elastic dough. Flour your hands and the work surface and roll into 16 dumplings – don't make them too neat as rough edges make the dumplings lighter.

Step eight:
20 minutes before the end of cooking time for the stews, check the liquid levels and top up if necessary. Season to taste. Bring the stew back to the boil and carefully spoon the dumplings into the stew ensuring that they are covered by the liquid, cover and cook for 20 minutes.

To serve

Serve in deep bowls. Place two dumplings in the centre of each bowl and spoon the stew around the dumplings, sprinkle with a little chopped parsley and serve with some fresh, crusty bread for mopping up.

Pork/gammon dishes

Pork chops with almonds/potatoes with almond and parsnip stuffing and apple sauce

TIME TO PREPARE: 20 MINUTES
TIME TO COOK: 1 HOUR
SERVES: 4 (2 MEAT AND 2 VEGGIE)

A delicious recipe for a quick and filling midweek meal. The homemade apple sauce is a perfect accompaniment to the richness of the pork and the spicy baked potatoes stuffed with parsnip and almonds.

Ingredients

3 large baking potatoes
8 oz (225 grams) parsnips
1 oz (25 grams) vegetarian margarine
1 teaspoon (5 ml) ground cumin
2 tablespoons (30 ml) fresh coriander
   (or 2 teaspoons [10 ml] of dried)
1 tablespoon (15 ml) sunflower oil
2 lean pork chops
4 oz (110 grams) low fat crème fraiche
Juice and zest of 1 lemon
4 oz (110 grams) almond flakes
4 oz (110 grams) Cheddar cheese
1 large free range egg
2 large cooking apples
2 oz (50 grams) brown sugar
Salt and Pepper

Health note

Pork is a fairly fatty meat so trim all visible fat to reduce the level of saturated fat. High in fibre and complex carbohydrates and contains protein, calcium, iron, zinc, and folate, vitamins B, C, D, E and K.

Method

Step one:
Scrub the potatoes and prick them all over with a fork. Place on a baking sheet and put in the oven at 200 C/400 F/gas mark 6, cook for 1 hour. To test if cooked, pierce with a skewer or sharp knife, the centre should be soft and the skin crispy.

Step two:
While the potatoes are cooking prepare the pork chops. Line an oven dish large enough to hold the chops with foil and grease lightly.

Step three:
Put 1 tablespoon (15 ml) oil into a frying pan and heat over a medium heat. Season the chops with salt and pepper and fry them in pan until they are nicely browned on both sides. Remove the chops from the pan and place in the oven dish. Add the lemon juice and zest to the pan and half the coriander, stir to mix and add 2 oz (50 grams) of the crème fraiche. Stir well and cook for 2 minutes. Pour the sauce over the chops, sprinkle with 2 oz (50 grams) of the almonds and cover the dish with a layer of foil. Place the chops in the hot oven and bake for 45 minutes.

Step four:
Peel the cooking apples, remove the core and cut into chunks. Place in a saucepan with the sugar and cover with 1″ (2.5 cm) cold water, bring to the boil and cook over a low heat for 15–20 minutes until the apples are softened and the liquid has been absorbed. Check the flavour and, if the sauce is too tart, add a little more sugar to taste. Mash the apples or blend roughly in a blender, so that you still have some chunks of apple, and return to the pan to keep warm.

Step five:
Put a medium-sized pan of water on to boil. Peel the parsnips, cut them into chunks and add to the pan. Boil for 15–20 minutes until tender. Drain off the water, then add the remainder of the crème fraiche, vegetable margarine, cumin, coriander, some salt and freshly ground pepper and mash well.

Step six:
When the jacket potatoes are cooked, remove them from the oven and allow them to cool for 5 minutes. When cooled cut in half lengthways and scoop out most of the flesh. Add this to the parsnip mixture, mix well and season with salt and black pepper. Beat the egg and grate the cheese. Stir this into the potato mixture with 1 oz (25 grams) almonds.

Step seven:
Spoon the potato mixture back into the potato shells and sprinkle over the remainder of the almonds. Put the potatoes back in the oven to cook for a further 15 minutes.

To serve

Serve with a dark green vegetable such as broccoli or curly kale.

Quick tip

You can use a jar of good quality apple sauce to save time. This recipe also works well with chicken or turkey breasts.

Spanish pork/Quorn with tomatoes and olives

TIME TO PREPARE: 15 MINUTES
TIME TO COOK: 1½ HOURS
SERVES 8 (4 MEAT AND 4 VEGGIE)

Ideal for a late supper as it can be prepared in advance and left to cook slowly in the oven. It needs nothing more than some fresh, crusty french bread to mop up the juices.

Ingredients

1½ lb (700 grams) lean shoulder of pork
8 Quorn pork-style ribsters
4 tablespoons (60 ml) olive oil
2 x 14 oz (400 grams) tins
  chopped tomatoes
4 tablespoons (60 ml) chopped fresh basil
4 oz (110 grams) pitted black olives
1 large Spanish onion
1 clove garlic
1 lb (450 grams) tomatoes
1 large green and 1 large red pepper
2 tablespoons (60 ml) sun dried tomato purée
1 teaspoon (5 ml) dried oregano
1 teaspoon (5 ml) paprika

Health note

Trim as much fat from the pork as possible to reduce the saturated fat. High in protein and carbohydrate and provides vitamins A, B, C E, folate and selenium.

Method

Step one: Cut the pork into 2" (5 cm) cubes. Cut the Quorn into 2" (5 cm) pieces.

Step two:
Put 2 tablespoons (30 ml) olive oil in a frying pan and fry the pork gently until browned on all sides. Remove the pork from the pan with a slotted spoon and place in a casserole dish. Clean the pan, put another 2 tablespoons (30 ml) olive oil into the pan and lightly fry the Quorn for 2–3 minutes, turning halfway through cooking. Remove the Quorn from the pan with a slotted spoon and place in a casserole dish.

Step three: Peel the onion and garlic and chop very finely. Add to the oil in the pan and fry gently for 5 minutes until softened.

Step four: De-seed the peppers and cut into ½" wide (1.25 cm) strips. Add the peppers to the pan with the paprika and oregano and fry lightly.

Step five: Peel the tomatoes and cut into quarters. Add the tinned tomatoes, fresh tomatoes, basil, olives and tomato purée to the pan and stir. Bring to a gentle boil and simmer gently for 15 minutes until the sauce has thickened.

Step six: Pour half the sauce over the pork and the other half over the Quorn. Cover with a lid or foil and cook in the oven for at least 1 hour on 170C/325F/gas mark 3. If you wish to cook this for longer cook for 15 minutes at 170 C/325F/gas mark 3 then reduce the oven temperature to 150C/300 F/gas mark 2 and cook for at least 2 hours.

To serve

Serve with crusty French baguettes and a simple green salad.

Quick tip

You can use a good quality tomato sauce for pasta and simply add a tin of chopped tomatoes and some chopped peppers. Also works well with chicken and Quorn chicken-style pieces.

Pork /vegetable biryani with vegetable curry

TIME TO PREPARE: 20 MINUTES
TIME TO COOK: 45 MINUTES
SERVES 8 (4 MEAT AND 4 VEGGIE)

This is an impressive dish to serve at a dinner party. Biryani is a traditional Indian dish of rice layered with meat or vegetables. It is quite dry and needs to be served with a vegetable curry sauce to complement it. There are quite a lot of ingredients to assemble, but it is straightforward and easy to prepare and cook.

Ingredients

For the biryani:
1 lb (450 grams) lean shoulder of pork
2 x 14 oz (400 grams) tins chickpeas
8 tablespoons (120 ml) sunflower oil
12 fl oz (350 ml) skimmed milk
3 lb (1350 grams) old potatoes
1 lb (450 grams) large carrots
1 lb (450 grams) green beans
8 oz (225 grams) okra
8 oz (225 grams) baby corn
16 oz (450 grams) basmati rice
4 tablespoons (60 ml) medium curry paste
2 small green chillies
2" (5cm) piece root ginger
4 cloves garlic
4 tablespoons (60 ml) fresh coriander
2 tablespoons (30 ml) fresh mint
1 teaspoon (5 ml) cumin seeds
2" (5 cm) piece of cinnamon stick
1 teaspoon (5 ml) saffron powder
6 cardamom pods
6 oz (175 ml) low fat natural yoghurt
3 tablespoons (45 ml) tomato purée
4 large onions
4 oz (110 grams) unsalted cashew nuts
4 oz (110 grams) sultanas
4 large free range eggs
Salt and pepper

Health note

Trim the fat from the pork to reduce the saturated fat. I have also replaced the traditional ghee (clarified butter) with sunflower oil. The combination of rice, nuts and chickpeas provides a perfect protein, high in fibre, complex carbohydrates and a good source of vitamins and minerals.

For the vegetable curry sauce:

2 tablespoons (30 ml) sunflower oil

1 large onion

2 cloves garlic

14 oz (400 grams) tin chopped tomatoes

2 tablespoons (30 ml) medium curry paste

3 courgettes

3 tomatoes

1 large red and 1 large green pepper

Salt and pepper

Method

Step one:

To make the vegetable curry sauce, place 2 tablespoons (30 ml) oil in a large, heavy based pan and heat over a medium heat. Chop onions and garlic finely, add them to the pan and fry gently for 5 minutes until softened. Add the tinned tomatoes and curry paste and stir. Cook gently for a further 5 minutes.

Step two:

Quarter the tomatoes, cut the courgettes into 1" (2.5 cm) slices, de-seed the peppers and cut into 2" (5 cm chunks). Add the vegetables to the curry sauce and cook over a low heat for 20 minutes until the vegetables are tender. Remove from the heat, season well with salt and freshly ground black pepper, and leave to stand covered while you cook the biryani.

Step three:

Remove the seeds from the chillies (best done under cold, running water) and chop finely. Peel and grate the ginger. Peel the garlic and chop finely. Finely chop the coriander and mint. Slice the onions thinly. Cut the potatoes and carrots into 2" (5 cm) chunks.

Step four:

Put 2 tablespoons (30 ml) sunflower oil into a large, heavy based saucepan and heat through gently. Add the sliced onions and fry gently until softened and golden brown, add a teaspoon (5 ml) salt to the pan and then mash the onions. Add the curry paste, tomato purée, chillies, ginger, garlic, coriander and the mint and stir well. Cook the mixture over a gentle heat for 5 minutes.

Step five:

Put half the mixture into another heavy based pan. Add the diced pork and half the potatoes to one pan and the chickpeas, the remainder of the

Continued on next page

potatoes, the carrots, green beans, baby corn and okra to the other pan. Return the pans to the heat and add a tablespoon (15 ml) sunflower oil to each. Cook gently over a medium heat for about 10 minutes, turning the meat and vegetables from time to time, until the pork and vegetables are nicely browned.

Step six:
Place a large pan of salted water on the hob to boil. When boiling add the rice, the cumin seeds, cinnamon stick and cardamom pods and cook over a medium heat for 5 minutes. Drain the rice, cover with a lid and leave to stand for 5 minutes then, if you prefer, you can remove the whole spices.

Step seven:
Add half the rice to the pork pan, and the remaining half to the vegetable pan and stir gently so that the rice and vegetables are thoroughly mixed.

Step eight:
Mix the milk and yoghurt with the saffron. Make holes in the rice mixture in both pans, use a metal skewer to do this, and pour half the milk mixture into the holes in each pan. Sprinkle a little sunflower oil over the surface of each pan, season well with salt and black pepper then cover with foil or a well fitting lid. Cook on the hob over a very low heat for 35–45 minutes. Check after 35 minutes, the rice should be tender and the pork and vegetables should be cooked through.

Step nine:
Place 1 tablespoon (15 ml) sunflower oil in a small saucepan and heat through gently. Add the cashew nuts and sultanas and fry gently for 2–3 minutes. Using a slotted spoon remove the nuts and sultanas from the pan and place them on a plate lined with kitchen paper to drain.

Step ten:
Hard boil the eggs, peel them and cut into quarters.

Step eleven:
Warm through the vegetable curry for 5 minutes before serving.

To serve

Garnish the biryani dishes with the nuts and sultanas, the quartered eggs and a little chopped coriander; serve the vegetable curry in a separate dish. Serve with poppadoms, mango chutney and cucumber raita (see recipe on p. 347)

Gammon steaks with pineapple/vegetarian 'bacon' and pineapple muffins

TIME TO PREPARE: 10 MINUTES
TIME TO COOK: 20 MINUTES
SERVES: 4 (2 MEAT AND 2 VEGGIE)

This classic family favourite is very quick and easy to prepare and cook.

Ingredients

2 unsmoked gammon steaks
1 tablespoon (15 ml) sunflower oil
4 fl oz (120 ml) pineapple juice
1 tablespoon (15 ml) cornflour
6 rings of pineapple (fresh or tinned)
2 English breakfast muffins
4 fl oz (120 ml) pizza sauce (see recipe on p. 345)
4 slices vegetarian bacon
4 oz (110 grams) Cheddar cheese

Health note

Trim most of the visible fat from the gammon to reduce the saturated fat, and grill rather than fry. High in protein and a good source of vitamin B and zinc.

Method

Step one:
Pre-heat the grill to high. Snip the remaining fat on the gammon steaks at 1" (2.5 cm) intervals then brush with a little sunflower oil and season with some black pepper. Grill the gammon steaks under the hot grill for 3–4 minutes each side until browned.

Step two:
Mix the cornflour with the pineapple juice and pour into a frying pan, heat through gently until the sauce thickens, and then add the gammon steaks and two of the pineapple rings. Turn the heat to the lowest setting.

Step three:
Brush the vegetarian bacon with a little oil and cook under the hot grill for one minute on each side. Split the muffins in two and toast the outside of each muffin under the grill until lightly browned. Turn over and spoon 1 tablespoon pizza sauce onto the cut side of each muffin, then top each muffin with a slice of the veggie bacon. Grate the cheese, sprinkle over the muffins and top each one with a pineapple ring. Put under the grill and cook

Continued on next page

under a medium heat until the cheese is golden and bubbling.

To serve

Place a gammon steak on two plates, pour over the pineapple sauce and top with a pineapple ring. Put two muffin halves on two more plates. Serve with crispy French fries, peas and sweetcorn.

Classic/vegetarian cassoulet

TIME TO PREPARE: 15 MINUTES
TIME TO COOK: 45 MINUTES
SERVES: 8 (4 MEAT AND 4 VEGGIE)

The classic version of the cassoulet calls for an abundance of fatty meat, pork and sausage. Although my version is much lighter, it still makes a warming, filling supper.

Ingredients

1lb (450 grams) lean shoulder of pork
4 rashers unsmoked streaky bacon
8 vegetarian Lincolnshire-style sausages
4 rashers vegetarian bacon
4 tablespoons (60 ml) olive oil
2 medium yellow onions
4 cloves garlic
2 x 14 oz (400 grams) tins butter beans
2 x 14 oz (400 grams) tins kidney beans
2 x 14 oz (400 grams) tins chopped tomatoes
4 fl oz (120 ml) vegetable stock
2 large red peppers
2 tablespoons (30 ml) each fresh sage, parsley
    and thyme (if fresh are unavailable use
    ½ teaspoon [2.5 ml] each of dried)
1 teaspoon (5 ml) dried oregano
2 teaspoons (10 ml) paprika
4 tablespoons (60 ml) sun dried tomato purée
Salt and black pepper to taste

Health note

The pork and beans make this a high protein dish. If you serve the cassoulet with rice it creates a perfect protein for vegetarians. Provides vitamins B, C and E.

Method

Step one:
Chop the onions and the garlic finely. De-seed the peppers and chop into small dice. Finely chop the fresh herbs. Cut the pork into 2" (5 cm) cubes. Cut the bacon into 1" (2.5 cm) pieces. Cut the vegetarian sausages into 2" (5 cm) slices and the vegetarian bacon into 1" (2.5 cm) pieces.

Step two:
Put 2 tablespoons (30 ml) of the oil into a frying pan over a medium heat.

Continued on next page

Add the cubed pork and the bacon to the pan and fry gently for about 5 minutes until the pork is browned on all sides and the bacon is crispy. Put the pork, bacon and the cooking oil into a casserole dish.

Step three:
Clean the pan and add 1 tablespoon (15 ml) of the oil. Warm through over a medium heat then add the vegetarian sausages and bacon and fry gently for about 5 minutes until the sausages are evenly browned on all sides and the bacon is crispy. Put the sausages, bacon and cooking oil into another casserole dish.

Step four:
Put 1 tablespoon (15 ml) of the oil into a large, heavy based saucepan. Warm through gently over a medium heat and then add the onions, peppers, paprika and garlic. Cook gently for five minutes until the onion has softened but not browned. Add the stock, tomatoes, herbs and the beans. Season well with salt and black pepper and bring gently to the boil. Turn down the heat to a gentle simmer and stir in the tomato purée.

Step five:
Pour half the tomato and bean sauce over the pork and the other half over the veggie sausages. Cover both casseroles with foil or a lid and cook in a medium oven 180C/350F/gas mark 4 for about 45 minutes.

To serve

Serve with brown rice or some crusty bread.

Gammon/creamy cheese and leek flan

TIME TO PREPARE: 15 MINUTES
TIME TO COOK: 30 MINUTES
MAKES TWO 9" (22.5 CM) FLANS

This tasty flan is quick and easy to prepare and makes a satisfying midweek supper when served with vegetables or a salad. It is also excellent served cold for picnics or as part of a buffet.

Ingredients

20 oz (550 grams) wholemeal shortcrust pastry (see recipe below or use chilled or frozen)
8 oz (225 grams) cubed gammon
4 large leeks
2 oz (50 grams) butter or vegetable margarine
8 medium free range eggs
6 fl oz (175 ml) organic milk
6 fl oz (175 ml) low fat crème fraiche
10 oz (275 grams) Cheddar cheese
2 teaspoons (10 ml) paprika
2 teaspoons (10 ml) freshly grated nutmeg
2 teaspoons (10 ml) English mustard
Salt and black pepper to taste

Health note

High in protein and carbohydrate, this dish provides Vitamins A, B, C, E, folate and calcium.

Method

Step one:
Lightly grease two 9" (22.5 cm) flan tins. Divide the pastry in two and roll each half out to form a circle about 12" (30 cm) in diameter. Line the tins with the pastry, prick the base of the pastry all over with a fork and put in the fridge to chill.

Step two:
Put 1 tablespoon (15 ml) of butter or margarine into a frying pan and melt gently over a low heat. Add the gammon cubes and cook gently for about 5 minutes. Remove from the heat.

Step three:
Slice the leeks thinly. Grate the cheese.

Continued on next page

Step four:
In a large frying pan melt the remainder of the butter over a gentle heat and add the leeks. Fry gently for about 5 minutes until tender, remove from the heat and sprinkle over the paprika and the grated nutmeg, stir well and allow them to cool.

Step five:
Crack the eggs into a mixing bowl and beat lightly, add the milk, mustard and crème fraiche and beat well, then season with salt and black pepper.

Step six:
Take the flans out of the fridge and sprinkle half the grated cheese over each flan. Spread the gammon over just one flan. Place a layer of leeks over the flans and pour on the egg mixture. Bake in the oven on 200 C/400 F/gas mark 6 for 30 minutes.

To serve

Allow the flans to cool slightly before slicing. Serve with a mixed salad or seasonal vegetables. If taking on a picnic, leave the flan in the tin and wrap tightly with foil.

WHOLEMEAL SHORTCRUST PASTRY

MAKES 20 OZ (550 GRAM)

Ingredients

14 oz (400 grams) wholemeal flour
4 teaspoons (20 ml) baking powder
7 oz (200 grams) butter or baking margarine
4–5 tablespoons (60–75 ml) cold water
Pinch of salt

Method

If using a food processor simply place all the ingredients in the processor and mix until the sides of the bowl are clean and a dough is formed. If making by hand sift the flour and salt into a large mixing basin. Chop the fat into small cubes and add to the flour. Lightly rub the fat into the flour with your fingertips until the mixture resembles fine breadcrumbs. Gradually add the cold water, mixing and kneading all the time until you have a soft dough that leaves the sides of the bowl clean. Chill the dough in the fridge for at least 30 minutes before using.

Sausage dishes

Traditional sausage/veggie sausage and mash with onion gravy

TIME TO PREPARE: 10 MINUTES
TIME TO COOK: 20 MINUTES
SERVES: 4 (2 MEAT AND 2 VEGGIE)

The classic sausage and mash served with savoury onion gravy.

Ingredients

For the sausages:
4 lean pork or beef sausages
4 Lincolnshire-style vegetarian sausages
Tablespoon (15 ml) sunflower oil
For the mash:
2 lb (900 grams) potatoes
    (Desirée or King Edwards)
1 teaspoon (5 ml) English mustard
1 oz (25 grams) butter
1 fl oz (30 ml) milk
Salt and pepper to taste
For the gravy:
2 tablespoons (30 ml) sunflower oil
1 large yellow onion
1 oz (25 grams) plain flour
¾ pint (450 ml) vegetable stock
1 teaspoon (5 ml) gravy browning
Salt and pepper to taste

Health note

Choose lean sausages to reduce the fat content of this dish. High in protein, fibre and carbohydrate this dish provides vitamins A, B, C and E and folate.

Method

Step one:
Prick the sausages all over with a fork. Lightly brush with a little sunflower oil. Cook under a hot grill for 10 minutes, turning frequently to ensure they are evenly browned.

Step two:
Boil a large pan of water with a teaspoon of salt.

Step three:
Peel the potatoes and cut into chunks. Add to the pan and boil for 20 minutes until tender.

Step four:
Drain the potatoes well, return them to the saucepan, add the butter, milk and mustard and mash well. Season with salt and pepper and whisk for a minute or two until the mash is creamy.

Step five:
Peel and thinly slice the onion. Heat the oil gently in a large, heavy based frying pan. Add the onion and cook over a medium to high heat until the onions have softened and turned brown (don't burn them as this makes the gravy taste horrible).

Step six:
Add the flour and stir thoroughly to mix. Gradually stir in the stock. Add the gravy browning, season with salt and pepper. Cook over a low heat for 5 minutes.

To serve

Serve with some lightly steamed spring greens or cabbage.

Sausage/veggie sausage and apple casserole

TIME TO PREPARE: 10 MINUTES
TIME TO COOK: 20 MINUTES
SERVES: 4 (2 MEAT AND 2 VEGGIE)

This dish is best made with delicately flavoured pork or turkey sausages and for vegetarians Quorn Bramley bangers.

Ingredients

4 lean pork or turkey sausages
4 Quorn Bramley apple bangers
2 tablespoons (15 ml) olive oil
5 fl oz (150 ml) dry cider
10 fl oz (300 ml) vegetable stock
14 oz (400 grams) tin butter beans
2 large crisp eating apples
   (Granny Smith or Braeburn work well)
1 medium onion
1 teaspoon (5 ml) dried sage
3 tablespoons (45 ml) plain flour
Salt and pepper to taste

Health note

Keep the fat content low by choosing lean sausages. This dish is a good source of vitamins A, B and E.

Method

Step one:
Brush the sausages and veggie sausages with a little olive oil, and grill for ten minutes under a medium grill, turning frequently, until browned all over.

Step two:
Slice the onion thinly. Wash and core the apples and cut into quarters.

Step three:
Put 1 tablespoon (15 ml) olive oil into a heavy based frying pan. Add the onions and sage and fry gently for 5 minutes until the onion has softened. Add the flour and stir to mix. Cook for a further 2 minutes over a gentle heat. Gradually stir in the cider and vegetable stock until the sauce thickens. Add the apples and butter beans, season well with salt and freshly ground black pepper and cook uncovered for 5 minutes.

Step four:
Cut the cooked sausages and veggie sausages into 2" (5 cm) slices and put into separate casserole or oven dishes. Pour half the apples and sauce over each dish. Cover and cook in the oven on 200C/400F/gas mark 6 for 20 minutes.

To serve

Serve with buttered noodles and a green leafy vegetable.

Creole/veggie sausage gumbo

TIME TO PREPARE: 15 MINUTES
TIME TO COOK: 45 MINUTES
SERVES: 4 (2 MEAT AND 2 VEGGIE)

Gumbo is a spicy stew of meat or seafood served in a bowl over a bed of plain steamed rice. It is quick and simple to prepare and makes an unusual supper dish.

Ingredients

4 spicy lean pork sausages
4 vegetarian Lincolnshire-style sausages
4 tablespoons (60 ml) olive oil
2 tablespoons (30 ml) plain flour
1 large yellow onion
4 cloves garlic
2 red peppers
4 stalks celery
1 pint (600 ml) vegetable stock
4 fl oz (120 ml) white wine
2 bay leaves
2 teaspoons (10 ml) Creole seasoning (see recipe below)
2 tablespoons (30 ml) fresh flat leaf parsley
Salt and pepper

For the Creole seasoning:
2 tablespoons (30 ml) each of the following:
    onion powder, garlic powder, dried oregano,
    dried basil
1 tablespoon (15 ml) each of the following:
    dried thyme, black pepper, white pepper,
    cayenne pepper, celery seeds
5 tablespoons (75 ml) sweet paprika

Health note

Keep the fat content down by using lean sausages. This dish is high in carbohydrates and provides vitamins A, B, C, E and folate.

Method

Step one:
To make the Creole seasoning put all the ingredients together in a blender or mixing bowl and blend or mix well. Store the Creole seasoning in a glass storage jar.

Step two:
Prick the sausages and veggie sausages all over with a fork and brush with a little olive oil and Creole seasoning. Grill under a medium grill for 10 minutes, turning frequently, until lightly browned on all sides.

Step three:
Peel onions and garlic and chop finely. De-seed the peppers and chop into small dice. Chop the celery into small dice. Finely chop the parsley.

Step four:
Put a large heavy based saucepan on the hob. Add the oil and heat gently over a low heat until hot, then add the flour a little at a time, stirring quickly to make a paste. Continue to stir and cook until the paste turns a light brown.

Step five:
When the paste is the colour and consistency of peanut butter, quickly add the onions, peppers, garlic and celery and stir thoroughly. Cook the mixture over a low heat for a further 5 minutes stirring constantly.

Step six:
Gradually stir in the vegetable stock and white wine until you have a thick sauce. Bring to the boil and season well with salt and black pepper.

Step seven:
Slice the sausages and veggie sausages into 2" (5cm) slices and place into separate oven dishes. Sprinkle with parsley and add a bay leaf to each dish. Pour half the Creole sauce over each dish, cover with foil or a lid and cook in the oven on 180C/350F/gas mark 4 for 45 minutes.

To serve

Serve in deep bowls filled one-third full with plain boiled rice and pour over the Gumbo.

Sausage/veggie sausage toad in the hole

TIME TO PREPARE: 5 MINUTES
TIME TO COOK: 30 MINUTES
SERVES: 4 (2 MEAT AND 2 VEGGIE)

The traditional combination of puffy, golden batter and succulent sausages makes a delicious and filling supper.

Ingredients

4 lean pork sausages
4 vegetarian sausages
4 tablespoons (60 ml) sunflower oil
6 oz (175 grams) plain flour
2 medium free range eggs
10 fl oz (300 ml) skimmed milk
Salt and white pepper

Health note

Use lean sausages to lower the fat content.

Method

Step one:
You will need two oblong roasting tins measuring approximately 11" x 7" (28 x 18 cm). Prick the sausages all over with a fork and put the veggie sausages into one tin and the pork sausages into the other. Pour 2 tablespoons (30 ml) oil over each and put into the oven at 200C/400F/gas mark 6. Cook for 10 minutes, turning occasionally to ensure the sausages are evenly browned.

Step two:
Sift the flour, salt and white pepper into a mixing bowl. Make a well in the centre and break the eggs into it. Stir with a fork until the egg is incorporated into the flour. Add the milk a tablespoon (15 ml) at a time, stirring well until you have a smooth batter that is the consistency of single cream.

Step three:
When the sausages have cooked for 10 minutes remove the trays from the oven and pour half the batter over each. Return the trays to the oven and increase the heat to 220C/425/gas mark 7 and cook for a further 20 minutes until the batter is well risen and golden brown.

To serve

Cut each toad in two. Serve with roast or mashed potatoes and a green vegetable.

Sausage/veggie sausage goulash

TIME TO PREPARE: 15 MINUTES
TIME TO COOK: 30 MINUTES
SERVES: 4 (2 MEAT AMD 2 VEGGIE)

This traditional Hungarian peasant dish is quick and easy to prepare and can be left to cook slowly.

Ingredients

4 lean pork or beef sausages
4 vegetarian sausages
2 large yellow onions
1 clove garlic
2 tablespoons (30 ml) olive oil
1 tablespoon (15 ml) plain flour
1 tablespoon (15 ml) paprika
14 oz (400 grams) tin chopped tomatoes
1 red and 1 green pepper
5 fl oz (150 ml) low fat crème fraiche
1 tablespoon (15 ml) lemon juice
Salt and pepper

Health note

Keep the fat content low by using lean sausages and by exchanging the traditional sour cream for low fat crème fraiche.

Method

Step one:
Prick the sausages all over with a fork and brush each with a little olive oil. Place under a medium grill and grill for 10 minutes, turning frequently, until they are lightly browned on all sides.

Step two:
Peel and roughly chop the onions and the garlic, de-seed the peppers and slice into strips.

Step three:
Put the remainder of the oil into a large, heavy based saucepan and warm over a gentle heat. Add the onions, garlic, peppers and paprika, and cook over a medium heat for 5 minutes until the onion is softened. Add the flour, stir well and cook for a further 5 minutes.

Continued on next page

Step four:
Add the chopped tomatoes, season well with salt and pepper, stir and cook for a further 5 minutes.

Step five:
Slice the sausages and veggie sausages into 2" (5 cm) slices and place in two separate casserole dishes. Pour half the tomato sauce over each dish and cover with foil or a lid and cook in the oven on 200C/400F/gas mark 6 for 30 minutes. (If you want to leave this for longer turn the heat down to 140C/275F/gas mark 1 at the end of the 30 minutes cooking time).

Step six:
Mix the lemon juice with the crème fraiche.

To serve

Just before serving stir half the crème fraiche mixture into each casserole and sprinkle a little paprika over the top. Nice served with plain brown rice or pasta and a green leafy vegetable.

Minced meat dishes

Shepherd's/gardener's pie

TIME TO PREPARE: 15 MINUTES
TIME TO COOK: 45 MINUTES
SERVES: 8 (4 MEAT AND 4 VEGGIE)

Traditionally shepherd's pie is made with lamb and cottage pie with beef. I also have two vegetarian recipes. Gardener's pie, a savoury lentil and vegetable mix which has a light texture and flavour, the other I call vegetarian shepherd's pie, as the rich soy mince mix is more in keeping with the traditional dish. I have given both recipes and leave you to decide which is your favourite.

COTTAGE/SHEPHERD'S PIE

Ingredients

1lb (450 grams) lean ground minced beef
  or lamb
1 tablespoon (15 ml) cornflour
1 pint (600 ml) beef stock
2 teaspoons (10 ml) tomato purée
14 oz (400 grams) tin chopped tomatoes
2 tablespoons (30 ml) fresh flat leaf parsley
1 large yellow onion
2 stalks celery
2 carrots
Salt and pepper to taste

Health note

Keep the fat content to a minimum by using lean mince and by dry-frying and skimming off any excess fat.

Method

Step one:
Peel and chop the onion finely. Peel and dice the carrots, dice the celery and finely chop the parsley.

Step two:
Put the minced meat into a large, heavy based frying pan and fry very gently for 5 minutes until the mince is lightly browned. Add the onion, carrots and celery and cook for a further 5 minutes until the onion is softened and season with salt and pepper.

Step three:
Stir in the cornflour and gradually add the beef stock. Add the tinned tomatoes, tomato purée and parsley, and cook for a further 10 minutes.

Step four:
Pour the mixture into an oven dish. Top with the mashed potato (see recipe below). Bake in the oven on 190 C/375 F/gas mark 5 for 30 minutes until the top is crispy and golden.

GARDENER'S PIE – LENTIL VERSION

Ingredients

8 oz (225 grams) red lentils
2 teaspoons (10 ml) Vegemite
   (or other vegetarian yeast extract)
2 teaspoons (10 ml) tomato purée
14 oz (400 grams) tin chopped tomatoes
1 pint (600 ml) vegetable stock
2 tablespoons (30 ml) fresh flat leaf parsley
2 tablespoons (30 ml) sunflower oil
1 large yellow onion
2 stalks celery
2 carrots
1 red and 1 green pepper
Salt and pepper

Method

Step one:
Peel and finely chop the onion. Peel the carrots and chop all the vegetables into small dice.

Step two:
Put the oil into a large, heavy based frying pan and heat over a gentle heat. Add the onions, celery, carrot and peppers and cook gently for 5 minutes until the onion has softened.

Step three:
Add the lentils to the pan and stir, cook gently for a further 5 minutes, stirring frequently to ensure the lentils do not stick.

Step four:
Add the vegetable stock, Vegemite, tomatoes, tomato purée and parsley and season with salt and pepper. Bring to the boil then turn down the heat and simmer for 10 minutes.

Continued on next page

Step five:
Pour the mixture into an oven dish and top with the mashed potato (see recipe below). Bake in the oven on 190C/375F/gas mark 5 for 20 minutes until the top is crispy and golden.

SOYA MINCE VERSION

Ingredients

1 lb (450 grams) chilled soya mince
1 tablespoon (15 ml) sunflower oil
1 large yellow onion
2 stalks celery
2 carrots
1 pint (600 ml) vegetarian gravy (see recipe on p. 137)
2 teaspoons (10 ml) Vegemite
2 teaspoons (10 ml) tomato purée
14 oz (400 grams) tin chopped tomatoes
Salt and pepper

Method

Step one:
Put a large, heavy based saucepan on the hob, add the oil and heat through gently.

Step two:
Chop the onion, dice all the vegetables, and add to the pan. Cook over a medium heat for 5 minutes.

Step three:
Add the soya mince, gravy, Vegemite, tomato purée and tomatoes and season with salt and black pepper, cook over a medium heat for 20 minutes.

MASHED POTATO TOPPING

Ingredients per pie

3lbs (1350 grams) Maris Piper potatoes
1 fl oz (30 ml) milk
1 oz (25 grams) butter or vegetarian margarine
Salt and white pepper

Method

Step one:
Fill a large saucepan ⅔ full with water and add a pinch of salt.

Step two:
Peel the potatoes and cut into large chunks. Cook in the boiling water for 20 minutes until tender.

Step three:
Drain all the water off and add the butter, milk and salt and pepper to taste. Mash or whisk until creamy.

Quick tip

Any leftover mince/lentil/soya mixture makes a tasty filling for stuffed peppers.

Meat/vegetable lasagne

TIME TO PREPARE: 10 MINUTES
TIME TO COOK: 65 MINUTES
SERVES: 8 (4 MEAT AND 4 VEGGIE)

I have two recipes for vegetarian lasagne. One is traditional, using a soya mince filling and the other using a mix of vegetables and tomatoes.

Ingredients

16 sheets no pre-cook lasagne
1 quantity meat lasagne sauce
   (see recipe below)
1 quantity vegetable or vegetarian
   lasagne sauce (see recipe below)
1 quantity cheese sauce (see recipe below)

Health note

The meat, cheese, veggie mince and cheese provide a high level of protein. The pasta provides carbohydrates and fibre, a good source of calcium and vitamins A, B, C and D.

MEAT SAUCE FOR PASTA

Ingredients

8 oz (225 grams) lean minced beef
2 tablespoons (30 ml) olive oil
1 large yellow onion
2 cloves garlic
4 fl oz (120 ml) beef stock
14 oz (400 grams) tin chopped tomatoes
2 tablespoons (30 ml) fresh basil (or 2 teaspoons [10 ml] of dried)
1 teaspoon (5 ml) dried oregano
2 tablespoons (30 ml) sun dried tomato purée

Method

Step one:
Peel the onion and garlic and chop finely. Finely chop the basil.

Step two:
Put a large, heavy based saucepan on the hob and pour in the oil. Heat gently over a low heat then add the onions and garlic. Cook over a low heat for 5 minutes until the onion has softened.

Step three:
Add the minced beef to the pan and stir, cook over a medium heat for a further 5 minutes until the beef has browned on all sides.

Step four:
Add the stock, tomatoes, tomato purée, basil and oregano to the pan, season with salt and pepper and bring to the boil stirring frequently. Turn down the heat and cook, uncovered, for 30 minutes until the sauce thickens.

VEGETARIAN SAUCE FOR PASTA

Ingredients

8 oz (225 grams) chilled soya mince
2 tablespoons (30 ml) olive oil
1 large yellow onion
2 cloves garlic
4 fl oz (120 ml) vegetable stock
1 tablespoon (15 ml) Vegemite
14 oz (400 grams) tin chopped tomatoes
2 tablespoons (30 ml) fresh basil (or 2 teaspoons [10 ml] of dried)
1 teaspoon (5 ml) of dried oregano
2 tablespoons (30 ml) sun dried tomato purée
Salt and pepper

Method

Step one:
Peel the onion and garlic and chop finely. Finely chop the basil.

Step two:
Put a large, heavy based saucepan on the hob and pour in the oil. Heat gently over a low heat then add the onions and garlic. Cook over a low heat for 5 minutes until the onion has softened.

Step three:
Add the soya mince to the pan and stir, cook over a medium heat for a further 5 minutes.

Step four:
Add the stock, Vegemite, tomatoes, tomato purée, basil and oregano to the pan, season with salt and pepper, bring to the boil stirring frequently. Turn down the heat and cook, uncovered, for 30 minutes until the sauce thickens.

Continued on next page

VEGETABLE SAUCE FOR PASTA

Ingredients

1 large yellow onion
2 tablespoons (30 ml) olive oil
2 cloves garlic
14 oz (400 grams) tin chopped tomatoes
2 tablespoons (30 ml) fresh basil (or 2 teaspoons [10 ml] of dried)
2 tablespoons (30 ml) tomato purée
1 teaspoon (5 ml) dried oregano
2 medium courgettes
2 stalks celery
2 carrots
1 red and 1 green pepper
8 baby sweetcorn
Salt and pepper

Method

Step one:
Peel the onions and garlic and chop finely. Dice all the vegetables into ½"
(1.25 cm) dice

Step two:
Put a large, heavy based saucepan on the hob. Pour in the oil and warm
through over a low heat. Add the onions and garlic and cook on low heat for
5 minutes until the onion has softened.

Step three:
Add the remainder of the fresh vegetables and cook for a further 5 minutes.

Step four:
Add the tinned tomatoes, basil, oregano and the tomato purée and season
with salt and pepper. Bring to the boil, then lower the heat and simmer
uncovered for 30 minutes.

CHEESE SAUCE

Ingredients

Makes enough for the two lasagnes
2 oz (50 grams) butter
1 oz (25 grams) plain flour
1 pint (600 ml) milk
3 oz (75 grams) Cheddar cheese
3 oz (75 grams) mozzarella cheese
Salt and pepper

Method

Step one:
Coarsely grate the Cheddar cheese and chop the mozzarella into small cubes.

Step two:
In a medium-sized saucepan, melt the butter slowly over a gentle heat and, gradually stir in the flour. Cook gently over a low heat for 3 minutes.

Step three:
Add the milk 1 tablespoon at a time, whisking all the time until it has all been added, season with salt and black pepper.

Step four:
Stir the cheese into the sauce and continue to cook over a low heat, stirring constantly, until the cheese is melted.

TO ASSEMBLE THE LASAGNE
You will need two oven dishes.
Step one:
Grease the oven dishes with a little butter. Spread a layer of the meat sauce over one dish and a layer of the vegetarian sauce over the other dish.

Step two:
Top the sauce in each dish with four sheets of lasagne. Add another layer of the meat/vegetable sauce to each dish and top this with another four lasagne sheets. Pour half the cheese sauce over each dish.

Step three:
Place the dishes, uncovered, into the oven and bake at 190 C/375 F/gas mark 5 for 30 minutes until the top is golden and bubbling.

Continued on next page

To serve

The lasagne is rich and filling and needs only a crisp green salad, a tomato salad or some lightly steamed green vegetables as an accompaniment.

Quick tip

The sauces in this recipe can be used to make a variety of other dishes such as moussaka, spaghetti bolognaise, cannelloni, penne pasta bake, and the cheese sauce is perfect for pasta carbonara or macaroni cheese.

Meat/vegetarian spaghetti bolognaise

TIME TO PREPARE: 15 MINUTES
TIME TO COOK: 30 MINUTES
SERVES: 8 (4 MEAT AND 4 VEGGIE)

I use the same sauce for bolognaise as for the previous lasagne dishes. This sauce is incredibly versatile and freezes well, so if you make extra simply freeze it and use for another pasta dish, a pizza topping or as a filling for jacket potatoes or peppers.

Ingredients

1 quantity meat sauce for pasta
(see recipe on p. 226)
1 quantity vegetarian/vegetable sauce
for pasta (see recipe on p. 227)
1 lb (450 grams) spaghetti
1 tablespoon (15 ml) olive oil
4 oz (110 grams) fresh parmesan cheese
(grated or shaved)
Salt

Health note

A good source of protein, iron, fibre, carbohydrates and vitamins A, B, C and D.

Method

Step one:
Begin by making the meat/vegetable sauce for the pasta.

Step two:
Fill a large saucepan 2/3 full of water and add 1 teaspoon (5 ml) salt and 1 tablespoon (15 ml) olive oil. Bring to the boil.

Step three:
Stand the spaghetti in the water, as it cooks it will soften into the pan. When it has softened, give it a good stir to prevent sticking. Continue to cook on a high heat so that the water is constantly boiling, stirring from time to time. If using standard spaghetti it will usually take around 12 minutes to cook, but some varieties cook more quickly – check the instructions on the pack. When you think the spaghetti is cooked, remove a strand from the pan and bite into it, it should be soft on the outside but still slightly chewy in the middle.

Continued on next page

Step four:
When the spaghetti is cooked drain in a colander to remove all the water then rinse with boiling water. Add a little olive oil or butter if liked.

To serve

Spoon the spaghetti onto plates and top with a ladle of meat/vegetable sauce. Serve the parmesan separately for sprinkling. I would serve this with a crisp, green salad and some garlic bread.

Meat/vegetable moussaka

TIME TO PREPARE: 20 MINUTES
TIME TO COOK: 30 MINUTES FOR THE SAUCE + 45 MINUTES FOR THE MOUSSAKA
SERVES: 8 (4 MEAT AND 4 VEGGIE)

Another recipe that uses the meat/vegetable sauce for pasta with just a couple of added ingredients. I use half potato, half aubergine in this recipe, but you can either use all aubergine or all potato as you prefer.

Ingredients

1 quantity meat sauce for pasta
   (see recipe on p. 226)
1 quantity vegetarian sauce for pasta
   (see recipe on p. 227)
4 fl oz (120 ml) red wine
2 teaspoons (10 ml) cinnamon
2 tablespoons (30 ml) olive oil
2 large aubergines
2 large baking potatoes
1 oz (25 grams) plain flour
2 oz (50 grams) butter
1 pint (600 ml) milk
2 large free range eggs
2 teaspoons (10 ml) freshly grated nutmeg
Salt and black pepper

Health note

A good source of protein, iron, fibre, carbohydrates, calcium and vitamins A, B, C and D.

Method

Step one:
Make the meat and vegetarian sauces. Add half the wine and 1 teaspoon (5 ml) of cinnamon to each pan of sauce and leave to cook gently while you prepare the remainder of the dish.

Step two:
Cut the aubergines into 1″ (2.5 cm) thick slices. Spread them out on a plate or some kitchen roll and sprinkle lightly with a little salt (this removes any bitterness and also stops the aubergines soaking up so much oil). Peel the potatoes and cut into 1″ (2.5 cm) thick slices.

Continued on next page

Step three:
Boil a pan of water, add the potatoes and cook for 2 minutes. Remove from the heat, drain and rinse with cold water to stop the potatoes cooking further.

Step four:
Rinse the aubergines. Put a heavy based frying pan on the hob and add the oil. Heat gently and add four or five slices of aubergine (just enough to cover the base of the pan). Fry the aubergines gently until browned on one side then turn them over and fry until browned on the other. Continue until you have browned them all. When cooked, remove the aubergines from the pan with a slotted spoon and drain on kitchen paper.

Step five:
Make the sauce by melting the butter in a heavy based saucepan. Gradually add the flour, mixing it into the butter and cook gently for 3 minutes. Next gradually add the milk a little at a time, stirring constantly, season with salt and pepper. Cook over a low heat for 3 minutes. Remove the sauce from the heat. Crack the eggs into a mixing bowl and beat them, then gradually beat them into the sauce.

Step six:
You will need two oven dishes. Lightly grease the dishes to prevent sticking and pour a layer of meat/vegetarian sauce over the base of each dish. Next add a layer of aubergines, then another layer of meat/vegetable sauce. Finish off with the layer of potatoes then top this with the sauce. Grate the nutmeg over the top of the sauce and bake the moussaka in the oven on 190C/375F/gas mark 5 for 45 minutes.

To serve

Moussaka is a meal in itself and needs little more than a crisp green salad as an accompaniment.

Spaghetti with meatballs/vegetarian meatballs

TIME TO PREPARE: 20 MINUTES
TIME TO COOK: FOR THE SAUCE 2 HOURS + 1 HOUR FOR THE MEATBALLS
SERVES: 4 (2 MEAT AND 2 VEGGIE)

The secret of the simple tomato sauce that is served with these tasty meatballs is in the long, slow cooking. This sauce is very versatile and can be used to top pasta, pizza, grilled meats and vegetables etc so it is worth making up a batch and chilling or freezing it until needed.

Ingredients

8 meatballs (see recipe below)
8 vegetarian meatballs (see recipe below)
1 quantity Italian pasta sauce
  (see recipe below)
1lb (450 grams) spaghetti

Health note

A good source of protein and iron, fibre, carbohydrate, vitamins A, B, C and D.

MEATBALLS

Ingredients

8 oz (225 grams) lean minced beef
8 oz (225 grams) Quorn or soya mince
1 large green pepper
2 medium free range eggs
1 large yellow onion
3 cloves garlic
2 tablespoons (30 ml) fresh basil
2 teaspoons (10 ml) dried oregano
6 oz (175 grams) wholemeal breadcrumbs
4 tablespoons (60 ml) tomato purée
4 tablespoons (60 ml) plain flour seasoned
  with salt and pepper
8 tablespoons (120 ml) sunflower oil
Salt and pepper

Continued on next page

Method

Step one:
Peel and finely chop the onion and garlic. De-seed the pepper and chop into fine dice. Chop the basil very finely. Break the eggs into a bowl and beat lightly.

Step two:
Put the minced beef into a mixing bowl and add half the onion, garlic, peppers, herbs, breadcrumbs, tomato purée and egg and mix thoroughly with a fork, season well with salt and pepper.

Step three:
Put the vegetarian mince into a mixing bowl and add the remaining onion, garlic, peppers, herbs, breadcrumbs, tomato purée and egg. Mix thoroughly with a fork and season well with salt and pepper.

Step four:
Use the flour to coat your hands and work surface, and make eight meatballs from the meat mixture and eight balls from the veggie mixture. Coat the meatballs and the veggie balls with a little flour.

Step five:
Put half the oil into a large frying pan and heat gently. Cook three or four beef meatballs at a time, frying them gently for about 5 minutes until they are browned all over. Using a slotted spoon remove the meatballs from the frying pan onto a plate lined with kitchen paper.

Step six:
Clean the pan and warm the remaining oil over a gentle heat. Fry the veggie balls over a medium heat for about 5 minutes until browned all over. Using a slotted spoon remove the from the frying pan onto a plate lined with kitchen paper.

ITALIAN TOMATO SAUCE:

Ingredients

2 lb (900 grams) plum tomatoes (or 2 x 14 oz [400 grams] tins of chopped tomatoes)
1 large yellow onion
3 cloves garlic
4 tablespoons (60 ml) fresh basil (or 2 teaspoons [10 ml] of dried)
2 teaspoons (10 ml) oregano
1 tablespoon (15 ml) olive oil

1 tablespoon (15 ml) extra virgin olive oil
2 tablespoons (30 ml) sun dried tomato purée
1 teaspoon (5 ml) sugar
Salt and pepper

Method

Step one:
Peel and finely chop the onions and garlic. Finely chop the basil. If you are using fresh tomatoes, place them in a bowl of boiling water for 5 minutes, then remove them and peel, remove the seeds and chop the flesh roughly.

Step two:
Put 1 tablespoon (15 ml) olive oil into a large, heavy based pan and warm on a medium heat. Add the onions and garlic and cook for 5 minutes over a low heat until the onion is softened.

Step three:
Add the tomatoes, herbs, tomato purée and sugar, stir well and bring to a gentle boil. Turn the heat down to the lowest setting, cover and cook for at least 2 hours.

Step four:
When the sauce has finished cooking stir in 1 tablespoon extra virgin olive oil, this gives the sauce a gloss and an extra richness.

To serve

Put the meatballs in a casserole or oven dish and the veggie meatballs in another oven dish. Pour half the sauce over each dish, cover tightly with foil or a lid and bake in the oven for 1 hour on 190C/375F/gas mark 5. 15 minutes before the meatballs are cooked, cook the spaghetti, according to the pack instructions. Ladle onto plates. Add meatballs, spoon the sauce over and garnish with a little chopped basil. Serve with some parmesan cheese and a green salad.

Quick tip

You can save time by making the sauce in advance or using a good quality bought pasta sauce. You can also buy the meatballs ready-made and Quorn make a vegetarian version called Swedish-style balls which work very well with this recipe.

Spicy beef/spicy chickpea enchiladas

TIME TO PREPARE: 25 MINUTES
TIME TO COOK: 15 MINUTES
SERVES: 4 (2 MEAT AND 2 VEGGIE)

A traditional Mexican dish of tortillas, filled with a delicious filling of spicy mince/chickpeas, vegetables and cheese.

Ingredients

4 oz (110 grams) lean minced beef
14 oz (400 grams) tin chickpeas
4 large tortillas
1 large yellow onion
1 large red onion
1 red and 1 green pepper
16 pitted black olives
2 cloves garlic
1 small red chilli
1 teaspoon (5 ml) cumin
1 teaspoon (5 ml) oregano
2 x 14 oz (400 grams) tins chopped tomatoes
2 tablespoons (30 ml) sunflower oil
8 oz (225 grams) Cheddar cheese
Salt and pepper

Health note

A good source of protein, iron, fibre, calcium and vitamins A, B, C and D.

Method

Step one:
Peel and finely chop the yellow onion and garlic. De-seed the peppers and slice into thin strips. Wash the chilli and remove the seeds (best done under running water) then chop finely. Chop the olives, peel the red onion and slice thinly, grate the cheese.

Step two:
Heat a large, heavy based saucepan, add the sunflower oil and heat gently. Add the yellow onion, garlic, chilli and red and green pepper and fry gently for 5 minutes until the onion has softened.

Step three:
Add the tomatoes, cumin and oregano, season with salt and pepper and cook for a further 15 minutes uncovered.

Step four:
Put the minced beef into a non-stick frying pan and dry fry over a gentle heat for 5 minutes until browned. Using a slotted spoon remove the mince from the pan onto a plate lined with kitchen paper.

Step five:
Drain the chickpeas and mash lightly with a fork.

Step six:
You will need two oblong or square oven dishes. Spoon a layer of the tomato sauce over the base of each dish. Lay the tortillas out on the work surface and spread a layer of the tomato sauce over each tortilla (reserve some for the topping). Spoon the minced meat onto two of the tortillas and the chickpeas onto the other two tortillas, sprinkle the tortillas with a few slices of red onion and half the cheese. Roll the tortillas up into a cigar shape.

Step seven:
Place the meat tortillas in one dish and the chickpea tortillas in the other dish. Spoon the remainder of the tomato sauce over the tortillas, and then sprinkle over the remaining cheese and the chopped black olives. Bake in the oven on 180C/350F/gas mark 4 for 15 minutes.

To serve

Serve with a salad of shredded lettuce and grated carrot and some spicy tomato salsa (see recipe on p. 272)

Quick tip

You can replace the tomato sauce with two tubs of bought spicy tomato salsa mixed with a small tin of tomato purée. You can make an alternative dish by using the tomato/mince/chickpea/cheese mixture to fill some taco shells.

Home-made beefburgers/veggie burgers

TIME TO PREPARE: 15 MINUTES + 30 MINUTES CHILLING TIME
TIME TO COOK: 15 MINUTES
SERVES 8 (4 MEAT AND 4 VEGGIE)

Home-made burgers contain less fat and additives than shop-bought and take just minutes to prepare and cook. Prepare some in advance and chill or freeze for later use. Perfect for barbeques, or served with salad, as a light lunch or supper dish.

Ingredients

1 lb (450 grams) lean minced beef
1 lb (450 grams) chilled Quorn or soya mince
5 tablespoons (75 ml) sunflower oil
2 red onions
2 teaspoons (10 ml) dried mixed herbs
2 teaspoons (10 ml) English mustard powder
2 small free range eggs
4 oz (110 grams) wholemeal breadcrumbs
Dash of vegetarian Worcester sauce
4 tablespoons (60 ml) flour seasoned
    with salt and pepper
Salt and freshly ground black pepper

Health note

A good source of protein, iron and Omega 6 fatty acids.

Method

Step one:
Peel and finely chop the onion. Heat 1 tablespoon (15 ml) of oil in a heavy based frying pan, add the onion and fry gently for 5 minutes until softened.

Step two:
Place the minced beef in a large mixing bowl and add half the onion, herbs, mustard powder, egg, breadcrumbs and Worcester sauce. Mix thoroughly and season well with salt and black pepper.

Step three:
Place the vegetarian mince into a large mixing bowl and add the remainder of the onion, herbs, mustard powder, egg, and the breadcrumbs. Mix thoroughly, season well with salt and pepper.

Step four:
Coat your hands and the work surface with flour and form the burger mix into four even meat patties and four even vegetarian patties. Chill the burgers in the fridge for 30 minutes.

Step five:
When the burgers have chilled place the remainder of the oil in a large, heavy based frying pan and fry them over a medium heat for 5 minutes on each side. Using a slotted spoon remove from the pan and drain on kitchen paper.

To serve

Serve as a light lunch or supper with salad or inside a burger bun with lettuce, relish and sliced red onion.

Fish dishes

Wild salmon baked with herb butter/pine nut and herb stuffed tomatoes

TIME TO PREPARE: 5 MINUTES
TIME TO COOK: 10 MINUTES
SERVES: 4 (2 FISH AND 2 VEGGIE)

Wild salmon is a little more expensive than farmed, but is free of artificial colouring and additives. Although this dish takes just minutes to prepare and cook it is special enough to serve at a dinner party.

Ingredients

2 wild salmon fillets
2 large beefsteak tomatoes
3 oz (75 grams) butter
Juice and zest of 1 lemon
2 carrots
4 baby sweetcorn
1 leek
3 tablespoons (45 ml) fresh coriander
2 tablespoons (30 ml) fresh parsley
2 tablespoons (30 ml) white wine
4 oz (110 grams) wholemeal breadcrumbs
1 clove garlic
4 oz (110 grams) pine nuts
Salt and pepper

Health note

Fish is low in fat and high in protein and Omega 3 fatty acids. The pine nuts also provide protein.

Method

Step one:
Cut the carrots into julienne strips. Cut the leek into three and shred finely lengthways. Cut the corn in half lengthways. Finely chop the herbs and garlic. Place the pine nuts in a dry frying pan over a very low heat, stirring constantly until they begin to turn brown.

Step two:
You will need two ovenproof dishes. Cut two pieces of foil to 12" (30 cm) x 12" (30 cm), lay one piece in an oven dish and place half of the carrots, leeks and corn in the centre of the foil. Place a salmon fillet on top of the vegetables and sprinkle with a quarter of the herbs. Add ½ tablespoon (7.5 ml) lemon juice and

1 tablespoon (15 ml) white wine, season with salt and pepper. Make a parcel of the foil by pulling two edges towards the centre and make a 1" (2.5cm) pleat in the top, then fold a similar pleat in the remaining two sides so that you have a sealed parcel. Follow the same method to make the second parcel.

Step three:
Soften 2 oz (25 grams) butter and mash into it a quarter of the herbs. Divide the butter in two and roll into a ball, then pat down until you have two thick circles. Chill in the fridge.

Step four:
Melt the remaining 1 oz (25 grams) butter in a frying pan over a low heat. Add the chopped garlic and fry gently for 30 seconds, then add the breadcrumbs, the remainder of the herbs, the lemon zest, 1 tablespoon (15 ml) lemon juice and the pine nuts. Cook over a medium heat, stirring gently with a fork, until the breadcrumbs begin to turn crispy and golden.

Step five:
Reserve a tablespoon (15 ml) of the breadcrumbs for later. Slice the lid of the tomatoes almost, but not quite, through. Scoop out the seeds and the flesh and mash them with the breadcrumb mixture, season with salt and freshly ground black pepper then return the mixture to the tomatoes.

Step six:
Bake the salmon and the tomatoes in the oven on 200C/400F/gas mark 6 for 15–20 minutes.

To serve parcels, sprinkle the remaining breadcrumbs over the salmon and place a knob of herb butter on each. Close the parcels and serve the salmon in the parcels. The fish and the tomatoes make a delicious light supper served with the Jewelled Summer tabbouleh (see recipe on p. 98) or with some plain boiled rice that has been mixed with sweetcorn and peas.

Pan fried tuna/grilled haloumi cheese on roasted Mediterranean vegetables

TIME TO PREPARE: 5 MINUTES
TIME TO COOK: 20 MINUTES
SERVES: 4 (2 FISH AND 2 VEGGIE)

A simple midweek meal, bursting with the flavours of the Mediterranean, prepared and cooked in under half an hour. Haloumi cheese is a firm goat's cheese that can be grilled or fried without dissolving.

Ingredients

2 fresh tuna steaks
4 x 2" (5 cm) thick slices haloumi cheese
8 fl oz (250 ml) Italian tomato sauce
   (see recipe on p. 344) or a jar of
   tomato sauce for pasta
4 tablespoons (60 ml) olive oil
2 teaspoons (10 ml) dried oregano
2 tablespoons (30 ml) basil pesto
4 tomatoes
2 cloves garlic
2 green peppers
2 red peppers
2 courgettes
2 small red onions
Salt and pepper

Health note

The tuna is high in protein and Omega 3 fatty acids and low in fat. The cheese provides protein and calcium. The vegetables provide vitamin C, carotenes, folate, fibre and carbohydrate.

Method

Step one:
Begin with the roasted vegetables. Quarter the tomatoes, de-seed and quarter the peppers, cut the courgettes into 2" (5 cm) chunks, peel and quarter quarter the onions, and peel and chop the garlic. Put the vegetables into an ovenproof dish and spoon over 2 tablespoons (10 ml) olive oil, sprinkle with the garlic and oregano and season with salt and pepper. Cover with foil and bake in the oven at 200C/400F/gas mark 6 for 20 minutes.

Step two:
Mix the remaining 2 tablespoons (30 ml) olive oil with the basil pesto and brush the tuna and haloumi cheese on both sides with the oil. Pre-heat the grill and place the cheese on the grill rack. Grill for 5 minutes each side.

Step three:
Put the remainder of the oil into a non-stick frying pan and gently fry the tuna for 5 minutes on each side.

Step four:
Warm the tomato sauce on the hob or in the microwave.

To serve

Place the tuna steak or grilled cheese on top of the vegetables on individual plates and spoon over the tomato sauce. Serve with pasta, rice or new potatoes.

Luxury fish/creamy tofu and sweetcorn pie

TIME TO PREPARE: 15 MINUTES
TIME TO COOK: 50 MINUTES
SERVES: 4 (2 FISH AND 2 VEGGIE)

You can use any mixture of white fish/shellfish to make this classic dish. The tofu and sweetcorn pie is just as creamy and appetising as the fish version.

Ingredients

4 oz (110 grams) firm tofu
1 small red pepper
4 oz (110 grams) tin sweetcorn
2 tablespoons (30 ml) sunflower oil
2 tomatoes
8 oz (225 grams) cod fillet (skin removed)
4 oz (110 grams) cooked and peeled prawns
2 large leeks
2 stalks celery
1 small yellow onion
1 pint (600 ml) milk
1 tablespoon (15 ml) cornflour
6 fl oz (175 ml) white wine
2 oz (50 grams) Cheddar cheese
2 tablespoons (30 ml) fresh flat leaf parsley
2 tablespoons (30 ml) fresh chives
1 bay leaf
1 teaspoon (5 ml) smoked paprika
   (use ordinary paprika if you don't have smoked)
2 lbs (900 grams) new potatoes
Salt and pepper

Health note

The fish is high in protein and Omega 3 fatty acids and low in fat. Tofu is high in protein and low in fat. This dish is a good source of calcium and vitamins A, B and C.

Method

Step one:
Finely chop the onion. Slice the leeks finely. De-seed the pepper and dice. Chop the celery into dice. Slice the tomatoes. Wash the herbs and chop finely. Grate the cheese.

Step two:
Scrub the potatoes and boil in salted water for 10 minutes. Drain, rinse with cold water and cool.

Step three:
Put the cod into an oven dish, pour over 1 tablespoon (15 ml) white wine and season with salt and pepper. Cook in the oven for 10 minutes on 200C/400F/gas mark 6.

Step four:
While the cod and potatoes are cooking, make the sauce by putting 1 tablespoon (15 ml) sunflower oil into a medium sized, heavy based pan. Heat gently then add the onions, leeks, peppers, celery, sweetcorn and paprika. Cook over a gentle heat for about 5 minutes until the vegetables begin to soften. Add the cornflour and stir into the vegetables, then add the remainder of the white wine and herbs, gently bring to the boil stirring constantly. Gradually stir in the milk and add the bay leaf, season with salt and pepper and simmer for 5 minutes.

Step five:
When the potatoes are cool cut them into thin slices. Remove the fish from the oven and flake it apart with a knife and fork. Add the prawns and pour over half of the white wine sauce. Layer half of the tomatoes over the dish and sprinkle half the cheese on top of this. Now layer half the potato slices on the top then brush with a little sunflower oil, season with salt and pepper.

Step six:
Mash the tofu and blend or stir it into the remainder of the white wine sauce. Pour the mixture into another oven dish and top with the remaining tomatoes, cheese and potatoes and then brush with a little sunflower oil, season with salt and pepper.

Step seven:
Place the pies on an oven tray and bake in the oven on 200C/400F/gas mark 6 for 25 minutes until the potatoes are browned and crispy.

To serve

Serve with a dark green vegetable such as broccoli.

Seafood/vegetable Paella

TIME TO PREPARE: 15 MINUTES
TIME TO COOK: 1 HOUR
SERVES: 4 (2 FISH AND 2 VEGGIE)

A traditional Spanish dish, paella is a wonderfully rich, golden mixture, made with medium grain rice that has been infused with saffron, a piquant sauce known as sofrito, and a mixture of fresh seafood and/or vegetables. You can replace the seafood with other fish such as haddock, cod, salmon, scallops, or you can use a mixture of fish and chicken or chicken and spicy sausage.

Ingredients

1 red onion
1 red and 1 green pepper
4 cloves garlic
2 tablespoons (30 ml) fresh flat leaf parsley
14 oz (400 grams) tin chopped tomatoes
8 large raw prawns (peeled and deveined)
1 squid tube (cut into rings)
6 fresh mussels (scrubbed and de-bearded)
5 tablespoons (75 ml) olive oil
2 teaspoons (10 ml) paprika
6 oz (175 grams) medium grain rice
10 fl oz (300 ml) hot vegetable stock
4 oz (110 grams) peas
2 oz (50 grams) fine green beans
6–8 florets cauliflower
4 medium, free range eggs
1 pinch saffron threads
2 lemons
Salt and pepper

Health note

Fish is high in protein and Omega 3 fatty acids and low in fat. Rice provides fibre, calcium, iron, B vitamins, and calcium and when mixed with the peas it provides a perfect protein. The vegetables provide more fibre, carbohydrate and vitamin C.

Method

Step one:
Peel and finely chop the onion and garlic. De-seed the peppers and cut into small dice. Finely chop the parsley. Cut the lemons into quarters. Cook the eggs in boiling water for 8 minutes then cool under running water; when cool peel and quarter them. Cook the peas, green beans and cauliflower in boiling, salted water for 3–4 minutes.

Step two:
First make the sofrito. You will need a large, shallow frying pan or skillet. Pour
2 tablespoons (30 ml) olive oil into the pan and heat gently, add the onion,
parsley, and three cloves chopped garlic, stir and cook over a gentle heat for
5 minutes. Add the tomatoes and paprika, stir and continue to cook over a
low heat for about 20 minutes until the liquid has been absorbed and the
sauce thickens. Pour the sofrito into a bowl and clean the pan.

Step three:
While the sofrito is cooking prepare the seafood. Place the mussels in a saucepan
(the mussels should all be closed at this point) and just cover them with boiling
water. Cover the pan and simmer on a low heat for 5 minutes (the mussels should
all be open at this point – discard any that remain unopened). Drain the mussels.
Heat 1 tablespoon (15 ml) olive oil in the frying pan and add the remaining
chopped garlic and the prawns. Cook over a medium heat for 2 minutes, stirring
frequently. Add the squid rings and cook for a further 2 minutes. Using a slotted
spoon, remove the seafood from the pan and drain on kitchen paper. Discard the
oil and clean the pan. Put the cooked seafood on a plate and cover with foil.

Step four:
Heat 2 tablespoons (30 ml) olive oil in the frying pan and add the chopped
peppers and cook for 5 minutes over a gentle heat.

Step five:
Pour the sofrito into the pan with the peppers and add the rice, stir well to
ensure all the grains are coated and cook over a low heat for 1 minute. Add the
hot vegetable stock, the saffron, a teaspoon (5 ml) salt and a good shake of
freshly ground black pepper, stir well and bring to the boil. Simmer over a
medium heat, uncovered, for 10 minutes. Do not stir the rice anymore but move
the pan around the heat to ensure that all the rice is cooked. Lower the heat and
cook for a further 15 minutes without stirring, turn the heat up to medium/high
for the last 2 minutes to lightly toast the rice on the bottom of the pan.

Step six:
Transfer the rice into two warmed serving dishes. To one dish add the seafood,
gently pushing it into the rice and then scatter half the peas over the top. To
the other dish add the cauliflower and the green beans, gently pushing them
into the rice then scatter over the remainder of the peas. Cover both dishes
with foil and allow the paella to rest for 5 minutes before serving.

To serve

Sprinkle the paellas with a little lemon juice and garnish with the lemon wedges
and the egg quarters. Traditionally, paella is eaten straight from the dish.

Penne Nicoise with tuna

TIME TO PREPARE: 10 MINUTES
TIME TO COOK: 20 MINUTES
SERVES: 4 (2 FISH AND 2 VEGGIE)

This is a really simple but tasty supper dish that can be prepared and cooked in under half an hour.

Ingredients

1 quantity Italian tomato sauce
   (see recipe on p. 236) or 1 large
   jar tomato sauce for pasta
7 oz (200 grams) tin tuna
8 oz (225 grams) fine green beans
4 oz (110 grams) grated Cheddar cheese
16 pitted black olives
1 lb (450 grams) penne pasta
1 tablespoon (15 ml) olive oil
Salt and pepper

Health note

The tuna is high in protein, low in fat and a good source of Omega 3 fatty acids. The cheese provides protein and calcium.

Method

Step one:
Begin by making the sauce. If you are using sauce you have already prepared or bought, simply warm through over a gentle heat.

Step two:
Boil a large pan of water and add 1 teaspoon (5 ml) salt and 1 tablespoon (15 ml) olive oil and add the penne. Bring the water back to the boil and cook for 12–15 minutes or according to pack instructions, stirring frequently. While the pasta is cooking top and tail the beans and steam them over the pasta or cook for 5 minutes in some boiling, salted water.

Step three:
Drain the pasta, add the green beans and olives and pour on the tomato sauce. Divide the pasta in two. Drain the tuna and mix into one half of the pasta, stirring well. Heat through over a medium heat for 2 minutes.

To serve

Spoon the pasta into serving bowls and sprinkle with grated cheese. Nice served with garlic bread and a green salad.

Spicy pan fried cod/Indian eggs with Indian potatoes

TIME TO PREPARE: 15 MINUTES
TIME TO COOK: 20 MINUTES
SERVES: 4 (2 FISH AND 2 VEGGIE)

This dish is incredibly quick to cook and makes a tasty supper dish – much cheaper and healthier than an Indian take away.

Ingredients

2 x 6 oz (175 grams) cod fillets or steaks
4 large free range eggs
8 spring onions
3 tablespoons (45 ml) olive oil
1 teaspoon (5 ml) ground ginger
2 teaspoons (10 ml) turmeric
1 teaspoon (5 ml) chilli powder
6 tablespoons (90 ml) fresh coriander
Salt and black pepper
2 lb (900 grams) potatoes
2 tablespoons (30 ml) curry paste
2 packets ripened on the vine cherry tomatoes (with vine and stalks on)

Health note

The fish is high in protein and low in fat. The eggs are also a good source of protein. The potatoes are a good source of fibre and carbohydrates.

Method

Step one:
Finely chop the spring onions. Peel the potatoes, cut into 1" (2.5 cm) cubes. Boil the potatoes for 5 minutes until tender. Mix one tablespoon (15 ml) of the oil with the ginger, turmeric, chilli powder and 4 tablespoons of the coriander.

Step two:
Drain the potatoes and mix in the curry paste and the remaining tablespoon (15 ml) of coriander, season with salt and pepper. Put the potatoes into an ovenproof dish and bake on 200C/400F/gas mark 6 for 15 minutes.

Step three:
Rub half the oil and spice mix into both sides of the cod and season with salt and pepper. Put 1 tablespoon (15 ml) of the oil into a frying pan and warm over a gentle heat. Add the cod and fry gently for 5–7 minutes each side until the fish flakes easily.

Continued on next page

Step four:
Wash the tomatoes, leaving the stalks and the vine in place. Season them with salt and pepper and put them in an oven dish. Bake in the oven with the potatoes for 10 minutes.

Step five:
Pour the remainder of the oil into another frying pan and heat gently. Add the spring onions and fry gently for 2 minutes. Beat the eggs in a mixing bowl and then beat in the remainder of the oil and spice mix, season with salt and pepper. Add the eggs to the onions in the pan and cook over a low heat, stirring constantly, until the eggs appear set but still moist, this should take about 5 minutes.

To serve

Serve the cod and the egg mixture, spoon on the spiced potatoes and add a bunch of roasted cherry tomatoes to each plate.

Thai style fishcakes/corn fritters with spicy dipping sauce

TIME TO PREPARE: 15 MINUTES
TIME TO COOK: 20 MINUTES
SERVES: 4 (2 FISH AND 2 VEGGIE)

These fish cakes and corn fritters are a mouth-watering combination of fresh crab meat and prawns/sweetcorn mixed with traditional Thai spices and herbs, served with a sweet and spicy dipping sauce.

Ingredients

1 quantity fish cakes (see recipe below)
1 quantity corn fritters (see recipe below)
1 quantity dipping sauce (see recipe below)

Health note

Fish is high in protein and low in fat. The corn is an excellent source of fibre.

FISHCAKES

Ingredients

2 oz (50 grams) wholemeal breadcrumbs
1 slice dry bread
1 oz (25 grams) plain flour
2 tablespoons (30 ml) sunflower oil
2 fl oz (50 ml) milk
3 oz (75 grams) fresh or tinned crab meat
3 oz (75 grams) peeled, cooked prawns
1 large free range egg
2 shallots or spring onions
1 stalk lemon grass
1 teaspoon (5 ml) chilli powder
1 tablespoon (15 ml) fresh coriander
2 teaspoons (10 ml) desiccated coconut
Zest of 1 lime
Salt and pepper

Method

Step one:
Add the desiccated coconut to the milk. Break the bread into chunks and add to the milk then leave to soak. Peel and finely chop the shallots or onions.

Continued on next page

Remove the woody stalk from the lemon grass and chop finely. Chop the coriander finely. Separate the egg yolk from the white.

Step two:
Flake the crab meat and put it into a mixing bowl. Chop the prawns and add them to the crab, add the egg yolk, shallots or onions, lemon grass, chilli powder, lime zest and coriander and mix well. Squeeze the soaking bread dry and add it to the mixture, season with salt and pepper and stir well.

Step three:
Sprinkle the flour onto one plate and the breadcrumbs onto another. Whisk the egg white with 1 teaspoon (5 ml) water. Flour your hands and form the crabmeat mixture into four balls, then pat each ball into a fish cake shape. Dip each fish cake in the flour, covering the cake completely, then dip in the egg white and the breadcrumbs.

Step four:
Heat the oil in a frying pan over a medium to high heat. Fry the fish cakes for 2–3 minutes on each side until the coating is crisp and golden. Using a slotted spoon remove the fish cakes from the pan and drain them on kitchen paper.

SWEETCORN FRITTERS

Ingredients

8 oz (225 grams) tin sweetcorn
1 medium free range egg
2 oz (50 grams) plain flour
1 teaspoon (5 ml) chilli powder
2 tablespoons (30 ml) fresh coriander
1 teaspoon (5 ml) ground ginger
2 shallots or spring onions
2 teaspoons (10 ml) desiccated coconut
Zest of 1 lime
4 tablespoons (60 ml) sunflower oil
Salt and pepper

Method

Step one:
Finely chop the onion and coriander. Drain the sweetcorn and put it into a large mixing bowl with all the ingredients except the sunflower oil. Mix well and season with salt and pepper.

Step two:
Heat the oil in a frying pan over a medium heat until quite hot. Drop 1 tablespoon of the batter at a time into the oil, cooking 2–3 fritters at a time, ensuring that you keep them apart in the pan. Fry for 4–5 minutes each side until golden brown. You should be able to make about 10 fritters in all. Using a slotted spoon remove the fritters from the pan and drain on kitchen paper. Keep them warm while you fry the remainder of the fritters.

DIPPING SAUCE:

Ingredients

8 oz (225 grams) brown sugar
5 fl oz (150 ml) water
5 fl oz (150 ml) white wine vinegar
2 cloves garlic
1 teaspoon (5 ml) hot chilli sauce
1 teaspoon (5 ml) ground ginger
1 tablespoon (15 ml) fresh coriander

Method

Step one:
Peel the garlic, wash the coriander and chop them finely.

Step two:
Put a medium saucepan on the hob and add the sugar, water, vinegar and garlic. Bring to the boil, stirring until the sugar has dissolved. Turn the heat to low and simmer gently for 10 minutes until the liquid turns syrupy.

Step three:
Remove the pan from the heat and add the chilli sauce, the ginger and the coriander.

To serve

Place fish cakes and fritters on plates, pour the dipping sauce into small bowls. Serve with a crisp green salad, some crudités for dipping and garnish with lemon wedges.

Pizzas

Pizza dough

TIME TO PREPARE: 15 MINUTES
  (+ 1 HOUR PROVING TIME IF YOU ARE MAKING YOUR OWN DOUGH)
TIME TO COOK: 15 TO 20 MINUTES
Each pizza generously serves four

No shop-bought pizza can compare with the taste and delicious aroma of a home-baked pizza. This recipe for pizza dough is straightforward and easy to make, but I often use a pizza dough mix or buy a pizza base if I am short of time. You can top a pizza with just about anything and I have included some of the more popular and traditional recipes.

PIZZA DOUGH

Ingredients

8 oz (225 grams) plain flour
1 teaspoon (5 ml) salt
¼ teaspoon (1.25 ml) sugar
1.5 teaspoons (7.5 ml) dried yeast
1 medium free range egg
4 fl oz (120 ml) lukewarm water
1 teaspoon (5 ml) olive oil

Health note

A source of fibre, calcium, iron, B vitamins and folate. The toppings add additional nutrients such as vitamin C and lycopene in the tomatoes.

Method

Step one:
Pour the lukewarm water into a measuring jug and add the sugar, stirring until it dissolves, then add the yeast and whisk for a minute. Leave the mixture to ferment for 15 minutes.

Step two:
Sift the flour and salt together into a large mixing bowl. Beat the egg. When the yeast is ready make a well in the centre of the flour and pour in the yeast mixture and the beaten egg. Mix with a fork until you have a dough, then knead with your hands. When the dough is ready it should be stretchy and leave the sides of the bowl clean; if the dough is stiff add a little more warm water, if it is too wet add a little more flour.

Step three:
Flour your hands and work surface and knead the dough for about 10 minutes. The best way to do this is to pull the dough or stretch it away from the centre then bring it back to the centre and knead back to a ball. Keep doing this and the dough will gradually become elastic and pliable.

Step four:
Put the dough back in the mixing bowl and rub the surface with the olive oil. Cover the bowl with cling film and put in a warm place for 1 hour to allow it to rise. (I find the best place for this is in my top oven with the lower oven turned to the lowest heat setting).

Step five:
At the end of an hour the dough should have doubled in size. You need to knock the air out of the dough by punching it (quite satisfying), then knead the dough again for about 5 minutes.

Step six:
Flour the work surface again and roll the dough out into a large circle or oblong to fit your pizza tin. Brush the tin with olive oil and sprinkle some flour over it to prevent the dough sticking. Then line the tin with the dough and fold any extra dough over to form a lip (this makes a lovely crust).

Quick tip

You can make and freeze your own pizza bases for later use. Simply make the pizza as shown above and bake blind in the oven on 200C/400F/gas mark 6 for 10 minutes. Allow to cool and wrap in cling film then foil, and freeze.

Pizza Margherita

A classic mixture of ripe tomatoes and melting cheese topped with aromatic herbs.

Ingredients

1 pizza base (see recipe above or
    use a ready prepared base)
1 quantity pizza sauce
    (see recipe p. 345 or use 1 jar
    good quality pizza topping)
4 large ripened on the vine tomatoes
2 oz (50 grams) mozzarella cheese
2 oz (50 grams) Cheddar cheese
1 teaspoon (5 ml) dried oregano.
Salt and pepper

Health note

Provides protein, calcium, vitamins A, B and C.

Method

Step one:
Make the pizza base and use it to line a 10" (25 cm) pizza tin or tray. Spread the pizza sauce over the pizza base.

Step two:
Slice the tomatoes thinly and layer them over the pizza, cut the mozzarella cheese into thin slices and layer this over the tomatoes, grate the Cheddar cheese and sprinkle over the pizza. Sprinkle over the oregano, some salt and freshly ground black pepper. Bake in a hot oven 220C/425F/gas mark 7 for 15–20 minutes. When the pizza is cooked the base should come away from the tin easily and be lightly browned on the bottom.

Pizza Marinara

For seafood lovers a tasty topping of tuna, prawns, anchovies and sardines creates a healthy option pizza.

Ingredients

1 quantity pizza dough
   (see recipe above) or 1 pizza base
1 quantity pizza sauce
   (see recipe p. 347) or 1 jar good
   quality pizza topping
3oz (75 grams) tin of tuna in brine
2 oz (50 grams) peeled cooked prawns
6 small anchovies
1 small tin sardines
6 black olives – stones removed
1 teaspoon (5 ml) oregano
2 tablespoons (30 ml) chilli oil
Salt and pepper

Health note

A good source of Omega 3 fatty acids and protein.

Method

Step one:
Line a 10" (25 cm) round or oblong pizza tray with the pizza dough and top with the pizza sauce.

Step two:
Drain the tuna and sardines and mash them together. Remove any bones. Spread the tuna and sardine mix over the pizza and then scatter over the prawns. Top with the anchovies and the olives, and sprinkle over the oregano and chilli oil then season with salt and pepper. Bake in a hot oven 220C/425F/gas mark 7 for 15–20 minutes.

Hawaiian/vegetarian Hawaiian pizza

The mix of savoury ham and sweet juicy pineapple is especially popular with children.

Ingredients

1 quantity pizza dough (see recipe p. 260)
1 quantity pizza sauce(see recipe p. 345)
1 large red pepper
2 oz (50 grams) sliced ham/Quorn
    ham-style slices
4 oz (110 grams) tin pineapple chunks
2 oz (50 grams) mozzarella cheese
Salt and pepper

Health note

Provides protein, calcium, vitamins A, B and C.

Method

Step one:
Use the pizza dough to line a 10" (25 cm) round or square pizza tray. Top with the pizza sauce.

Step two:
Slice the red pepper into thin strips and scatter across the pizza. Cut the ham or vegetarian ham into 1" (5 cm) squares and scatter across the pizza. Top with the pineapple chunks and thin slices of mozzarella cheese, season with salt and pepper. Bake in a hot oven 220C/425F/gas mark 7 for 15–20 minutes.

Spicy chicken/Spicy Quorn pizza

Indian spices and Italian cuisine seem an odd mix but they work together deliciously.

Ingredients

1 quantity pizza dough
   (see recipe p. 260)
1 quantity pizza sauce
   (see recipe p. 345)
2 oz (50 grams) chicken tikka fillets/
   Quorn tandoori pieces
1 tablespoon (15 ml) fresh coriander
1 green pepper
1 red onion
Salt and pepper

Health note

Provides low fat protein, fibre, carbohydrates, vitamins A, B, C and D.

Method

Step one:
Use the pizza dough to line a 10" (25 cm) round or square pizza tray.

Step two:
Chop the onion, pepper and the coriander finely. Chop the chicken tikka fillets/ Quorn tandoori pieces into ½" (1.25 cm) pieces. Sprinkle the onion and pepper over the pizza. Sprinkle over the chicken or Quorn and top this with the chopped coriander, season with salt and pepper. Bake in a hot oven on 220C/425F/gas mark 7 for 15–20 minutes.

6

PARTY FOOD AND SNACKS

By making your own party food you can reduce the high salt and fat content contained in many of the commercially prepared foods. You can also mix some of the more calorific dishes with raw vegetables, crudités, coleslaw and salads to reduce fat and calories and improve the nutrient content of your buffet table.

Dips to share

Spicy cheese and tomato dip with nachos

TIME TO PREPARE: 10 MINUTES
TIME TO COOK: 15 MINUTES
SERVES: 4 TO 6

This warm, creamy dip makes a lovely starter to share with friends and is a popular centre piece on a party table.

Ingredients

1 large red onion
1 tablespoon (15 ml) olive oil
3 cloves garlic
4 large tomatoes
4 tablespoons (60 ml) white wine
8 oz (225 grams) Cheddar cheese
1 tablespoon (15 ml) chilli sauce
4 fl oz (120 ml) of low fat crème fraiche
1 small bunch fresh coriander
Salt and freshly ground black pepper
To serve: tortilla chips, pitta breads, crudités

Health note

Provides protein, calcium, vitamins A, B, C and E.

Method

Step one:
Finely chop the onions and garlic, peel and finely chop the tomatoes, finely chop the coriander, grate the cheese.

Step two:
Put a large, heavy based saucepan on a low heat and add the oil. Warm through and cook the onions and garlic over a low heat for 5 minutes until softened.

Step three:
Add the tomatoes, coriander, white wine and chilli sauce to the pan and cook for a further 5 minutes.

Step four:
Add the crème fraiche to the pan and stir, bring to the boil and then add the cheese, cook for a further 5–10 minutes stirring constantly until the cheese has melted, season with salt and black pepper.

To serve

Serve in a large bowl garnished with a few coriander leaves and lots of warmed tortilla chips, slices of toasted pitta bread and crudités for dipping.

Quick tip

To keep the dip warm you can either place the bowl over a bain marie of hot water or serve it in a slow cooker with the heat turned low.

Creamy lentil dhal with toasted pitta fingers

TIME TO PREPARE: 10 MINUTES
TIME TO COOK: 15 MINUTES
SERVES: 4 TO 6

A creamy dip of red lentils cooked with Indian spices and served with toasted pitta fingers. It is quick and easy to prepare and can also be served as an accompaniment to curries or as a filling for baked potatoes or stuffed peppers.

Ingredients

12 oz (350 grams) red lentils
1 teaspoon (5 ml) each ground turmeric, mild chilli powder and garam masala
1" (2.5 cm) piece fresh ginger
2 cloves garlic
1 tablespoon (15 ml) sunflower oil
1 yellow onion
2 pints (1.2 litres) hot vegetable stock
6 pitta breads

Health note

A good source of protein, B vitamins, iron and zinc.

Method

Step one:
Finely chop the onion and garlic. Peel the ginger and grate finely.

Step two:
Put a large, heavy based saucepan on the hob and pour in the oil. Warm over a gentle heat and add the onions, garlic, ginger and spices. Cook over a gentle heat for 5 minutes until the onion has softened.

Step three:
Add the lentils to the pan and stir, cook for a further 5 minutes stirring constantly to ensure the lentils do not stick.

Step four:
Add the vegetable stock and bring to the boil, then lower the heat and simmer for 15 minutes until the lentils have softened into a thick, lumpy dip.

To serve

Serve the dip in individual bowls as a starter or in a large bowl for a buffet, garnished with a little chopped coriander or some flaked almonds, with some toasted pitta breads cut into fingers.

Tomato salsa dip with crispy potato wedges

TIME TO PREPARE: 10 MINUTES
TIME TO COOK: 20 TO 25 MINUTES
SERVES: 4

Salsa is a combination of chopped vegetables and herbs or spices. It makes a tasty, low fat dip and is an excellent way to add extra vegetables to lunch or main course dishes.

Ingredients

4 ripe tomatoes
1 red onion
1 small red or green chilli
2 tablespoons (30 ml) chopped fresh coriander
1 tablespoon (15 ml) white wine vinegar
Salt and freshly ground black pepper to taste
For the potato wedges:
2 large baking potatoes
1 tablespoon (15 ml) sea salt
1 tablespoon (15 ml) olive oil
2 teaspoon (5 ml) chilli powder
Freshly ground black pepper

Health note

A good source of vitamin C, carotenes, folate, fibre and carbohydrates.

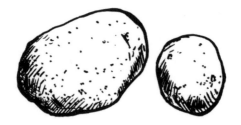

Method

Step one:
Peel and roughly chop the tomatoes and onions, cut the chilli in half lengthways and remove the seeds (do this under a running tap to avoid burning yourself).

Step two:
Combine the salsa ingredients in a small mixing bowl, season with salt and pepper and mix well. Cover and chill in the fridge until needed.

Step three:
Scrub the potatoes and cut each into eight wedges.

Step four:
Pour the oil into a mixing bowl and add the salt, chilli powder and some freshly ground black pepper. Dip each wedge into the oil mixture.

Step five:
Put the potato wedges onto a shallow baking tray and cook in the oven at 200C/400F/gas mark 6 for 20–25 minutes until the potatoes are crispy on the outside and soft inside.

To serve

Pour the salsa into a bowl and place this in the centre of a large plate. Pile the potatoes around the plate ready for dipping.

Warm tomato salsa

Ingredients

1 large red pepper
1 large yellow pepper
4 large tomatoes
1 red onion
2 cloves garlic
1 teaspoon (5 ml) chilli sauce
2 tablespoons (30 ml) chopped fresh coriander
Salt and freshly ground black pepper to taste

Method

Step one:
De-seed and chop the peppers into small dice. Peel and dice the tomatoes. Finely chop the onions and garlic.

Step two:
Put the tomatoes, onions, peppers, garlic, chilli sauce and 2 tablespoons (30 ml) chopped coriander into a small saucepan, season well with salt and pepper and stir thoroughly. Cook over a low heat for 5 minutes until just warmed through.

Hummus with pitta bread

TIME TO PREPARE: 5 MINUTES
SERVES: 4 TO 6

Hummus is a creamy, garlicky dip made from chickpeas and tahini, a paste made from sesame seeds. We often use it instead of butter or margarine in sandwiches.

Ingredients

16 oz (450 grams) tin chickpeas
2 tablespoons (30 ml) tahini
1 tablespoon (15 ml) cold water
2 cloves garlic
Juice and zest of 1 lemon
Salt and freshly ground black pepper
To serve: pitta bread, bread sticks, crudités

Health note

Chickpeas are a good source of protein, fibre, iron and zinc and sesame seeds provide calcium, iron, magnesium and zinc.

Method

Step one:
Put all the ingredients into a blender and blend until a thick paste is formed.

To serve

Serve in individual bowls with toasted pitta bread, breadsticks and crudités.

Quick tip

You can now buy low fat, low salt hummus. Ring the changes by adding some smoked paprika, basil pesto or chopped herbs to the hummus.

Guacamole

TIME TO PREPARE: 5 MINUTES
SERVES: 4 TO 6

A rich, creamy dip from Mexico made from avocados.

Ingredients

2 ripe avocados
2 tablespoons (30 ml) lime juice
1 small onion
1 jalapeno pepper
Salt and pepper to taste

Health note

Avocados are a good source of vitamin E, B6, folic acid, vitamin C and monounsaturated fat.

Method

Step one:
Peel the avocados, remove the stone and roughly mash the flesh in a bowl, add the lime juice and stir thoroughly.

Step two:
Peel and finely chop the onion. Wash the jalapeno pepper, cut it in half and remove the seeds (best done under running water) and chop finely.

Step three:
Add the onion and pepper to the guacamole and season with salt and pepper. This is best served immediately. If you are making it in advance place a sheet of cling film directly on top of the avocado and then cover the bowl with another sheet of cling film.

To serve

Serve as a dip in individual bowls with tortilla chips and lime or lemon wedges. Guacamole is also served as an accompaniment to Mexican dishes such as fajitas.

Pico de Gallo

TIME TO PREPARE: 10 MINUTES
SERVES: 4 TO 6

A traditional Mexican salsa of crunchy vegetables served in a piquant sauce, traditionally served with fajitas.

Ingredients

2 large tomatoes
1 large onion
2 cloves garlic
½ cucumber
6 radishes
2 tablespoons (30 ml) fresh coriander
2 small green or red chillies
1 tablespoon (15 ml) white wine vinegar
1 tablespoon (15 ml) lime juice
Salt and pepper to taste

Health note

A good source of vitamin C, betacarotenes and antioxidants.

Method

Step one:
Peel the tomatoes and chop finely. Chop the onion and garlic very finely. Peel the cucumber, slice in half lengthways and remove the seeds then chop into small dice. Top and tail the radishes and chop into small dice. Chop the coriander finely.

Step two:
Wash the chillies and, holding them under a running tap, cut them in half lengthways and remove the seeds. Chop them very finely.

Step three:
Put the diced vegetables, herbs and chillies into a bowl with the vinegar and lime juice. Season to taste with the salt and pepper and store in a sealed container in the fridge until needed.

To serve

This salsa tastes better if the flavours are left to develop overnight. Serve as an accompaniment to Mexican dishes such as fajitas or as a dip with tortilla chips.

Savoury bites on toast

I like to serve all these savoury little toasts with pre-dinner drinks – they are much nicer and far healthier than the usual crisps and nuts.

Grilled sardine/vegetable bruschettas

TIME TO PREPARE: 10 MINUTES
TIME TO COOK: 15 MINUTES
SERVES: 8 (4 SARDINE AND 4 VEGGIE)

These moreish bruschettas are a delicious blend of sweet Mediterranean vegetables/succulent sardines piled onto warm, garlicky French toast.

Ingredients

4 fresh sardines filleted
   and with heads removed
2 red and 2 yellow peppers
2 small courgettes
2 small red onions
2 tomatoes
2 cloves garlic
4 tablespoons (60 ml) olive oil
Small bunch basil
2 tablespoons (30 ml) basil pesto
Salt and pepper
1 French baguette

Health note

Sardines are a good source of Omega 3 fatty acids and are high in protein. Also provide fibre, carbohydrates, vitamins A, B, C and E and folate.

Method

Step one:
De-seed and quarter the peppers, quarter the onions, crush the garlic. Slice the courgettes into four lengthways.

Step two:
Brush the sardines with a little olive oil and grill under a hot grill for 4–5 minutes then turn and grill for a further 4–5 minutes.

Step three:
Place the vegetables into an oven dish and drizzle over the remainder of the olive oil, season with salt and pepper and bake in the oven at 200C/400F/gas mark 6 for 15 minutes.

Step four:
Cut the baguette into 2" (5cm) thick diagonal slices rub both sides with the garlic and then lightly toast on both sides.

Step five:
Spread a little of the basil pesto on each toast and top with the roasted vegetables.

Step six:
Place a grilled sardine on top of four of the baguette slices.

To serve

Cut into bite sized fingers, garnish with the basil leaves and serve warm.

Taramasalata toasts

PREPARATION: 5 MINUTES
SERVES: 4 TO 6

A savoury Greek dip traditionally made from tarama, the roe of the carp fish. Unless you are lucky enough to have a good deli or fishmonger nearby you will have to use the jars of cod roe available in supermarkets, even so the end result is much nicer than the ready-made products.

Ingredients

7 oz (200 grams) smoked cod roe, skin removed (you can use a jar of cod roe if you can't find fresh)
1 small ciabatta loaf
1 small onion
Juice of 2 lemons
Zest of a lemon
5 fl oz (150 ml) olive oil
1 tablespoon (15 ml) fresh, chopped parsley
Salt and pepper to taste

Health note

A good source of monounsaturated fats.

Method

Step one:
Slice the ciabatta bread into 1" (2.5 cm) thick slices. Remove the crusts from three slices of the bread and soak these in water. Peel and finely chop the onion.

Step two:
Squeeze out the excess water from the bread and place it in a blender or mixing bowl with the roe, the onion and the lemon zest. Mash or blend until you have a thick paste, season with salt and pepper.

Step three:
Gradually blend or whisk in the olive oil and lemon juice until you have a smooth dip.

Step four:
Lightly toast the remainder of the ciabatta bread on both sides.

To serve

Serve the dip in a bowl surrounded by fingers of ciabatta toast, or pipe a little dip onto each toast and garnish with chopped parsley.

Cheese and apple toasts

TIME TO PREPARE: 10 MINUTES
TIME TO COOK: 5 MINUTES
SERVES: 4 TO 6 AS A SNACK OR LIGHT LUNCH, OR MAKES 12 MINI TOASTS.

These make a nice winter snack or light lunch and are very popular with children.

Ingredients

6 x 2" (5cm) thick slices
   wholemeal bread
3 Braeburn or Cox apples
6 oz (175 grams) Cheddar cheese
4 tablespoons (60 ml) apple sauce
   (see recipe on p. 199)
Freshly ground black pepper

Health note

A good source of protein, calcium and selenium, also provides fibre, carbohydrate and vitamins A, B and E.

Method

Step one:
Core the apples and slice into ½" (1.25 cm) thick slices. Grate the cheese.

Step two:
If you are making the mini toasts cut two circles from each slice of bread with a cookie cutter. If not making the mini toasts leave the slices whole. Lightly toast the bread on one side only.

Step three:
Spread the untoasted side of each slice with apple sauce and top with a slice of apple and some grated cheese.

Step four:
Place the toasts on a grill pan under a hot grill for 4–5 minutes until the cheese has melted. Grind some black pepper over the toasts if liked.

To serve

Serve immediately while still hot.

Fun fork food

Having a party, don't give in to the temptation to buy a pack of 50 frozen mini sausage rolls, pizza, quiche etc. They are invariably expensive and tasteless. Home-made party food is inexpensive and easy to prepare in advance. The secret of good fork food is to provide savoury, bite-sized morsels that are easy to eat.

Making your own party food will reduce the fat and salt content of typical party foods.

Pissaladière (French onion tart)

TIME TO PREPARE: 30 MINUTES
TIME TO COOK: 25 MINUTES
MAKES: 1 12" X 8" (30 CM X 20 CM) TART

Pissaladière is traditionally served in the South of France and is similar to pizza. I bake these in a large, shallow oven tray and then cut them into 2" (5 cm) squares. You can add different toppings to the basic recipe such as cheese and grated tomato, or tuna and anchovies, spicy sausage, ham and pineapple etc.

Ingredients

1 quantity pizza dough (see recipe on p. 260)
2 lb (900 grams) Spanish onions
4 tablespoons (60 ml) olive oil
2 cloves garlic
4 oz (110 grams) pitted black olives
1 large red pepper
1 teaspoon (5 ml) dried oregano
Salt and black pepper

Method

Step one:
Make the pizza dough and put it in a warm place to rise. Thinly slice the onions and chop the garlic. Slice the olives in two. De-seed the pepper and slice into thin strips.

Step two:
Put a large, heavy based saucepan on the hob and pour in the olive oil. Add the onions and garlic, cook over a gentle heat for 25 minutes until the oil has been absorbed and the onions are soft and jammy.

Step three:
Lightly grease the baking tray. Roll out the pizza dough and line the tray with it. Spread the onions over the dough and season with salt and pepper.

Step four:
Sprinkle the red pepper, olives and the oregano over the pizza and bake in the oven at 200C/400F/gas mark 6 for 20–25 minutes.

To serve

Cut the pizza into 2" (5 cm) squares and serve warm or cold.

Spicy sausage/vegetarian sausage rolls

TIME TO PREPARE: 15 MINUTES + 30 MINUTES CHILLING
TIME TO COOK: 25 MINUTES
MAKES: 24 SAUSAGE ROLLS AND 24 VEGETARIAN SAUSAGE ROLLS

Hot sausage rolls are a predictable but always welcome choice at any party. You may want to omit the spices if cooking for children.

Ingredients

Pastry:
16 oz (450 grams) plain flour
12 oz (350 grams) hard vegetable margarine (suitable for baking)
    that has been chilled in the freezer for 20 minutes
1 teaspoon (5 ml) salt
Cold water
Sausage meat:
16 oz (450 grams) lean pork sausage meat
1 medium yellow onion
1 teaspoon (5 ml) chilli powder
1 teaspoon (5 ml) English mustard powder
1 teaspoon (5 ml) dried sage
2 tablespoons (10 ml) raw egg
Salt and pepper
Vegetarian sausage meat:
16 oz (450 grams) vegetarian sausages
1 medium yellow onion
1 teaspoon (5 ml) chilli powder
1 teaspoon (5 ml) English mustard powder
1 teaspoon (5 ml) dried sage
2 tablespoons (10 ml) raw egg
Salt and pepper
Glaze:
1 free range egg
1 tablespoon (15 ml) milk

Method

Step one:
The secret to making good flaky pastry is to chill all the ingredients in the fridge for 30 minutes before using and to run your hands under the cold tap

Continued on next page

to ensure they are cold before handling the pastry. Sift the flour and salt into a large mixing bowl. Using a coarse grater, grate the margarine directly into the bowl. Mix the margarine into the flour using a palette knife until the mixture resembles breadcrumbs. Add the cold water 1 tablespoon (15 ml) at a time and knead it into the dough with your hands. Keep adding the water until you have a firm dough that leaves the sides of the bowl clean. Wrap the dough in cling film and put it in the fridge for 30 minutes to chill.

Step two:
While the dough is chilling make up the fillings. Peel and finely chop the onion. Place all the ingredients for the pork sausage meat into a bowl, season with salt and pepper and mix well with a fork. Place all of the ingredients for the vegetarian sausage meat into another bowl – you will need to mash up the sausages with a fork or blender, season with salt and pepper then mix well to combine.

Step three:
When the pastry is chilled divide it in two. Flour your hands and the work surface and roll out one half of the pastry thinly into an oblong shape. Cut the pastry in three long strips. Roll the pork sausage meat into three long sausage shapes and place these in the centre of each strip.

Step four:
To make the glaze beat the egg with the milk and brush the egg mixture down the length of one edge of the pastry. Roll the pastry over to form a sausage roll shape and press down along the edges to seal. Keeping the sealed edge on the bottom cut the roll into 2" (5 cm) long sausage rolls. Using some kitchen scissors snip two small diagonal cuts in the top of each sausage roll and brush with the remainder of the egg.

Step five:
Repeat Steps 3 and 4 for the vegetarian sausage rolls.

Step five:
Place the sausage rolls on a lightly greased oven tray and bake in the oven at 220C/425F/gas mark 8 for 20–25 minutes until golden. Allow to cool slightly before serving.

To serve

Best served warm straight from the oven. When serving vegetarian and non-vegetarian food at a buffet I always line the plates or dishes with green serviettes to denote the vegetarian version and red serviettes for the non-vegetarian version.

Spicy beef/vegetable samosas

TIME TO PREPARE: 20 MINUTES
TIME TO COOK: 1 HOUR
MAKES 15 BEEF SAMOSAS AND 15 VEGETABLE SAMOSAS

Samosas are crisp, little pastry triangles that are filled with a spicy meat or vegetable filling.

Ingredients

1 packet filo pastry defrosted
1 free range egg
4 oz (110 grams) very finely ground minced beef
2 lb (900 grams) old potatoes
3 oz (75 grams) frozen peas
2 oz (50 grams) sweetcorn (tinned or frozen)
1 teaspoon (5 ml) each coriander powder, cumin and turmeric
1 small red onion
2 cloves of garlic
2 small green chillies
2 tablespoons (30 ml) each fresh coriander and mint
Juice of 1 lemon
Sunflower oil for deep frying
Salt and pepper to taste

Method

Step one:
Peel the potatoes and cut into cubes. Boil for 20 minutes until tender.

Step two:
Put the peas and sweetcorn in a metal steamer or sieve, place over the potatoes and steam for 7–8 minutes.

Step three:
Finely chop the onion and garlic. De-seed the chillies and chop finely. Crack the egg into a cup and beat lightly with a fork. Finely chop the fresh herbs.

Continued on next page

Step four:
Put the beef in a non-stick frying pan with half the onion and garlic and dry fry for 10 minutes over a gentle heat. Remove with a slotted spoon and drain on kitchen paper.

Step five:
Drain the cooked potatoes and mash them, add the peas, sweetcorn, onions, garlic, herbs, spices, lemon juice and chillies to the potatoes and mix well, season with salt and pepper to taste. Divide the mixture in two. Add the minced beef to one half of the mixture.

Step six:
Take one strip of filo pastry at a time, brush with the beaten egg and place 1 tablespoon (15 ml) of the filling 2/3 of the way along the pastry. Fold the end 1/3 of the pastry over the filling diagonally, then fold the remainder of the pastry around this to form a sealed triangle.

Step seven:
Heat the oil in a wok or deep frying pan and deep fry the samosas in batches until they are golden brown on the outside (should take about 5 minutes per batch). Drain on kitchen paper.

To serve

These can be served warm or cold and are nice with some sweet chilli dipping sauce (p. 255) or cucumber raita (p. 347).

Wild salmon/courgette and herb tartlets

TIME TO PREPARE: 10 MINUTES + 30 MINUTES RESTING TIME
TIME TO COOK: 20 TO 25 MINUTES
MAKES: 12 SALMON AND 12 COURGETTE TARTLETS

Pastry that is crisp and light as a feather topped with a creamy, herby filling.

Ingredients

Pastry:
8 oz (225 grams) plain flour
1 teaspoon (5 ml) salt
4 oz (110 grams) block vegetable margarine (suitable for baking)
4 fl oz (120 ml) cold water
Fillings:
6 oz (175 grams) tin of wild, red salmon
6 oz (175 grams) courgettes
1 tablespoon (15 ml) butter
2 oz (50 grams) Cheddar cheese
1 small yellow onion
1 tablespoon (15 ml) each fresh flat leaf parsley and coriander
4 medium free range eggs
10 fl oz (300 ml) crème fraiche
5 fl oz (150 ml) milk
Salt and pepper

Method

Step one:
You will need two mince pie or tartlet tins that hold 12 tarts each. Grease the tins with a little sunflower oil and sprinkle them with flour.

Step two:
Begin by making the pastry. Sift the flour and salt into a bowl. Chop the margarine into small cubes and lightly rub into the pastry with your fingertips (or do this in a food processor if you have one). When the pastry resembles fine breadcrumbs add the water a tablespoon at a time until you have a firm dough that leaves the sides of the bowl clean. Cover the dough with cling film and chill in the fridge for 30 minutes.

Continued on next page

Step three:
Cut the courgettes into matchstick size lengths and slice into matchstick size pieces. Peel and finely chop the onion. Finely chop the herbs. Grate the cheese. Drain and mash the salmon, removing any bones, skin and gristle.

Step four:
Crack the eggs into a mixing bowl and beat them lightly, add the herbs, milk and crème fraiche, season with salt and freshly ground black pepper and beat well.

Step five:
Put 1 tablespoon butter into a small pan and melt over a gentle heat, add the onion and courgettes and cook for 5 minutes then allow them to cool.

Step six:
When the pastry is chilled remove it from the fridge and roll out thinly. Cut out 24 circles with a mince pie or tartlet cutter and use these to line the baking tins. Put a layer of grated cheese into the base of half the tarts then a layer of courgettes and onions. Fill the other tarts with the salmon. Fill each case ⅔ full with the egg mixture. Bake in the oven at 180C/350F/gas mark 4 for 20–25 minutes until the quiches are risen and golden and firm to the touch.

To serve
These can be served warm or cold.

Mini pizzas

TIME TO PREPARE: 30 MINUTES + 30 MINUTES PROVING TIME.
TIME TO COOK: 8 TO 10 MINUTES
MAKES: 24 MINI PIZZAS

These bite-size pizzas are popular with adults and children alike. You can use a variety of toppings, but I have included here the traditional cheese and tomato topping.

Ingredients

1 quantity pizza dough (see recipe on p. 260)
1 quantity pizza sauce (see recipe on p. 345)
2 oz (50 grams) Cheddar cheese
2 teaspoons (10 ml) dried oregano
12 pitted black olives

Method

Step one:
Begin by making the dough and put it in a warm place to rise.

Step two:
Make the pizza sauce. Grate the cheese. Cut the olives in half.

Step three:
When the dough is ready, roll it on a floured work surface as thinly as possible. Cut 24 circles from the dough with a cookie cutter.

Step four:
Place the pizza circles on a greased baking sheet. Spread 1 teaspoon (5 ml) of pizza sauce onto each circle then top with a little grated cheese and a sprinkle of oregano. Place half an olive in the centre of each pizza. Bake the pizzas in the oven at 200C/400F/gas mark 6 for 8–10 minutes.

To serve

Can be served warm or cold.

Lamb koftas/roasted squash koftas

TIME TO PREPARE: 30 MINUTES PLUS 30 MINUTES CHILLING TIME
TIME TO COOK: 30 MINUTES
MAKES: 8 LAMB KOFTAS AND 8 ROASTED VEGETABLE KOFTAS

These tasty koftas can be served as a light meal with salsa and some plain boiled rice, as barbeque food with salsa and a fresh salad, or as party food. You really need a food processor or blender to make these. If using wooden skewers make sure you soak them in cold water first to prevent them burning.

Ingredients

1 large Spanish onion
1½ lb (700 grams) butternut squash
1 lb (450 grams) lean minced lamb
15 oz (400 grams) tin chickpeas
2 teaspoons (10 ml) each ground cumin, paprika, ground ginger, ground cinnamon
Small bunch fresh coriander
Small bunch fresh mint
Juice and zest of 2 lemons
2 cloves garlic
1 free range egg
1 red pepper
5 oz (150 grams) quark or low fat cream cheese
4 fl oz (120 ml) natural yoghurt
6 oz (175 grams) chopped almonds
5 slices wholemeal bread
Salt and black pepper
16 wooden skewers soaked in cold water for 30 minutes

Health note

High in fibre and protein and relatively low in fat (buy lean lamb to reduce the fat content).

Method

Roasted vegetable koftas
Step one:
Pre-heat the oven to 180C/350F/gas mark 4.

Step two:
Cut the crusts off the bread and whiz up in a processor to make fine breadcrumbs.

Step three:
Peel and de-seed the squash and cut it into 2" (5 cm) chunks.

Step four:
Mix the spices together in a small bowl. Peel the onion and chop finely.

Step five:
Place the squash in a large roasting tray, sprinkle with half the spices and season with salt and black pepper. Roast in the oven for 30 minutes – when cooked the squash should be tender but not browned. Allow to cool.

Step six:
Drain the chickpeas and put into a blender or food processor with half the lemon juice and rind and blend until smooth. Add the cooled squash and half the fresh coriander to the chickpeas and blend for about 1 minute. The mixture should be thick with small lumps, not a purée.

Step seven:
De-seed the red pepper and chop into small dice. Add the red pepper, half the onion, the egg, the quark or cream cheese, ⅓ of the almonds and ⅔ of the breadcrumbs to the squash mixture. Stir well, season with salt and black pepper to taste and put in the fridge to chill for 30 minutes.

Step eight:
While the vegetable koftas are chilling you can prepare the mixture for the lamb koftas if making (see below).

Step nine:
Once the vegetable kofta mixture has chilled remove it from the fridge and divide into eight. Flour your hands and the worktop and roll each kofta into a ball between your hands. Place the ball onto the worktop and roll into a sausage shape. Mould each sausage shape around a skewer to form the koftas. Mix the remaining breadcrumbs with the remainder of the almonds and spread out on a plate. Roll each kofta across the plate to cover with the almond/breadcrumb mixture. Put back in the fridge to chill for at least 5 minutes or until needed. The koftas can be cooked on a barbeque or a medium high grill. Each kofta will take around 5 minutes to cook. Turn frequently to avoid burning.

Method

Lamb Koftas
Step one:
Peel the garlic and chop finely. Put the lamb into the food processor or blender with the garlic, the remainder of the spices, fresh coriander, lemon juice and rind, onion and yoghurt, season with salt and pepper. Blend to a thick paste.

Step two:
Divide the mixture into eight as with the vegetable koftas, form into sausage shapes and mould around the remaining eight skewers.

Step three:
Chop the mint finely and spread out on a plate. Roll each kofta in the mint. Chill for at least 5 minutes or until needed.

Step four:
When the koftas are chilled cook them on the barbeque or under a medium hot grill. Each kofta will take 7–8 minutes to cook, turn frequently and baste with a little oil if necessary.

To serve

Serve with plain boiled rice and some tomato salsa (see recipe on p. 272) as a light meal, or with pitta breads, a fresh green salad and the salsa at a barbeque, or put the salsa in two bowls and place each bowl in the middle of a large serving platter. Line the platter with chopped iceberg lettuce and place the koftas around the plate. Garnish with lemon wedges and chopped coriander.

Nibbles

Spicy roasted cashew nuts

TIME TO PREPARE: 5 MINUTES
TIME TO COOK: 20 MINUTES

These are very moreish so make plenty!

Ingredients

1lb unsalted cashew nuts
1 tablespoon (15 ml) sunflower oil
2 tablespoons (30 ml) soya sauce
2 tablespoons (30 ml) chilli sauce

Method

Step one:
Pour the oil into a shallow baking tin, add the nuts and stir well to ensure the nuts are well coated with oil. Roast in the oven at 180C/350F/gas mark 4 for 15 minutes, turning occasionally.

Step two:
Remove the nuts from the oven and sprinkle them with the soya sauce and the chilli sauce. Return them to the oven and cook for a further 5 minutes. At the end of cooking time stir them again and leave them to cool in the tin.

To serve

Serve just warm or cold. The nuts can be stored in an airtight container until needed.

Quick tip

You can use any nuts or combinations of nuts in this recipe.

Vegetable crisps

TIME TO PREPARE: 10 MINUTES
TIME TO COOK: 20 MINUTES

These crunchy vegetable crisps are perfect for parties, nibbles and lunchboxes and contain much less fat and salt than standard crisps. A food processor is useful for slicing the vegetables.

Ingredients

2 large baking potatoes
2 large parsnips
2 sweet potatoes
2 tablespoons (30 ml) olive oil
Salt and freshly ground black pepper

Method

Step one:
Peel all the vegetables and slice very thinly.

Step two:
Put the oil into a large mixing bowl and add the sliced vegetables, season well with salt and pepper then mix well to ensure all the vegetables are coated with the oil.

Step three:
Lay the vegetables out on a large baking tray (you may have to cook them in batches) and bake in the oven on 200C/400F/gas mark 6 for 20 minutes until crisp and browned. Remove from the oven and drain on kitchen paper.

To serve

These are nice served in bowls with some mixed dips.

Quick tip

If you want to pack the crisps in lunch boxes or for picnics make a little bag for them out of greaseproof paper.

7

ENTERTAINING AND SPECIAL OCCASIONS

One of the most important things about entertaining is to make your guests feel welcome immediately they arrive. Although the food plays an important role, your guests have come to see you and are far more interested in catching up on all your latest news than they are in your ability to carve a rose out of a radish. So give yourself a break, choose menus that can be prepared as far as possible in advance, and always greet your guests with a welcoming drink or cocktail as soon as they arrive. I have given ideas for some alcoholic and-non alcoholic cocktails as I find that these are a sure ice breaker at any event.

You will, no doubt, have noticed that I have not provided a dessert section. I rarely make rich, complicated desserts – for who needs the hassle of making a cheesecake or gateau after you have already prepared and cooked a delicious meal? I tend to offer fresh fruit, good quality ice cream and sometimes a cheese board. I have included recipes in the entertainment section for some simple desserts that are quick and easy to prepare.

Summer Entertaining

Lazy summer brunch

MENU

ST CLEMENT'S SMOOTHIE (P. 31)

⬿

KEDGEREE (P. 37)
CONTINENTAL BREAKFAST (P. 43)

⬿

BLOODY MARY/VIRGIN MARY COCKTAILS (SEE BELOW)

For me the perfect summer brunch is a light yet delicious feast that can be cooked in advance and will not spoil if guests arrive and eat at different times. The smoothie is sharp and tangy and contrasts well with the smoky creaminess of the kedgeree.

BLOODY MARY COCKTAILS:
You will need tall, slim glasses. Fill the glass ⅓ full with ice then add a measure of vodka, top up the glass with tomato juice, add a dash of Worcester sauce (for non vegetarians only), tabasco and sprinkle with celery salt. Add a stick of celery (leaves still on) to stir.

To make the Virgin Mary cocktail simply omit the vodka.

A tapas evening

MENU

TEQUILA SUNRISE COCKTAILS/MOCKTAILS (SEE BELOW)
VEGETABLE CRISPS (P. 299)
SALSA DIP (P. 272)

⁂

JUG OF SANGRIA (SEE BELOW)
FRESH LEMONADE (SEE BELOW)
SPANISH OMELETTE (P. 57)
WHITE BEAN AND ONION SALAD (P. 84)
TOMATO AND ONION SALAD (P. 83)
MIXED GREEN SALAD
HERBED OLIVES/CRUSTY BREAD

⁂

RIOJA
SPANISH PASTA WITH CHORIZO SAUSAGE (P. 96)
SPANISH PASTA WITH SPICY VEGETARIAN SAUSAGE (P. 96)
SPANISH PORK/QUORN WITH TOMATOES AND OLIVES
PAELLA/VEGETABLE PAELLA (P. 250)
PINE NUT AND HERB STUFFED TOMATOES (P. 244)
ROASTED VEGETABLES (P. 246)

⁂

MIXED FRUIT PLATTER
VANILLA ICE CREAM

What could be more exciting than a tapas evening, redolent of summer holidays, with spicy food and big jugs of sangria? Set the scene by laying the table with a colourful cloth and napkins, red and yellow work well, dim the lights and light lots of big church candles.

Tapas is a traditional Spanish meal that consists of small servings of lots of different dishes. The tradition arose when Spanish bartenders used to put little saucers over their customers' wine glasses to keep out the flies! Gradually they began to put little morsels of salty, savoury foods on those saucers in order to keep their customers in the bar and drinking.

There are a lot of dishes to prepare but most can be made in advance. With tapas you would serve half the usual portion size and lay the food out buffet-style for guests to help themselves to a little of everything. After such a rich

Continued on next page

meal a complicated dessert is not required and a platter of fresh tropical fruit such as pineapple, mango, melon, strawberries and grapes served with some good quality vanilla ice cream will perfectly complement the meal.

TEQUILA SUNRISE COCKTAILS:
You need tall, slim glasses. Dip the rim of the glass in water and then in caster sugar, fill the glass ⅓ with ice then add some orange and lemon slices, a measure of grenadine syrup and a measure of tequila, top up the glass with orange juice. Do not stir. The grenadine should rise up through the cocktail to create the sunrise effect.

TEQUILA SUNRISE MOCKTAILS
Follow the recipe above but simply omit the tequila.

SANGRIA:
You will need a large jug ⅓ filled with ice. Add some sliced oranges and lemons and fill ⅓ with sangria, add two measures of brandy and top up with lemonade.

FRESH LEMONADE:
Slice 3 lemons and place in a saucepan with 6 oz (175 grams) sugar and 1¾ pints (1 litre) of water. Bring to the boil and stir until the sugar is dissolved. Turn the heat down and cook for 5 minutes then allow the lemonade to cool and refrigerate until cold.

A stunning barbeque

MENU

JUG OF PIMMS (SEE BELOW)
COLD BEER
FRESH FRUIT JUICE
❧

HOT STEAK BAGUETTE (P. 106)
VEGETARIAN STEAK BAGUETTE (P. 106)
LAMB KEBABS (P. 184)
TURKEY/MEDITERRANEAN VEGETABLE KEBABS (P. 159)
MINTED COUSCOUS (P. 184)
TOMATO AND ONION SALAD (P. 88)
TRADITIONAL COLESLAW SALAD (P. 91)
❧

BOWL OF FRESH SUMMER BERRIES
VANILLA ICE CREAM
SUMMER PUDDING GREEK YOGHURT (P. 32)

Barbeques are the ideal occasion to gather a crowd of friends and family to dine al fresco. Because the British weather does not always comply with our plans I have suggested menus that can be cooked and enjoyed just as easily indoors as out.

The recipe for success with barbeques is to prepare everything in advance and keep refrigerated until you are ready to cook. The couscous and the coleslaw can be prepared a day in advance and will keep well, as will the summer pudding Greek yoghurt. If you are having lots of children at the BBQ you may want to include some homemade beef burgers/veggie burgers (p. 240) and some chilli hot dogs/vegetarian chilli dogs (p. 119).

JUG OF PIMMS:
Fill a cold jug ⅔ full with ice, add some sliced fruit such as oranges, apples and strawberries and some mint leaves. Fill the jug ⅓ full with Pimms and top up with lemonade.

For non-drinkers make up a jug of fresh, mixed fruit juice such as orange, lemon and lime, add ice and fresh fruit and top up with lemonade.

A summer picnic

MENU

FRESH LEMONADE (P. 304)
WHITE WINE
༒
MEXICAN TORTILLA (P. 62)
JEWELLED SUMMER TABBOULEH (P. 98)
༒
CHEDDAR AND APPLE STUFFED PITTAS (P. 108)
MOZZARELLA, BASIL AND TOMATO ON OLIVE FOCACCIA (P. 122)
SALAMI/SMOKY HAM WRAPS (P. 116)
TRADITIONAL COLESLAW SALAD (P. 91)
༒
QUICK BAKE PEACH MUFFINS (P. 27)
FRESH FRUIT

Picnics, whether for children or adults, are about having fun eating in the open air, on the beach, in the countryside, at the park or simply in the garden. Keep the food simple; remember to pack a rug and plenty of bats, balls, buckets and spades.

The wraps and the pittas are perfect picnic fare for children who, if they are anything like mine, will want to eat on the run. The muffins lend some sweetness without any stickiness from melted chocolate or icing.

The tortilla can be made the day before and allowed to cool in the fridge: you can then cut it into bite-sized squares and pack it into a polythene tub. The pitta bread should be toasted and sliced then wrapped in foil, the Cheddar and apple filling should be made on the day and packed in a tub. The tabbouleh and the coleslaw will benefit from being made a day or two in advance and can be packed into polythene tubs. The focaccia rolls and the wraps should be made up on the day of the picnic and wrapped in greaseproof and then foil. The muffins can be made the day before and stored in a polythene tub.

Summer dinner party

MENU

KIR ROYALE (SEE BELOW)
CRANBERRY FIZZ (SEE BELOW)

꩜

SALAD NICOISE/SALAD DU JARDIN (P. 82)
FRESH FRENCH BAGUETTE

꩜

RED OR ROSÉ WINE
LAMB CHOPS/VEGETABLE GRILLS PROVENÇAL (P. 190)
NEW POTATOES WITH FRESH MINT
JULIENNE CARROTS WITH FINE GREEN BEANS

꩜

BOWL OF FRESH RASPBERRIES WITH CRÈME FRAICHE
PLATTER OF CONTINENTAL CHEESES (P. 43)

꩜

FRENCH COFFEE (P. 44)
BRANDY

This menu is perfect for a warm summer evening when dinner can be eaten al fresco and guests can linger and chat over coffee and brandy.
Kir is served in France as an aperitif.

KIR ROYALE:
You will need a bottle of cassis (blackcurrant liqueur) and a bottle of champagne or sparkling white wine. Fill a champagne glass ¼ full with cassis and top up with the wine or champagne.

CRANBERRY FIZZ:
Fill a glass ⅓ full with ice then ½ fill with cranberry juice and top up with sparkling water or lemonade.

Winter Entertaining

Warming winter brunch

MENU

MIXED BERRY SMOOTHIES (P. 29)

∽

ENGLISH MUFFIN PIZZAS (P. 35)
HASH BROWNS (P. 39)
FRESH COFFEE (P. 44)

∽

FRENCH TOAST WITH CINNAMON AND APPLES (P. 33)

∽

BLOODY MARY/VIRGIN MARY COCKTAILS (P. 302)

What could be more pleasant than arising to the smell of fresh coffee, baking bread and warm cinnamon wafting through the house? Set the scene by lighting the fire, making the house warm and cosy, and providing lots of Sunday papers and magazines to while away a lazy Sunday.

As with the summer brunch I have chosen dishes that can be prepared in advance, quickly assembled, and cooked as and when guests arrive. You can make the pizza sauce and the hash browns in advance and refrigerate or freeze. The French toast can also be made a day in advance and stored in the fridge.

A Mexican evening

MENU

TEQUILA SUNRISE COCKTAILS/MOCKTAILS (P. 304)
TORTILLA CHIPS WITH WARM SALSA DIP (P. 274)

⚘

RED WINE OR MEXICAN LAGER
FAJITAS (P. 152)
SPICY BEEF/CHICKPEA ENCHILADAS (P. 238)
GUACAMOLE (P. 276)
PICO DE GALLO (P. 277)
WEDGE POTATOES (P. 272)
MEXICAN RICE SALAD (P. 94)

⚘

WARM FRUIT SALAD (SEE BELOW)
CREAMY VANILLA CUSTARD (SEE BELOW)

⚘

FRESH COFFEE (P. 44)
BRANDY

To save time on the day you can make the salsa dip, pico de gallo and Mexican rice salad the day before, the enchilada fillings can be cooked in advance and refrigerated until needed.

WARM FRUIT SALAD:

Mix together some cubed pineapple, peaches, nectarines, plums and apricots then place them in a saucepan with a little water, a stick of cinnamon, two tablespoons (30 ml) brown sugar and a couple of splashes of brandy or liqueur, bring to the boil and cook over a gentle heat for about 5 minutes until the fruit is warm and slightly softened.

CUSTARD:

Buy a large carton of fresh custard and mix with half that quantity of fresh single cream and a couple of drops of vanilla essence.

A curry evening

MENU

COLD WHITE WINE AND LAGER
FRESH LEMONADE (P. 304)
SPICY ROASTED CASHEW NUTS (P. 298)

∞

CREAMY LENTIL DHAL WITH PITTA FINGERS (P. 270)
LAMB/ROASTED SQUASH KOFTAS (P. 294)
CUCUMBER RAITA (P. 347)

∞

CREAMY CHICKEN/QUORN AND SPINACH CURRY (P. 146)
BEEF BALTI/CHICKPEA AND VEGETABLE BALTI (P. 172)
BASMATI RICE/NAAN BREADS

∞

EXOTIC FRUIT PLATTER (SEE BELOW)
MANGO SORBET

I have chosen fairly mild curries for entertaining but if you like something hotter you could choose the rogan josh on p. 188. The mixture of fresh fruit and cool sorbet is extremely refreshing after the spiciness of the curry.

The lemonade, peanuts, dhal, koftas and curries can all be made at least a day in advance and refrigerated, then simply warmed through on the day.

EXOTIC FRUIT PLATTER:

You will need a large serving plate. Cut a pineapple in quarters, cube the flesh and return it to the shell. Place two quarters at each end of the platter, fill the spaces in between with slices of fresh mango, guava, melon and banana. Serve with some good quality mango sorbet.

Winter dinner party

Menu

Mulled wine (see below)
Warm fruit cup (see below)
Spicy cheese and tomato dip (p. 268)
Nachos/breadsticks/ crudités
Grilled sardine/vegetable bruschettas (p. 280)

⤜

French burgundy wine
Beef Bourgignon/Tofu a la Bourgignon (p. 164)
Buttered tagliatelli
Steamed Broccoli

⤜

Caramelised oranges (see below)
Whisky cream custard (see below)

⤜

Fresh coffee (p. 44)
Brandy/Liqueurs

Welcome friends and family who have ventured out on a cold winter's evening, with a warming glass of mulled wine, seat them in front of a roaring fire and serve the warm dip, nibbles and bruschettas while you chat. Next produce a steaming casserole aromatic with wine and herbs and finish with some tart, caramelised oranges perfectly complemented by the slightly boozy custard.

Then return to the fireside to linger over coffee and brandy.

The cheese and tomato dip can be made in advance and reheated before serving. The casserole can be made a day or two in advance and refrigerated, reheat until piping hot before serving.

MULLED WINE:

Pour a bottle of French red Burgundy wine into a saucepan, add 1 stick of cinnamon, 3 whole cloves, a pinch of ginger, some orange and lemon slices and a couple of tablespoons (60 ml) of brandy. Warm through very gently, then remove from the heat and allow the spices to infuse for an hour or two. Remove the spices, then simply warm through gently before serving.

WARM FRUIT CUP:
Pour a carton of red grape juice and a carton of blackcurrant juice into a saucepan, add some orange and lemon slices and a pinch of cinnamon or a cinnamon stick, and a pinch of ginger. Warm through and serve.

CARAMELISED ORANGES:
Leaving the skin on, slice 8 whole oranges, discard the ends, cut the peel and the pith off the orange slices with a sharp knife. Put a heavy based frying pan on the hob and add 4 oz (110 grams) brown sugar and 2 oz (50 grams) butter, heat through gently until the butter melts and the sugar dissolves and caramelises, add the oranges and a splash of brandy or liqueur, heat through and serve.

WHISKY CUSTARD:
Buy a large carton of fresh custard and add half that amount again of fresh single cream, stir to mix and add a couple of splashes of whisky. Serve with the oranges.

Hot suppers
to come home to

I have set out below ideas for some easy meals that you can prepare and cook in advance for when you are going out and want to provide a hot supper for friends or family to come home to.

MENU ONE

SPICY PARSNIP AND APPLE SOUP (P. 65)
CRUSTY BREAD
⊗
COQ AU VIN/BURGUNDY STYLE CASSEROLE (P. 154)
⊗
BAKED APPLES (SEE BELOW)
VANILLA ICE CREAM

The parsnip and apple soup can be made in advance and simply warmed through for 5 minutes before serving. The casserole can be prepared in advance and left to cook long and slow while you are out. There is no need to cook additional vegetables as there are plenty in the main dish.

BAKED APPLES:
Simply core the required number of cooking apples and stuff them with some ready prepared sweet mincemeat (you could do this before you go out and refrigerate). Put them in the oven when you get home at 200C/400F/gas mark 6 for about 20 minutes. Serve with some good quality vanilla ice cream.

MENU TWO

WARM BACON, LENTIL AND RICE SALAD (P. 86)
⊗
IRISH STEW WITH DUMPLINGS (P. 193)
⊗
VANILLA ICE CREAM WITH WARM CHOCOLATE SAUCE (SEE BELOW)

The salad can be made in advance and reheated in the microwave on high for 2 minutes before serving. The stew can also be made in advance and left to cook long and slow. The dumplings can be made and refrigerated. When you get in simply bring the casserole up to the boil, drop in the dumplings and cook for about 20 minutes while you are eating your entrée.

CHOCOLATE SAUCE:
You will need 8 oz (225 grams) good quality (70% cocoa) dark chocolate and 4 fl oz (120 ml) fresh cream. Melt the chocolate in the microwave or over a bain marie and beat in the fresh cream. Pour over some good quality vanilla ice cream.

MENU THREE

GREEK SALAD (P. 78)

SHEPHERD'S PIE/GARDENERS PIE (P. 222)
BEEF GRAVY/VEGETABLE GRAVY (P. 170/P. 137)
MIXED VEGETABLES

FRESH FRUIT SALAD

Prepare the Greek salad in individual dishes and refrigerate before you go out. The shepherd's pie/gardener's pie and gravy can be made in advance and reheated until piping hot while you eat your entrée. You could use frozen mixed vegetables or prepare fresh before you go out. The fruit salad can also be prepared in advance.

Traditional celebrations

Many of us tend to entertain more during the traditional holidays of Easter, Christmas and New Year as families gather and friends drop by for a visit. At times like these it is even more important to make guests feel welcome and well-fed, which can leave the poor host/hostess under pressure, often having to prepare, cook and wash up after three meals a day, when he or she should be enjoying the festivities and having a relaxing break. With this in mind I have put together some simple, no-fail recipes, many of which can be prepared in advance and refrigerated or frozen until needed.

Easter

Easter, falling as it does in March or April, can be a difficult holiday to plan for. We have had Easters that are like deep midwinter – complete with snow – and others that bring a balmy early spring, warm enough to eat outside. These menus cover the Easter period, from Good Friday through to Easter Monday, and should be suitable whatever the weather does. I have tried to include recipes that cater for all eventualities and age groups such as children on school holidays, teenagers who are home from university and family visiting for the holidays.

Good Friday Menu

BREAKFAST:
FRUITY PANCAKES (P. 23),
APRICOT AND BANANA SMOOTHIES (P. 30)

⌇

LUNCH:
SPANISH OMELETTE (P. 57)
GREEN SALAD AND CRUSTY BREAD

⌇

DINNER:
LUXURY FISH/CREAMY TOFU AND SWEETCORN PIE (P. 243)
STEAMED LEEKS, CARROTS AND BABY SWEETCORN

⌇

DESSERT:
RASPBERRIES WITH MERINGUE AND CREAM

Everyone I know loves pancakes and they bring a sense of celebration to any occasion. The apricot and banana smoothies are perfect for young children, hung-over teenagers or anyone unable to face food early in the morning. At lunchtime prepare a huge Spanish omelette to make the most of all the young spring vegetables in season, the omelette is also nice served cold for late arrivals.

Traditionally, and for religious reasons, meat was avoided on Good Friday. Although most people no longer follow this tradition I have included a fish main course and a delicious vegetarian alternative for those who do.

RASPBERRIES WITH MERINGUE AND CREAM:

You will need a packet of meringue cases, fresh raspberries and a carton of crème fraiche into which you have stirred a couple of drops of vanilla essence. Crumble the meringue cases into a large serving bowl and add the raspberries, then pour over the crème fraiche and mix, garnish with some mint leaves. It looks messy but tastes delicious.

Easter Saturday Menu

BREAKFAST:
FULL ENGLISH BREAKFAST (P. 39)

⚬℣⚬

LUNCH:
AMERICAN CHEF'S SALAD (P. 80)

⚬℣⚬

DINNER:
SHEPHERD'S/GARDENER'S PIE (P. 222)
SERVED WITH GREEN BEANS, PEAS AND CARROTS

⚬℣⚬

DESSERT:
POACHED PEARS WITH CALVADOS ICE CREAM (SEE BELOW)

Easter Saturday is not really a traditional holiday and many people go about their business as usual. Cooking a full English breakfast gives you the opportunity to extend a really hearty welcome to weekend guests and family returning home for the holidays. After such a large breakfast all that is needed for lunch is a tasty salad. The chef's salad is quick and easy to prepare using up any leftover vegetables from the evening before. A hearty, home cooked, shepherd's/gardener's pie using seasonal ingredients will be warmly welcomed and can be reheated for any latecomers.

POACHED PEARS WITH CALVADOS ICE CREAM:

You will need a dessert pear per person, 1 oz (25 grams) sugar per pear, water, vanilla essence, vanilla ice cream and calvados.

Allow the ice cream to soften and then beat in 2 or 3 measures of the calvados, return to the freezer and freeze. Halve the pears, remove the pips and the core but retain the stalks. Poach them in a little water with the sugar until tender and serve while still warm with the ice cream.

Easter Sunday Menu

BREAKFAST:
BOILED EGGS WITH BUTTERED TOAST FINGERS

⬡

LUNCH:
LAMB CHOPS/VEGGIE LAMB STEAKS (P. 192)
WITH REDCURRANT SAUCE (P. 192)
ROASTED ROOT VEGETABLES (P. 139)
STEAMED SPRING GREENS

⬡

DESSERT:
ICE CREAM SUNDAE

⬡

SUPPER:
RED LENTIL AND CARROT SOUP WITH SESAME TOASTS (P. 69)
TRADITIONAL/VEGETARIAN CLUB SANDWICHES (P. 126)

Easter Sunday breakfast just has to be about eggs. When my children were small we would decorate ours by drawing on faces and designs. Seasonal lamb makes for a traditional Easter Sunday roast lunch. A fun way to serve the ice cream sundae is to provide various ice creams, chopped fruits, sauces and toppings and let guests, particularly children, assemble their own. Following a large lunch a simple yet satisfying supper of soup and sandwiches will fill up any empty corners.

Easter Monday Menu

BREAKFAST:
CONTINENTAL BREAKFAST (P. 43)

☙

LUNCH:
STUFFED PITTAS (P. 108)
TRADITIONAL COLESLAW SALAD (P. 91)

☙

DINNER:
POT ROAST BEEF (P. 174)
BUTTERBEAN AND SPRING VEGETABLE CASSEROLE (P. 174)

☙

DESSERT:
APRICOT FOOL WITH AMORETTI BISCUITS (SEE BELOW)

Bank Holiday Monday is often a day for family outings so I have suggested a quick and easy-to-prepare breakfast, followed by a simple lunch that can either be eaten at home or packed up for a picnic. Neither breakfast nor lunch relies on fresh bread, which is difficult to find at the end of a holiday weekend. The pot roast and the casserole can be prepared and left to cook long and slow while you are out. The apricot fool and amoretti biscuits provide a traditional hint of almonds and can be prepared in advance and refrigerated until needed.

APRICOT FOOL:

You will need a packet of amoretti fingers, 1lb (450 grams) apricots, 4 oz (110 grams) sugar, water and an 8 fl oz (250 grams) carton of whipping cream. Halve the apricots, remove the stone, and put the flesh in a pan with the sugar and enough water to barely cover them. Cook over a medium heat for 15 minutes until the sugar has dissolved and the apricots are soft. Blend or mash the apricots. Whip the double cream and fold into the apricots, pour into dessert glasses. Serve with the amoretti fingers.

Hallowe'en

The Hallowe'en celebration has grown in popularity in recent years, largely due to American television shows and clever marketing. That said, it is a wonderful excuse for a party to soften the blow of the end of autumn and the beginning of winter. Hallowe'en is also the ideal occasion for a fancy dress party and the perfect opportunity to offer warming drinks and nibbles to welcome home hungry trick or treaters.

A Hallowe'en party menu

WARM FRUIT PUNCH (SEE BELOW)

∝

TANGY SALSA DIP WITH POTATO WEDGES (P. 272)
SPICY CHEESE AND TOMATO DIP (P. 268)
BREADSTICKS AND CRUDITÉS FOR DIPPING

∝

PISSALADIÈRE (P. 286)
QUICK FRENCH BREAD PIZZA (P. 54)
MEXICAN TORTILLA (P. 62)
SPICY SAUSAGE/VEGGIE ROLLS (P. 282)

∝

WARM BACON/LENTIL AND RICE SALAD (P. 86)
CRUNCHY RED CABBAGE AND APPLE SALAD (P. 90)

∝

BAKED CARIBBEAN FRUIT SALAD
VANILLA ICE CREAM WITH TOFFEE SAUCE

Much of the party food can be prepared in advance. The salsa dip, pizza sauce, sausage/veggie rolls, bacon/lentil and rice salad and the red cabbage salad can all be made the day before. The cheese and tomato dip, pissaladière, pizza and tortilla can be made on the afternoon of the party and simply warmed through when guests arrive.

WARM FRUIT PUNCH:
Makes about 40 servings. You will need 2 cartons each of fresh orange juice, sweetened cranberry juice and pineapple juice, the juice of 6 fresh limes and 1 pint (600 ml) ginger ale. Simply mix all the ingredients together in a large saucepan and warm through. You can make an adult punch by adding white rum to taste.

BAKED CARIBBEAN FRUIT SALAD:
Serves 4 to 6. You will need 1 large pineapple, 3 large ripe bananas, 2 ripe mangos, 4 tablespoons (60 ml) rum or pineapple juice, good vanilla ice cream and a bottle of toffee sauce. Peel the pineapple, cut it in half lengthways and remove the core, then cut into cubes. Peel the bananas and chop into 2" (5cm) chunks, peel the mangos, cut them in half and remove the stone and then cut the flesh into cubes. Place the fruit in an ovenproof dish and poor over the rum or pineapple juice, cover with foil then bake in the oven for 15 minutes on 180C/350F/gas mark 4. Serve in small bowls with some vanilla ice cream and the toffee sauce.

To serve

To add some fun to the table hollow out a pumpkin and fill with the warm cheese dip. Surround with bowls of tortilla chips and bread sticks for dipping, serve the salsa in a deep bowl in the centre of a large round serving platter, circled by the potato wedges. Cut the pizza, pissaladière and the tortilla into fingers.

Fireworks night

Fireworks night is one of my favourite celebrations. I love venturing out on a cold winter's night to stand by a roaring bonfire, with a sparkler in one hand and a glass of mulled wine in the other, cheering as the fireworks light up the faces of small children dressed in cheerful bobble hats, scarves, gloves and Wellington boots.

A bonfire night menu

MULLED WINE (P. 313)
WARM FRUIT CUP (P. 324)

∞

MINI PIZZAS (P. 293)
SPICY BEEF/VEGETABLE SAMOSAS (P. 289)

∞

JACKET POTATOES WITH CHEESY SPICY BEAN MIX (P. 49)
CHILLI/VEGETARIAN CHILLI DOGS (P. 119)
HOMEMADE BEEF BURGERS/VEGGIE BURGERS (P. 240)
TRADITIONAL COLESLAW SALAD (P. 91)
MEXICAN RICE SALAD (P. 94)

∞

WARM CHOCOLATE FONDUE WITH FRESH FRUIT AND MARSHMALLOWS

Make the mulled wine and the fruit cup in advance and simply warm through when you are ready to serve.

Prepare and cook the mini pizzas and samosas in advance, these can be quickly warmed through in the oven and served as nibbles whilst you are warming through the jacket potatoes and cooking the burgers and the hot dogs. The jacket potato topping can be made in advance and chilled until needed, the potatoes can be left to cook on a low heat in the oven, then simply add the topping and heat through until piping hot. The sauce for the chilli dogs can be made in advance, as can the burgers and the salads.

CHOCOLATE FONDUE:
Serves 4 to 6. you will need 1lb (450 grams) good quality (70% cocoa) dark chocolate, 6 fl oz (175 ml) double cream, 1 teaspoon (5 ml) vanilla essence. Pour the cream into a heavy based saucepan and heat over a medium heat until hot but not boiling. Grate or chop the chocolate into small chunks and add to the cream, heat until melted then remove from the heat and stir in the vanilla essence. You will need to transfer the chocolate sauce to a fondue dish or keep it warm in an ovenproof dish over a heated plate warmer. Serve the fondue with strawberries, chunks of banana, wedges of apple and marshmallows for dipping.

Christmas

Christmas seems to become more complicated and pressurised every year and, if you are anything like me, you will read with mounting dismay all the articles showing us how to create the perfect, family Christmas. This seems to consist of Mum and Dad smiling happily at rosy cheeked children, exquisitely wrapped presents and a towering Christmas tree artistically decorated. A table laid with gleaming silver, shining crystal and linen napkins, sporting a perfectly bronzed turkey, surrounded by bright green Brussels sprouts and crispy roast potatoes completes the picture.

In the real world, Christmas isn't much like this – well, certainly not in our house! Mum and Dad are exhausted, the children hyper and the television is blaring. The tree takes up most of the sitting room; it isn't co-ordinated but is decorated with much loved ornaments, each child adding their favourites to the tree.

I believe that Christmas is stressful enough without having to worry about complicated and fussy menus. One useful tip I can pass on: some years ago I made the decision to serve Christmas dinner in the evening, rather than at lunchtime, and it revolutionised Christmas for me. I now have time to spend with the family, opening presents, enjoying a glass of Buck's fizz, instead of missing all the fun to peel mounds of potatoes and sprouts. I serve a light breakfast and lunch to make room for Christmas dinner with all the trimmings.

Christmas Eve Menu

MULLED WINE (P. 313)
WARM FRUIT PUNCH (P. 314)
❀
GAMMON AND LEEK FLAN (P. 209)
CHEDDAR CHEESE AND LEEK FLAN (P. 209)
CREAMY SPINACH AND NEW POTATO SALAD (P. 92)
TOMATO AND ONION SALAD (P. 88)
❀
HOT MINCE PIES (SEE BELOW)

This menu can be served either as a sit-down meal or as a buffet. You could prepare some extra nibbles such as the spicy roasted cashew nuts (p. 298), vegetable crisps (p. 299), with some salsa dip (p. 272) and some sausage rolls (p. 287) in case friends and family drop in.

MINCE PIES

Makes 12. You will need 4 oz (110 grams) plain flour, 2 oz (50 grams) vegetable margarine (suitable for baking), a pinch of salt and some cold water, 8 oz (225 grams) vegetarian mincemeat. To make the pastry, sift the flour and salt into a mixing bowl, grate or cube the margarine and add it to the bowl, rub the fat into the flour with your fingertips until it resembles fine breadcrumbs, sprinkle a little cold water over and quickly mix it in with a fork. Continue to add a little water at a time until you have a dough, finish the dough by rolling it into a ball with your hands then chill it in the fridge for half an hour. For the mincemeat, buy a jar of vegetarian mince meat, or make your own using vegetarian suet, add 1 tablespoon (30 ml) brandy and a grated dessert apple. When the pastry is chilled roll it out thinly and cut with mince pie cutters, grease a minced pie tin and line with pastry, add 1 teaspoon mincemeat, brush the edges of the pastry with a little milk or egg yolk and the put a pastry lid on, press firmly to seal and snip a small diagonal cut in the lid. Bake in the oven at 200C/400F/gas mark 6 for about 30 minutes until the pastry is crisp and golden. Allow to cool and dust with a little icing sugar.

Christmas Day menu

BREAKFAST:
BUCK'S FIZZ (SEE BELOW)
FRESH ORANGE JUICE
BOILED EGGS WITH TOAST

∽∾

LUNCH:
CHICKEN/SPRING VEGETABLE SOUP (P. 71)
BACON/VEGGIE BACON, LETTUCE AND TOMATO
SANDWICHES (P. 127)

∽∾

CHRISTMAS DINNER
PRAWN/MELON COCKTAIL (SEE BELOW)

∽∾

ROAST TURKEY DINNER/
MUM'S VEGGIE ROAST DINNER (P. 136)
HOMEMADE CRANBERRY SAUCE (P. 346)

∽∾

CHRISTMAS PUDDING
WITH BRANDY CREAM (SEE BELOW)
POIRE BELLE HÉLÈNE (SEE BELOW)

A simple breakfast of eggs and toast will settle any over-excited tummies; the buck's fizz lends an air of celebration and give the adults a much needed lift. As you will be preparing mountains of vegetables for the evening meal simply prepare a few extra to make a light yet nourishing soup to serve with the universally popular BLT sandwiches.

Christmas dinner begins with a simple, easy-to-prepare, first course that can be made in advance and chilled in the fridge until needed, followed by a sumptuous but uncomplicated roast dinner. It finishes with either the classic Christmas pudding, or a light yet luxurious fruity pudding.

BUCK'S FIZZ:
Makes about 12 servings. Simply mix a bottle of champagne or sparkling white wine with half that quantity of fresh orange juice and serve over ice.

PRAWN COCKTAIL:
Serves 4. You will need 4 tablespoons (60 ml) mayonnaise, 1 teaspoon (5 ml) tomato purée, 4 slices lemon, 4 slices cucumber, ¼ iceberg lettuce chopped finely and 4 oz (110 grams) cooked peeled prawns. Place the lettuce in four serving dishes and top with the prawns. Mix the mayonnaise and the tomato purée together and spoon over the prawns, then garnish with a twist of lemon and a slice of cucumber.

MELON COCKTAIL:
Serves 4. You will need ½ yellow honeydew melon and ½ galia melon, 4 slices orange and some mint leaves. Either use a melon baller or cut the melons into 1" (2.5 cm) cubes. Fill four serving dishes with the melon, garnish with the orange slices and the mint leaves.

For Christmas dinner use the roast chicken/Mum's veggie roast dinner on p. 136 but replace the chicken with a turkey, goose or whatever you plan to cook for the main course and adjust the timings accordingly.

CHRISTMAS PUDDING:
Buy a vegetarian Christmas pudding or make your own using vegetarian suet. Buy or make the pudding at least a month before Christmas, unwrap it then make holes in the pudding with a skewer and pour in a little brandy, whisky or sherry. Re-wrap in foil, repeat this process every week until Christmas.

BRANDY CREAM:
Simply whip up a carton of double or whipping cream until thick, sift in 1 tablespoon (15 ml) icing sugar and mix well, then add a tablespoon (15 ml) brandy.
To make the Poire Belle Hélène: (serves 4) you will need 4 large, ripe pears, 1 lemon, 2½ oz (60 grams) sugar, 8 fl oz (250 ml) water, good vanilla ice cream, 7 oz (200 grams) good quality dark chocolate (70% cocoa) and 2 tablespoons (30 ml) single cream. Place the water, sugar and the juice of the lemon in a saucepan, bring to the

boil then reduce the heat and simmer for 3 minutes. Peel the pears and rub with the cut lemon halves. Cut the pears in half, remove the core and add to the pan, cover and poach for 5 minutes. Melt the chocolate in the microwave or over a bain marie, remove from the heat and beat in the cream. Serve each person with two pear halves, with a scoop of ice cream in each half and pour the chocolate sauce over.

Boxing Day menu

BREAKFAST:
MUESLI AND FRESH FRUIT SUNDAE (P. 22)
ST. CLEMENT'S SMOOTHIES (P. 31)
⚬⚬

LUNCH:
AMERICAN CHEF'S SALAD (P. 80)
CRUSTY BREAD
⚬⚬

DINNER:
QUICK TURKEY AND CASHEW STIR FRY (P. 157)
CASHEW AND VEGETABLE STIR FRY (P. 157)
JEWELLED SUMMER TABBOULEH (P. 98)
⚬⚬

POACHED PLUMS (SEE BELOW)
WITH CHRISTMAS ICE CREAM (SEE BELOW)

This Boxing Day menu is light yet tasty, to tempt jaded appetites. The no-cook breakfast and lunch give the chef a break. It is also planned to use up all those leftovers. The St Clement's smoothies are bursting with vitamin C to combat any lingering hangovers. The muesli and fresh fruit sundaes are nutritious and perfect for using up leftover fruit. The chef's salad is also useful for using up leftover vegetables, cooked meats and cheeses. The quick turkey stir fry can be made with leftover turkey rather than fresh. The Jewelled summer tabbouleh perfectly complements the stir fry and is yet another way to use up leftover salad vegetables, herbs, fruit, etc.

POACHED PLUMS:
Serves 8. You will need 2lb (900 grams) plums, 2oz (50 grams) sugar and 4 fl oz (120 ml) water. Halve the plums and remove the stones. Pour the water into a saucepan and add the sugar, bring to the boil, add the plums and simmer gently for 5–10 minutes.

CHRISTMAS ICE CREAM:
Allow a carton of vanilla ice cream to become soft and beat in 8 oz (225 grams) leftover Christmas cake or pudding and 2 tablespoons (30 ml) brandy or whisky. Return to the freezer and freeze for at least 2 hours.

New Year's Eve

After the hustle and bustle of a family Christmas, New Year's Eve is a time for the adults to celebrate in style. I have suggested recipes for an elegant dinner party and for a cocktail party with fork food.

New Year's Eve Dinner Party

CHAMPAGNE COCKTAILS (SEE BELOW)

∞

DRY WHITE WINE
WILD SALMON AND HERB TARTLETS (P. 291)
COURGETTE AND HERB TARTLETS (P. 291)
MIXED LEAF SALAD
VINAIGRETTE DRESSING (P. 88)

∞

RED BURGUNDY WINE
BEEF BOURGUIGNON (P. 164)
TOFU À LA BOURGUIGNON (P. 164)
POTATOES BOULANGÈRE (SEE BELOW)
PETITS POIS AND BABY CARROTS

∞

SWEET WHITE WINE
TARTE TATIN (SEE BELOW)
VANILLA ICE CREAM

∞

CHEESE BOARD

∞

FRESH COFFEE (P. 44)
BRANDY/LIQUEURS

Start the evening by welcoming your guests with a champagne cocktail to break the ice and get everyone in a celebratory mood.

COCKTAILS:
Makes 6 servings. You will need a bottle of champagne, sugar cubes, thin slices of lemon and a bottle of angostura bitters. Place the sugar cubes in a bowl and pour over a little of the angostura bitters until they turn pink – then simply drop a sugar cube into a champagne glass, top up with champagne and garnish with a lemon twist.

The little tartlets make an elegant starter when served with a mixed leaf salad drizzled with a classic vinaigrette dressing. They can be prepared in advance and warmed through just before serving.

The hearty casserole will benefit from being made a day or two in advance, to allow the flavours to develop, then reheated until piping hot on the day. The potatoes boulangère perfectly complement the richness of the main course and can be cooked in the oven with the casserole.

POTATOES BOULANGÈRE:
Serves 4. You will need 2lb (900 grams) old potatoes, 1 large yellow onion, ¼ pint (150 ml) hot vegetable stock, ¼ pint (150 ml) milk, 2 oz (50 grams) butter, salt and black pepper. Use an attractive, ovenproof dish as the potatoes are served in the dish straight from the oven. Grease the dish. Peel the potatoes and slice thinly, peel the onion and chop finely, place a layer of potatoes on the bottom of the dish, sprinkle over some of the onion and season with salt and pepper, add another layer of potatoes and onion and season again, add one more layer of potatoes, season again and pour over the stock and the milk. Dot the potatoes all over with the butter. Bake in the oven at 180C/350F/gas mark 4 for 30–40 minutes until the potatoes are tender and the top is a golden brown. Note: if your dinner party is running late simply turn the oven to low and this dish will keep perfectly until you are ready.

TART TATIN:
Tart Tatin is basically an upside-down apple pie and is always popular when served with a good quality vanilla ice cream.

Serves 4 to 6. You will need 1lb (450 grams) cooking apples, 4 oz (110 grams) light brown sugar, 1 teaspoon (5 ml) ground cinnamon, 1lb (450 grams) shortcrust pastry (see p. 209). Liberally butter an 8" (20 cm) flan tin, then line the base of the tin with buttered greaseproof paper, sprinkle the base of the tin with the sugar and cinnamon, peel, core and thinly slice the apples and arrange them in circles on top of the sugar. Roll the pastry into a 1" (2.5 cm) thick circle and place this on top of the apples. Bake in the oven at 180C/350F/gas mark 4 for 30 minutes until the pastry is crisp and golden. Remove the tart from the oven and allow it to completely cool. When the tart is cold loosen around the edges with a palette knife, cover the tin with a plate and carefully invert the pie onto the plate. Remove the greaseproof paper and warm through gently before serving with the ice cream.

New Year's Eve Hot Buffet Menu

CHAMPAGNE COCKTAILS
BELLINI COCKTAILS (SEE BELOW)
KIR ROYALE (P. 307)

❧

SPICY ROASTED CASHEW NUTS (P. 298)
VEGETABLE CRISPS (P. 299)
WARM SALSA DIP (P. 272)

❧

GRILLED SARDINE/VEGETABLE BRUSCHETTAS (P. 280)
WILD SALMON AND HERB TARTLETS (P. 291)
COURGETTE AND HERB TARTLETS (P. 291)

❧

PAELLA/VEGETABLE PAELLA (P. 250)
PISSALADIÈRE (P. 286)
THAI STYLE FISH CAKES/CORN FRITTERS (P. 255)
WITH SPICY THAI DIPPING SAUCE (P. 255)
GREEN SALAD
TOMATO AND ONION SALAD (P. 88)

❧

HOMEMADE CHOCOLATE TRUFFLES

When you have more guests coming to dinner than you have seats the only alternative is a buffet and, in the cold mid-winter, I think it is nice to offer hot food. This can be difficult to manage as you will need to serve food that can be picked up, held on a small plate or in a small bowl and eaten easily. Provide some crisps and peanuts for your guests to nibble on while they drink their cocktails. The tartlets and bruschettas can be made in advance and served just warm (I used to ask my children to hand round plates of warm, savoury foods to encourage even the shyest of guests to eat).

The main course paella makes a stunning centre piece and both the paella and the pasta salad are easy to eat with just a fork. The fish cakes and fritters can be eaten with the fingers. The meal is perfectly rounded off by addictive, homemade chocolate truffles.

BELLINI COCKTAILS:

Fill a champagne glass ⅓ full with peach juice and top up with cold champagne. (If you can't find peach juice buy 2 tins of peaches, drain and liquidise).

CHOCOLATE TRUFFLES:

Makes 20. You will need 7oz (200 grams) good quality (70% cocoa) dark chocolate, 7 fl oz (200 ml) double cream, 1 oz (25 grams) butter, cocoa powder, crushed almonds and some chocolate vermicelli. Begin by grating or finely chopping the chocolate. Pour the cream into a heavy based saucepan and gently bring to the boil, remove from the heat and stir in the chocolate until melted (you may need to return the pan to the heat for a moment or two). Next whisk in the butter then allow the mixture to cool in the fridge for 2 hours. Dip a melon baller in hot water and scoop across the chocolate mix to make balls or scoop up a tablespoon of mixture and roll into a ball with your hands. Dip some of the truffles in cocoa powder, some in crushed almonds and some in chocolate vermicelli. Refrigerate for up to 2 days until needed. You can add some liqueur such as cointreau or Grand Marnier to the truffles at the point where you add the butter.

Parties

Party food should look beautiful, taste wonderful and be easy to eat. The key to good party food is to present a variety of colours, textures and flavours that complement each other. Displaying the food attractively is also important. The party cake or gateau should have centre stage in the middle of the buffet table. Wrap cutlery in a colourful serviette and place at each end of the table with a supply of plates, bowls and condiments. This avoids a queue building up. Set up a bar to serve drinks in a separate room where possible.

Serve vegetarian food on different coloured plates or serviettes (I always use green). Try to use a long table (a trestle table covered with a long cloth is perfect). Divide the table into three sections and arrange the same selection of foods in each section – again this prevents queues building up and presents a pleasing uniformity to the table.

Children's birthday party menu

FRESH LEMONADE (P. 304)
STRAWBERRY FIZZ (SEE BELOW)

❧

SPICY CHEESE AND TOMATO DIP (P. 268)
BREADSTICKS, CARROT AND CELERY STICKS
MINI PIZZAS (P. 293)
SPICY SAUSAGE ROLLS (P. 287)
VEGGIE SAUSAGE ROLLS (P. 287)
STUFFED MINI PITTAS (P. 108)
GRAPE AND CHEESE SALAD (SEE BELOW)
PEANUT BUTTER AND BANANA SANDWICHES (P. 129)
TRAFFIC LIGHT SANDWICHES (SEE BELOW)

❧

ICE CREAM SUNDAES (P. 322)

With a children's party it is doubly important to make the food both appealing and bite-sized, otherwise you will find that at best it is wasted, and at worst it is trampled into the carpet. Children are over-excited enough at a party without ingesting the additives contained in most soft drinks so I recommend making your own.

The dip, pizzas, sausage rolls and pitta mix can all be made in advance. You can buy mini pittas and simply fill with the mix just before the party begins. Make the peanut butter and banana sandwiches just before you intend to serve them. For a children's party I always cut the bread into fun shapes with a cookie cutter.

STRAWBERRY FIZZ:
Mix a carton of strawberry juice with a large bottle of sparkling water and add some sliced strawberries.

GRAPE AND CHEESE SALAD:
Cube some mild Cheddar and Edam cheese and mix with whole black and white seedless grapes. It is simple but it is one of the most popular children's party dishes I have served.

TRAFFIC LIGHT SANDWICHES:
Makes 16. You will need 8 slices brown bread and 8 slices white bread with the crusts removed, softened butter for spreading, Thousand island dressing, finely shredded dark green lettuce, 8 hard boiled eggs, 20 slices of tomato. Butter the bread then spread a little Thousand island dressing onto the brown bread slices which will form the bottom of the sandwich. Place some lettuce on the bottom

third of each brown bread slice, next place slices of hard boiled egg yolk on the middle third of the bread, finish off with slices of tomato on the top third of each slice.

Using a small cookie cutter cut three evenly spaced holes down one half of the white bread slice and another three down the other half. Place the white bread on top of the sandwich. You should find that the bottom hole is filled with green lettuce, the middle with yellow egg yolk and the top with red tomato to make the traffic lights (If not simply chop a little extra filling and use to fill the holes). Cut each sandwich in two lengthways.

Teenage birthday party

For a teenage birthday party you have to provide food that is cool (as in fashionable, not temperature) yet substantial enough to see them through to the early hours and to soak up the alcohol (if it is being served). If you decide to allow alcohol to be served, it is wise to serve plenty of non alcoholic alternatives for non-drinkers and drivers.

Teenage birthday party menu

NON ALCOHOLIC FRUIT CUP (P. 313)
TEQUILA SUNRISE MOCKTAILS (P. 304)

WEDGE POTATOES WITH WARM SALSA DIP (P. 272)
SPICY CHEESE AND TOMATO DIP WITH NACHOS (P. 268)
HOMEMADE PIZZAS (P. 260)
MEXICAN TORTILLA (P. 62)
TRADITIONAL COLESLAW SALAD (P. 91)
MEXICAN RICE SALAD (P. 94)
GREEN SALAD
PITTAS STUFFED WITH LAMB/AUBERGINE KEFTEDES (P. 111)

BELLY BUSTER (SEE BELOW)

BELLY BUSTER:
Belly busters are a sort of grown up version of an ice cream sundae and are great fun to make and eat. Serves about 8. You will need a large oval platter (the disposable foil ones are perfect), 1 carton chocolate ice cream, 1 carton strawberry ice cream, 1 carton vanilla ice cream, strawberry sauce and chocolate sauce, ice cream wafers, strawberries, cubes of pineapple, grapes, sponge fingers, meringue nests, white and chocolate Maltesers, chopped nuts, Smarties or M&Ms, an aerosol can of cream.

To assemble: place 4 scoops each of chocolate, strawberry and vanilla ice cream in the centre of the dish, now place another 3 scoops each on top of this, then 2, then 1 until you have a pyramid of ice cream scoops. Starting at one end of the platter place a pile of strawberries, then a pile of Maltesers, a pile of pineapple, a pile of crumbled meringue, a pile of grapes, more Maltesers and so on until the entire platter has been covered. Liberally spray with aerosol cream and sprinkle with chopped nuts, Smarties or M&Ms, and the ice cream sauces. Finish off by pushing the wafers and sponge fingers into the ice cream. Serve immediately and let party-goers help themselves to as much as they dare.

Grown up party food

Great parties begin with great party food and drink. Offer a cocktail or a bowl of punch to create an element of surprise. There is something for everyone in the following menu, a selection of fresh dips with crudités, sumptuous warm finger food, sandwiches with excitingly different fillings and big bowls of colourful salads.

Adult party menu

STRAWBERRY CHAMPAGNE PUNCH (SEE BELOW)

∞

A SELECTION OF DIPS
CREAMY LENTIL DHAL (P. 270)
HUMMUS (P. 275)
GUACAMOLE (P. 276)
CRUDITÉS, BREADSTICKS, PITTA FINGERS, TORTILLA CHIPS

∞

A SELECTION OF WARM FINGER FOOD
GRILLED SARDINE AND VEGETABLE BRUSCHETTAS (P. 280)
FRENCH ONION TART (P. 286)
WILD SALMON AND HERB TARTLETS (P. 291)
COURGETTE AND HERB TARTLETS (P. 291)
TARAMASALATA TOASTS (P. 282)

∞

A SELECTION OF SANDWICHES
MATURE CHEDDAR WITH QUICK APPLE CHUTNEY (P. 123)
SPICED EGG AND TOMATO (P. 124)
SMOKED SALMON/CREAM CHEESE WRAPS (P. 118)
PATÉ/VEGETABLE PATÉ WITH ONION MARMALADE (P. 130)

∞

A SELECTION OF SALADS
GREEK SALAD (P. 78)
TOMATO AND ONION SALAD (P. 88)
CRUNCHY RED CABBAGE SALAD (P. 90)
MEXICAN RICE SALAD (P. 94)

∞

A SELECTION OF DESSERTS
HOMEMADE CHOCOLATE TRUFFLES (P. 334)
MINI CHEESECAKES (SEE BELOW)
BAKED CARIBBEAN FRUIT SALAD (P. 325)
VANILLA ICE CREAM WITH TOFFEE SAUCE (P. 325)

The French onion tart and the tartlets can be made in advance and frozen, simply defrost and reheat before serving. Cut the tart into fingers or squares. The dips, crudités, red cabbage salad, Mexican rice salad and the chocolate truffles can be made the day before the party and refrigerated until needed. The apple chutney and the onion marmalade can be made several days in advance and stored in an airtight container in the fridge. To make the sandwiches use a variety of freshly sliced breads, white, wholemeal and granary and cut into triangles for best effect.

STRAWBERRY CHAMPAGNE PUNCH:
Makes 40 servings. You will need a large punch bowl, 1½ lbs (700 grams) strawberries, 8 oz (225 grams) sugar, water, 2 bottles rosé wine, juice of 2 lemons, 3 bottles champagne or sparkling wine. Begin by making an ice mould: use a jelly mould or bowl that will easily fit inside your punch bowl. Fill with water and add some sliced strawberries then freeze.

PUNCH:
Wash and hull the strawberries and place them in a saucepan, cover with 1" (2.5 cm) of water, bring to the boil and add the sugar. Cook for 3–4 minutes until the sugar has dissolved and the strawberries have softened, then remove from the heat and blend to a purée. Chill in the fridge for at least 2 hours. Chill the rosé wine and champagne for the same length of time.

Just before the party begins pour the lemon juice into the bowl, add the strawberry purée and the rosé wine and stir well. When the first guests begin to arrive add the champagne and stir gently, then add the ice mould.

MINI CHEESECAKES:
These are simplicity itself, but very popular. You will need a packet of digestive biscuits, 8 oz (225 grams) cream cheese, juice of ½ lemon, strawberry jam, apricot jam, blackcurrant jam and lemon curd. Whip the cheese with the lemon juice and spread it on to the biscuits then top with a little jam or lemon curd and voilà – a mini cheesecake.

BASIC RECIPES

Fresh fruit spreads produce a deliciously soft, fresh tasting, spread that contains much less sugar than normal jams and jellies. The consistency of the spread is less gelatinous than traditional jams due to the reduced sugar, and the finished product should resemble a thick, fruity sauce.

Strawberry spread

TIME TO PREPARE: 5 MINUTES
TIME TO COOK: 1 HOUR 10 MINUTES TO 1 HOUR 40 MINUTES
MAKES ABOUT 2 LB (900 GRAMS) JAM

Ingredients

2 lbs (900 grams) fresh strawberries
12 oz (350 grams) sugar
3 tablespoons (90 ml) lemon juice

Method

Step one:
Wash, hull and slice the strawberries then place in a large, heavy bottomed saucepan. Add the sugar and lemon juice and cook over a low heat for about 10 minutes. Put a saucer in the fridge to cool.

Step two:
When the strawberries have softened mash them lightly with a fork to release the juice. Reduce the cooking temperature to the lowest setting and cook uncovered for a further hour. After an hour has passed test the jam by taking a teaspoon (5 ml) of the spread and dropping it onto the cold saucer, it should form a soft gel, if not cook the jam for a further 30 minutes and test again.

Step three:
When cooked allow the jam to cool and then pour into sterilised jars or an airtight container and keep in the fridge for up to 2 weeks.

Quick tip

The jam can be frozen for up to 3 months and is a useful way to use up a glut of fruit. The same method will work for any soft berry fruit.

Apricot spread

TIME TO PREPARE: 15 MINUTES
TIME TO COOK: 1 HOUR 20 MINUTES

Ingredients

2 lbs (900 grams) ripe apricots
8 oz (225 grams) sugar
3 tablespoons (90 ml) lemon juice

Method

Step one:
Cut the apricots in half, remove the stones then chop the flesh roughly. Place them in a large, heavy based saucepan with the sugar and lemon juice.

Step two:
Cook over a medium heat for about 10 minutes. Remove the fruit from the heat and lightly mash with a fork to release the juice. Put a saucer in the fridge to cool.

Step three:
Return the fruit to the heat and lower the temperature to the lowest setting then cook for a further 20 minutes, remove from the heat after 20 minutes and stir. Cook for a further 30 minutes then remove the fruit from the heat again and drop a teaspoon of the jam onto the saucer. It should form a soft gel, if not stir the jam again and return to the heat for a further 20 minutes and test again. When cooked the fruit should form a soft gel when dropped onto the cold saucer.

Step four:
When cooked allow the jam to cool and store it in sterilised jars or an airtight container in the fridge for up to 2 weeks.

Quick tip

The jam can be frozen for up to 3 months and works well with peaches (you need to peel them before cooking), nectarines and plums.

Italian tomato sauce

TIME TO PREPARE: 5 MINUTES
TIME TO COOK: 30 MINUTES
SERVES: 4 TO 6

This classic tomato sauce can be used as the base for a number of different dishes including bolognaise, chilli con carne and moussaka. It makes a quick supper dish when simply poured over pasta and sprinkled with cheese.

Ingredients

1 large yellow onion
2 cloves garlic
2 tablespoons (30 ml) olive oil
1 small bunch basil
1 teaspoon (5 ml) dried oregano
2 x 14 oz (400 grams) tins of chopped tomatoes
Salt and freshly ground black pepper

Method

Step one:
Peel and finely chop the onion and garlic. Finely chop the basil.

Step two:
Pour the oil into a medium sized heavy based pan and heat over a gentle heat. Add the onions and garlic and cook over a low heat for 5 minutes.

Step three:
Add the chopped tomatoes and the basil and season with salt and pepper. Cook uncovered over a medium heat for about 30 minutes until the sauce has thickened.

Pizza sauce

TIME TO PREPARE: 5 MINUTES
TIME TO COOK: 1 HOUR
MAKES SUFFICIENT TO TOP 1 10" PIZZA, 4 FRENCH BREAD PIZZAS OR 24 MINI PIZZAS

Pizza sauce can be stored in an airtight jar or container in the fridge for up to a week. It also freezes well.

Ingredients

2 tablespoons (30 ml) olive oil
14 oz (400 grams) tin chopped tomatoes
½ teaspoon (2.5 ml) sugar
1 large onion
2 cloves garlic
1 teaspoon (5 ml) dried oregano
2 tablespoons (30 ml) fresh basil (or 1 teaspoon {5 ml} dried)
Salt and pepper

Method

Step one:
Peel and finely chop onions and garlic. Finely chop the basil.

Step two:
Put a large, heavy based saucepan on the hob and pour in the oil. Heat gently and add onions and garlic. Fry gently for 5 minutes until the onion is softened.

Step three:
Add the tomatoes, sugar and herbs to the pan and season with salt and freshly ground black pepper. Cook uncovered over a low heat for 1 hour. When the mixture is cooked it will resemble a thick tomato jam.

Cranberry sauce

TIME TO PREPARE: 5 MINUTES
TIME TO COOK: 5 MINUTES
MAKES ABOUT 1 LB (450 GRAMS) SAUCE

This traditional sauce is laced with ruby port for that true Christmas flavour.

Ingredients

12 oz (350 grams) fresh cranberries
8 fl oz (250 ml) boiling water
4 tablespoons (60 ml) ruby port
4 oz (110 grams) light brown sugar
1 teaspoon (5 ml) allspice

Method

Step one:
Roughly chop the cranberries and place in a large, heavy based saucepan, cover with boiling water, bring back to the boil and cook on high for about 5 minutes until all the cranberries have burst open.

Step two:
Remove the pan from the heat and stir with a wooden spoon, lightly mashing the berries against the side of the pan.

Step three:
Add the sugar and allspice to the cranberries and stir well to dissolve, if necessary return the pan to the heat for a moment or two.

Step four:
Stir in the port and allow the sauce to cool. The sauce will thicken as it cools. Pour into sterilised jars or an airtight container and keep in the fridge for up to two weeks.

Quick tip

Can be frozen for up to three months.

Cucumber raita

TIME TO PREPARE: 5 MINUTES

This refreshing dip is traditionally served with curries to cool the palate.

Ingredients

8 fl oz (250 ml) carton natural yoghurt
½ cucumber
1 small bunch fresh mint
Salt

Method

Step one:
Peel the cucumber, slice it in half lengthways and remove the seeds, then chop into small dice.

Step two:
Finely chop the mint. Pour the yoghurt into a mixing bowl and add the mint, cucumber and ½ teaspoon salt. Chill in the fridge until needed (use within 24 hours).

Croutons

TIME TO PREPARE: 5 MINUTES
TIME TO COOK: 30 MINUTES

Croutons are quick and easy to make and can be flavoured with different herbs and spices to add a satisfying crunch to soups, salads and dips.

WHOLEWHEAT CROUTONS

Ingredients

4 thick slices wholemeal bread
4 tablespoons (60 ml) olive oil
Salt and pepper

Method

Step one:
Remove the crusts from the bread and discard. Cut the bread into ½" (1.25 cm) cubes.

Step two:
Pour the olive oil into a bowl and season well with salt and freshly ground black pepper.

Step three:
Toss the bread in the olive oil and then lay it flat on an oiled baking sheet. Cook in the bottom of the oven on 150C/300 F/gas mark 2 for 30 minutes until the croutons are crispy.

Step four:
Serve immediately in soups or salads or store in an airtight container for 2–3 days.

Garlic croutons

Ingredients

4 thick slices white bread
4 tablespoons olive oil
1 garlic clove
1 teaspoon (5 ml) mixed herbs
Salt and freshly ground black pepper

Method

Step one:
Peel and finely chop the garlic. Remove the crusts from the bread and discard. Cut the bread into ½″ (1.25 cm) cubes.

Step two:
Pour the oil into a mixing bowl; add the herbs and garlic and season well with salt and pepper. Add the bread cubes, toss in the oil, herbs and garlic mixture.

Step three:
Lay the croutons flat on an oiled baking sheet and cook in the oven at 150C/300 F/gas mark 2 for 30 minutes until the croutons are crispy and golden.

Step four:
Serve immediately in soups or salads or store for 2–3 days in an airtight container.

CHAPTER

9

FOUR-WEEKLY MENU PLAN
AND SHOPPING LIST

The menu plan and shopping lists have been designed to cater for a family of four made up of two meat eaters and two vegetarians. You may need to adjust them to your own requirements. This four-week menu plan is suggested as an aid for the busy cook to provide a variety of healthy and interesting main course meals on a daily basis.

To ensure that you are eating a healthy diet it is important to eat from a variety of food groups daily. By cooking a proper evening meal every day you will be making a good start on the road to healthy eating. I have included a meat and vegetarian recipe for each meal, but if you can tempt your meat eaters away from meat, particularly red meat, once or even twice a week they will enjoy even greater health benefits – not to mention delicious food.

Keep up the good work by eating healthily throughout the day. Start by choosing a nutritious breakfast from the breakfast chapter and follow this with a delicious lunch from the lunch chapter. Vary your meals as much as possible to ensure an adequate intake of protein, carbohydrates, fats, essential vitamins and minerals. Chapter 1 sets out current guidelines for healthy eating and all the recipes contain a 'health note' to help you choose a nutritious and balanced diet.

Week 1:

Monday: chicken breasts/chicken-style fillets with warm tomato salsa (p. 144) served with new potatoes, broccoli and carrots.

Tuesday: gammon steaks with pineapple/'bacon' and pineapple muffins (p. 205) served with low fat oven chips or use frozen), peas and sweetcorn.

Wednesday: penne Niçoise with/without tuna (p. 252) served with grated cheese and a mixed salad of lettuce, tomatoes, cucumber, peppers, onions and a vinaigrette dressing (p. 88).

Thursday: sausage/veggie sausage and mash (p. 218) served with stir fried cabbage and leeks.

Friday: quick turkey and cashew stir fry/cashew and vegetable stir fry (p. 157) served with brown rice.

Saturday: wild salmon baked with herb butter/pine nut and herb stuffed tomatoes (p. 244) served with whole wheat pasta and Mediterranean vegetables (p. 246).

Sunday: Roast chicken/Mum's veggie roast dinner (p. 136).

SHOPPING LIST FOR WEEK 1:
Fish, meat/meat substitutes
4 free range boneless and skinless chicken breasts
2 thinly sliced turkey breast steaks
8 Quorn chicken-style fillets
2 unsmoked gammon steaks
4 slices vegetarian bacon
4 lean pork or beef sausages
4 Lincolnshire-style vegetarian sausages
2 wild salmon fillets

Vegetables, fruits and fresh herbs
2 lb (900 grams) potatoes (Desiree or King Edwards)
4 large Maris Piper or roasting potatoes
2 lb (900 grams) new potatoes
2 large sweet potatoes
2 large parsnips
2 red onions

6 large yellow onions
5 large leeks
Savoy cabbage or spring greens
5 lbs (2250 grams) carrots
2 lb (900 grams) broccoli
1 small white cabbage
3 bulbs garlic
1 large bunch fresh parsley
1 large bunch fresh coriander
3 sprigs each sage, rosemary and thyme
1 large bunch fresh basil
2" (5 cm) piece fresh ginger
12 oz (350 grams) fine green beans
12 baby corn cobs
4 red peppers
3 green peppers
3 yellow peppers
4 courgettes
8 large tomatoes
2 large beefsteak tomatoes
1 lettuce
1 cucumber
1 bunch celery
1 small bag bean sprouts
3 lemons
2 limes
6 rings pineapple (fresh or tinned)
1 large cooking apple

Dairy produce
12 oz (225 grams) Cheddar cheese
5 oz (150 grams) butter
2 eggs
Milk

Oils
Olive oil
Sunflower oil

Dried herbs and spices
Oregano
Dry English mustard
Bay leaves

Salt
Freshly ground black pepper

Dried goods
Cornflour
Vegetarian gravy browning
Vegetarian gravy granules
Sugar
1 lb (450 grams) penne pasta shapes
1 lb (450 grams) wholewheat pasta
1 lb (450 grams) long grain rice
1lb (450 grams) brown rice
Plain flour
4 oz (110 grams) unsalted cashew nuts
4 oz (110 grams) pine nuts

Tins/jars
3 x 14 oz (400 grams) tins chopped tomatoes
7 oz (200 grams) tin tuna in brine or spring water
Small tin or jar pitted black olives
8 oz (225 grams) tin sweetcorn
4 oz (110 grams) tin water chestnuts
Yeast extract

Bread
2 English breakfast muffins
8 thick slices wholemeal bread (for breadcrumbs)

Liquids (stocks, wine, fruit juice and sauces)
White wine
White wine vinegar
Dry sherry
Vegetable stock cubes (if not making your own)
4 fl oz (120 ml) pineapple juice
Chilli sauce
Dark soy sauce

Frozen
Low fat oven chips (if not making your own)
Peas

Week 2:

Monday: turkey/spicy veggie sausage and Mediterranean vegetable kebabs (p. 159) served with brown rice and a salad of raw spinach, sliced red onion, grated carrot and cucumber with vinaigrette dressing (p. 88).

Tuesday: pan fried cod/Indian eggs with Indian potatoes (p. 253) served with peas and roasted tomatoes.

Wednesday: homemade Hawaiian pizza (p. 264) served with traditional coleslaw salad (p. 91).

Thursday: shepherd's/gardener's pie (p. 222) with gravy/vegetarian gravy (p. 137) served with cauliflower and broccoli florets.

Friday: Paella/vegetarian paella (p. 250) served with a mixed green salad of lettuce, rocket, spinach and cucumber and a tomato and onion salad (p. 88).

Saturday: chicken breast in ciabatta bread/hummus in ciabatta bread with roasted vegetable salad (p. 148).

Sunday: roast beef/savoury loaf with roast potatoes and Yorkshire pudding (p. 168) served with Brussels sprouts and carrots.

SHOPPING LIST FOR WEEK 2:
Fish, meat/meat substitutes
2 thinly sliced turkey breast steaks
2 x 6 oz (175 grams) cod fillets or steaks
2 oz (50 grams) sliced ham
2 oz (50 grams) Quorn ham-style slices
8 oz (225 grams) lean ground minced beef or lamb
4 large raw prawns
1 squid tube (cut into rings)
6 fresh mussels
3 lb (1350 grams) joint sirloin of beef
1 lb (450 grams) vegetarian soy mince
4 oz (110 grams) hummus

Vegetables, fruits and fresh herbs
2 large Spanish onions
4 large yellow onions
6 large red onions
Bunch spring onions

6lbs (2700 grams) Maris Piper potatoes
1 small white cabbage
1 large cauliflower
1 lb (450 grams) Brussels sprouts
8 oz (225 grams) broccoli
6 oz (175 grams) fine green beans
4 lbs (1800 grams) carrots
1 lettuce
1 rocket
1 cucumber
1 bunch celery
2 packets ripened on the vine cherry tomatoes (with vine and stalks on)
8 large tomatoes
2 large beef steak tomatoes
4 green peppers
5 red peppers
1 yellow pepper
8 baby corn cobs
4 oz (110 grams) bean sprouts
3 bulbs garlic
2″ (5 cm) piece fresh ginger
4 lemons
2 limes
1 small red or green chilli
1 large bunch fresh coriander
1 bunch of fresh basil
1 large bunch of fresh flat leaf parsley
1 small bunch fresh chopped mint
6 sprigs fresh rosemary
1 small bunch fresh thyme
2 x 4 oz (110 grams) bag of fresh spinach

Dairy produce
12 large free range eggs
2 oz (50 grams) mozzarella cheese
Milk
Butter or vegetable margarine
2 oz (50 grams) silken tofu
4 fl oz (120 ml) carton natural yoghurt

Oils
Sunflower oil
Olive oil

Dried herbs and spices
Salt
Sea salt
Freshly ground black pepper
English mustard powder
Dried oregano
Ground ginger
Turmeric
Chilli powder
Cumin
Paprika
Saffron threads

Dried goods
4 oz (110 grams) unsalted cashew nuts
1 lb (450 grams) brown rice
6 oz (175 grams) medium grain rice
Plain flour
Cornflour
Beef stock cubes (if not making your own)
Vegetable stock powder (if not making your own)
8 oz (225 grams) packet dried red lentils
1 small packet sesame seeds
1 small packet caraway seeds
Dried yeast
Sugar

Tins/jars
4 oz (110 grams) tin water chestnuts
1 jar medium hot curry paste
1 jar Vegemite
4 oz (110 grams) tin pineapple chunks
5 x 14 oz (400 grams) tins tomatoes
2 tins of tomato purée
1 small jar clear honey

Bread
2 thick slices wholemeal bread (for breadcrumbs)
2 long ciabatta loaves (or 4 large ciabatta rolls)

Liquids (stocks, wine, fruit juice and sauces)
Soy sauce
White wine vinegar
Dry sherry (for gravy)

Frozen
Peas

Week 3:

Monday: Caribbean chicken/Quorn (p. 150) served with brown rice mixed with peas and sweetcorn.

Tuesday: Pan fried tuna/grilled haloumi cheese served on a bed of roasted vegetables (p. 246) served with potato wedges (p. 272).

Wednesday: Mexican chicken/ vegetarian fajitas (p. 152) served with traditional coleslaw salad (p. 91), guacamole and pico de gallo (p. 000) and some grated cheese.

Thursday: Lamb chops/veggie lamb steaks with redcurrant sauce (p. 192) served with new potatoes, green beans and julienne carrots.

Friday: jacket potatoes with tuna and spicy bean mix/ cheesy spicy bean mix (p. 49) served with a large mixed salad of salad leaves, grated carrot, sweetcorn, red onion and tomatoes.

Saturday: spaghetti bolognaise/vegetarian spaghetti bolognaise (p. 231) served with a large mixed salad of lettuce, rocket, spinach, tomatoes, onions and cucumber.

Sunday: Pot roast beef/butterbean and spring vegetable casserole (p. 174) served with mashed sweet potatoes.

SHOPPING LIST FOR WEEK 3:

Fish, meat/ meat substitutes
4 free range, skinless and boneless chicken breasts
4 oz (110 grams) firm tofu
4 lean lamb cutlets
4 Quorn lamb-style steaks
2 fresh tuna steaks
2lb (900 grams) joint silverside, top rump or rolled brisket
8 oz (225 grams) lean minced beef
8 oz (225 grams) chilled soya mince
8 oz (225 grams) Quorn chicken-style pieces

Vegetables, fruits and fresh herbs
2 lbs (900 grams) new potatoes
4 large baking potatoes

2 lb (900 grams) green beans

1 small white cabbage

1 bulb fennel

4 small shallots or button onions

8 baby carrots

1 bunch celery

4 oz (110 grams) chestnut mushrooms

2lb (900 grams) mixed root vegetables (potatoes, parsnips, turnips, swede)

2 large Spanish onions

5 bulbs garlic

6 large yellow onions

5 large red onions

1 large bag mixed salad leaves of rocket, spinach and watercress

1 iceberg lettuce

4 lbs (1800 grams) large tomatoes

1 lb (450 grams) plum tomatoes

2 cucumbers

8 baby sweetcorn

2 courgettes

5 red, 5 green and 5 yellow peppers

3 lbs (1350 grams) large carrots

4 oz (110 grams) fresh pineapple chunks or small tin pineapple

1" (2.5 cm) piece fresh ginger

5 small birds eye green or red chillies

1 bunch radishes

1 small bunch fresh coriander

1 large bunch fresh basil

2 sprigs each parsley, thyme and sage and two bay leaves

2 ripe avocados (omit if you are not making your own guacamole)

1 jalapeno pepper (omit if you are not making your own guacamole)

4 limes

1 lemon

1 large orange

8 oz (225 grams) fresh redcurrants

Dairy produce

4 oz (110 grams) fresh parmesan cheese (grated or shaved)

2 oz (50 grams) silken tofu

6 oz (175 grams) Cheddar cheese

4 x 2" (5 cm) thick slices haloumi cheese

Tub of fresh guacamole (if not making your own)

Tub of fresh tomato salsa (if not making the Pico de Gallo)

Oils
Sunflower oil
Olive oil
Extra virgin olive oil

Dried herbs and spices
Dried oregano
Ground cumin
Paprika

Dried goods
Cornflour
Brown sugar
White sugar
Dried barley
3 oz (75 grams) cashew nuts
1 oz (25 grams) dried coconut
1 lb (450 grams) brown rice
1 lb (450 grams) spaghetti
Beef stock cubes or powder (if you are not making your own)
Vegetable stock cubes or powder (if you are not making your own)
1 small packet sesame seeds
1 small packet caraway seeds

Tins/jars
2 x 8 oz (225 grams) tins sweetcorn in water
2 x 14 oz (400 grams) tins chopped tomatoes
1 small tin or tube sun dried tomato purée
Vegemite
1 small jar clear honey
1 small jar or tube basil pesto
2 x 16 oz (450 grams) tins butter beans
1 x 16 oz (450 grams) tin red kidney beans
1x 6oz (175 grams) tin tuna in brine or water

Bread
8 wheat flour tortillas

Liquids (stocks, wine, fruit juice and sauces)
¼ pint (150 ml) pineapple juice
White wine vinegar
Beef stock (if you are not making your own)
½ bottle Mexican beer or lager (use ordinary if you can't find Mexican)
4 fl oz (120 ml) red wine
½ pint (300 ml) dry cider

Frozen
Peas

Week 4:

Monday: Spanish-style chicken/tofu (p. 142) served with spinach tagliatelli and roasted vegetables (p. 104).

Tuesday: Mexican tortilla (p. 62) served with homemade chips (p. 166) and a large mixed salad of lettuce, rocket, spinach, tomatoes and red onions.

Wednesday: Crispy beef stir fry/marinated tofu stir fry (p. 180) served with stir fried greens (spinach, spring greens, Chinese cabbage, leeks etc.) and some brown rice mixed with chopped peppers, onions, peas and sweetcorn.

Thursday: Sausage/veggie sausage and apple casserole served with mashed sweet potatoes and broccoli.

Friday: jacket potatoes filled with prawn crunch/cottage cheese and herb crunch (p. 51) served with a mixed salad of lettuce, rocket, watercress, tomatoes, cucumber and traditional coleslaw salad (p. 91).

Saturday: creamy chicken/Quorn and spinach curry (p. 146) served with rice and cucumber raita (p. 347).

Sunday: pork chops with almonds/potatoes with almond and parsnip stuffing with homemade apple sauce (p. 198) served with new potatoes and braised red cabbage.

SHOPPING LIST FOR WEEK 4:

Fish, meat/meat substitutes
4 free range, boneless and skinless chicken breasts
2 lean pork chops
8 oz (225 grams) Quorn chicken-style pieces
12 oz (350 grams) tofu
8 oz (225 grams) lean sirloin steak
4 lean pork or turkey sausages
4 Quorn Bramley apple bangers
6 oz (175 grams) fresh cooked prawns

Vegetables, fruits and fresh herbs
2 medium Spanish onions
3 large red onions
2 medium yellow onions

1 large bunch spring onions
3 bulbs garlic
1 small white cabbage
1 red cabbage
3 leeks
4 large carrots
2 parsnips
1 bunch celery
3 lb (1350 grams) new potatoes
2 lb (900 grams) old potatoes
2 lb (450 grams) sweet potatoes
7 large baking potatoes
8 oz (225 grams) green beans
1 lb (450 grams) broccoli
4 red, 4 yellow and 3 green peppers
3 lbs (1350 grams) large tomatoes
4 medium courgettes
Lettuce
Rocket
Spinach
Spring greens
1 chinese cabbage
1 cucumber
1 small bag fresh bean sprouts
1 small bunch fresh basil
1 small bunch flat leaf parsley
1 small bunch chives
1 small bunch fresh coriander
1 small bunch fresh mint
2 lemons
1 lime
2" (5 cm) piece fresh ginger
2 stems lemon grass
4 large crisp eating apples (Granny Smith or Braeburn work well)
2 large cooking apples (if you are making your own apple sauce, otherwise buy a jar of low sugar apple sauce)

Dairy produce
6 large organic free range eggs
6 oz (175 grams) plain cottage cheese
Small carton silken tofu (if making your own tofu mayonnaise – otherwise buy a jar of low fat mayonnaise)
14 fl oz (400 ml) natural yoghurt
1 small tub vegetarian margarine
4 oz (110 grams) low fat crème fraiche

4 oz (110 grams) Cheddar cheese

Oils
Olive oil
Sunflower oil

Dried herbs and spices
Paprika
Smoked paprika
Ground cumin
Oregano
Salt and freshly ground black pepper
Chinese five spice powder
Dried sage

Dried goods
1 lb (450 grams) spinach tagliatelli
1 lb (450 grams) brown rice
1 lb (450 grams) basmati rice
2 oz (50 grams) salted peanuts
4 oz (110 grams) flaked almonds
2 small packs lightly salted tortilla chips
Cornflour
Plain flour
Brown sugar
2 tablespoons (30 ml) sesame seeds
1 tablespoon (15 ml) caraway seeds

Tins/jars
3 x 14 oz (400 grams) tins chopped tomatoes
1 oz (25 grams) black olives (stone removed)
8 oz (225 grams) tin sweetcorn
14 oz (400 grams) tin butter beans
1 small jar clear honey
1 jar green curry paste

Liquids (stocks, wine, fruit juice and sauces)
5 fl oz (150 ml) white wine or vegetable stock
Yellow bean sauce
Hot chilli sauce
Dark soy sauce
Rice wine or dry sherry
10 fl oz (300 ml) dry cider
4 fl oz (120 ml) vegetable stock

Frozen
Peas

Index